Under A Big Blue Star

Under A Big Blue Star

Exotic Voyages of a Deck Cadet

Phil Carroll

Shakspeare
EDITORIAL

First published by Shakspeare Editorial, UK, December 2022

For permissions contact: philipjcarroll@btinternet.com

ISBN pbk 978-1-7397590-8-7
      ebk 978-1-7397590-9-4

Designed and typeset www.ShakspeareEditorial.org

Dedicated to

My Wonderful Wife, Lynne

Contents

Figures

Glossary

Abaft	behind
Bajan	Barbadian; Blue Star traditionally employed Barbadian crews in several of its ships
Boilie	boiler suit
Bollard	a short, thick post on the ship's deck (or a quayside), to which ship's berthing ropes or wires were secured
Bosun	Boatswain, the non-officer in charge of the deck crowd (see below)
Box	slang for a standard 20 feet shipping container
Box boat	container-ship
Break bulk	goods that must be loaded individually (in bags, boxes, crates, drums, barrels), but not in either intermodal containers or in bulk
Bulkhead	a dividing wall or barrier between separate compartments inside a ship
Bulwark	an extension of a ship's sides above the level of the deck
Burma Road	within the hull, a passageway along the ship's length on its port and starboard sides used for access to holds on a container-ship and as a safe means of getting from the aft superstructure to the fo'c'sle in inclement weather
Capstan	a motor-powered broad revolving cylinder on its vertical axis used for winding or hauling in, or easing out, a rope or wire
Chiefy	Chief Engineer, in charge of the ship's engineering department
Chippy	ship's carpenter
Cofferdam	vacant space across the width of the ship between two watertight bulkheads to separate the engine room and fuel tanks
Courtesy ensign	when in foreign waters usually the national flag of that country is hoisted on the starboard outer halyard of a merchantman's main mast (usually atop the bridge)
Crowd	crew
Deck crowd	deck crew: Bosun and his Able Seamen

Deckies	deck department
Dhobying	laundry
Dings	engineers
Donkeyman	engineer's equivalent to seaman (interchangeable with greaser and motorman), although historically he was responsible for the steam donkey engine that powered a merchantman's cargo winches
Dunnage	timber boards laid singularly or in double pattern under cargo parcels to keep the surface of the cargo off the steel deck plate to provide air space around the cargo and prevent 'cargo sweat'
Duty mess	room used by crew to take meals during their watch while attired in grubby, greasy boilersuits or work-clothes; wearing of boilersuits in the Officers' Mess was strictly forbidden
Engine Room Storekeeper (ERS)	engineer's equivalent to Bosun
Fo'c'sle (forecastle)	the forward part of the ship
For'ard	the forward end of a ship
Fridgie	Chief Refrigeration Officer, engineer responsible for maintaining required temperatures in refrigerated cargo holds
Greaser	engineer's equivalent to seaman (interchangeable with donkeyman and motorman)
Heads	ship's toilets
House flag	a flag indicating the company that a ship belongs to
Jumbo derrick	a derrick designed to lift abnormally heavy cargo
Lampy	lamp-trimmer; in the old days, responsible for ensuring the wicks on ship's oil lamps yielded a clear, bright flame; electricity ended the role, but 'Lampy' retained as the senior AB below the Bosun
Lecky	Electrical Officer, responsible for the ship's electrical supplies and kit; usually two on board (Chief Lecky and 2nd Lecky)
Master or Old Man	Captain
Moll	a party girl found in Australian and New Zealand ports; attracted to parties aboard merchant ships; somewhat liberal in their favours
Monkey island	bridge roof deck

On the coast	a merchantman's period in several ports on a particular coast, such as Australia, New Zealand, or South America; in the old days, ships were 'on the coast' for months
Painter	seaman responsible for ship's paint locker
Poop deck	aft-most part of the upper deck/weather deck
Port side	left-hand side of the ship
Reefer	refrigerated cargo ship
Rule of the Road	shortened form of the 'International Regulations for Preventing Collision at Sea 1972'
Second Mate	watchkeeping deck officer responsible for all aspects of navigation
Sherbet	beer or lager, either in a can or draught
Skiddies	underpants
Skids	the dodgy, sometimes dangerous, part of any port town or city, filled with bars, clubs, cheap hotels; an area where merchant seaman became acquainted with whores
Smoko	an informal Australian term widely adopted in the Merchant Navy for morning/afternoon tea/coffee
Soogee/soojee	to clean or wash down a ship
Sparks	Radio Officer
Stand-by	the period between embarking a pilot until securely berthed at a wharf, and the reverse on departure
Stations	shipboard locations occupied by deck officers and crew during stand-by: fo'c'sle, poop deck or bridge
Starboard side	right-hand side of the ship
Tabnabs	cakes/biscuits provided for smoko by ship's cook (tea and tabnabs); not a daily occurrence, but a real treat!
The Mate	Chief Officer or Chief Mate, most senior deck officer after the Master, watchkeeper; responsible for cargo operations: loading, discharge, cargo plan
Third Mate	watchkeeping deck officer responsible for ship's safety and life-saving equipment (lifeboats, life rafts, emergency radios, hydrants, fire-hoses, fire extinguishers, etc)
Transit	first generation satellite navigation system, yielding a position roughly every 90 minutes
Twistlock	a standardised rotating connector for securing shipping containers in place on a container ship
Union purchase	a system of handling cargo where a pair of derricks are used in combination; the derricks are fixed using wire

	'preventers' (or guys) and the cargo runners coupled such that the load is swung from a position dockside vertically under one derrick to a position in the hold vertically under the second
Up the road	to go ashore
Weather deck	the uppermost deck on a ship which is exposed to the environment
Wharfie	stevedore or docker
Windlass	apparatus for hoisting an anchor from the seabed; usually also fitted with a drum-end used to haul in and ease out a ship's berthing ropes
Yellow brick road	route demarcated as safe for pedestrians to follow between dock gates and wharves, usually delineated by parallel yellow lines and yellow hashed lines across

Abbreviations

AB   Able Seaman
ACT   Associated Container Transportation
ADL   Automatic Data Logger
aka   also known as
ARPA   Automatic Radar Plotting Aid
BA   Buenos Aires
BGM   Bell Gravimeter
BSSM   Blue Star Ship Management Ltd
BSL   Blue Star Line
CPA   closest point of approach
CRE   Chief Refrigeration Engineer (Fridgie)
DNS   Decca Navigator System, a hyperbolic electronic position-fixing
        system; usually known as Decca Navigator
DR   dead reckoning or deduced reckoning, a means of projecting a
        ship's position on a chart using only course and speed
ECNA   east coast of North America
EDH   Efficient deck hand, a practical and theory course covering
        deck seamanship skills and ship knowledge; the qualifying
        examination for an Able Seaman's certificate in the merchant
        navy
EP   estimated position
GM   distance between ship's 'geometric height' and its 'centre of
        gravity'; critical in ship stability
GMDSS   Global Maritime Distress and Safety System; worldwide
        system of automated emergency signal communication for ships
        at sea developed by the International Maritime Organisation
        (IMO) as part of the SOLAS Convention; safety procedures,
        types of equipment, and communication protocols for safety
        and rescue operations of distressed ships, boats, and aircraft
GPS   global positioning system, or satnav
GSK   general ship knowledge; a catch-all examinable subject in the
        2nd Mate's syllabus
IALA   International Association of Marine Aids to Navigation and
        Lighthouse Authorities

IDL	International Date Line
IMO	International Maritime Organisation
IRGBR	Inner Route of the Great Barrier Reef
L&H	Lamport & Holt Line (aka Lean & Hungry)
MCR	machinery control room
MNTB	Merchant Navy Training Board
OCL	Overseas Containers Limited
OOW	Officer of the Watch
O/T	Officer Trainee, a graduate entry deck cadet – only BSSM recruited graduates
OTC	Officers' Training Corps
PACE	Pacific America Container Express
PDR	Precision Depth Recorder
POB	pilot on board
PTI	Physical Training Instructor
QM	Quartermaster
RN	Royal Navy
RNAD	Royal Naval Armament Depot
ROR	Rule of the Road, or International Regulations for Preventing Collisions at Sea 1972; the mariners' highway code
SINS	Ship's Inertial Navigation System
SOLAS	International Convention for the Safety of Life at Sea (1974); maritime treaty that sets minimum safety standards in the construction, equipment and operation of merchant ships
SR	Survey Recorder of the Watch
SWL	Safe Working Load
TEU	20-foot equivalent unit, a standard 20-foot container and the basis for measuring a container-ship's carrying capacity – the internationally recognised measure of a ship's container capacity
TPC	tonnes per centimetre
VHF	very high frequency, line of sight radio communications between ship and shore and inter-ship
WMO	World Meteorological Organisation
XO	Executive Officer

Acknowledgements

My wife, Lynne, encouraged me to pen these memoirs. Frequently, our general chit-chat led into one of my 'salty' dits from my seafaring days with Blue Star and in the Royal Navy. She suggested I write them down as, surely, former shipmates and fellow mariners would find my tales and anecdotes of interest and trigger nostalgia for their own past maritime career. As I completed each draft chapter, Lynne avidly read and offered her critique. It was gratifying that, as a landlubber, she grasped the specifics of my life at sea.

I'm greatly indebted to David Smiley (ex-Blue Star, ex-Master, and marine consultant) and Mick Slater (retired Warrant Officer Survey Recorder).

I established email contact with David early on in this writing 'process' via the Blue Star Facebook site where he advertised his own memoirs. I can recommend his book, *Beyond the Blue Horizon – an Autobiography*, which is filled with interesting and enjoyable tales from his long and varied seafaring career. His feedback on each of my draft chapters was invaluable.

I've known and respected Mick Slater since 1987, when we served first in HMS *Fox* and in HMS *Hecla* some five or six years later. Mick also kindly read every draft chapter and, being ex-Navy, offered a critical eye on my merchant navy life, somewhat different from that we experienced in the Royal Navy.

An absolutely invaluable source was the 'Blue Star Line & Associated Companies' Facebook site. A dull title, certainly, but its content is utterly brilliant. Fascinating reading and wonderful old photographs posted by 'ancient mariners' from the 1950s until Blue Star Ship Management's sad demise. Some members' names were familiar, having sailed with a few and recognising others. The comments, reminiscences and exchanges are fulsome, brilliant memories and anecdotes of what we collectively recount as the 'good old days', the happiest days of our lives. I posted some questions and members responded with great information, invaluable to me in scribbling these memoirs.

An equally brilliant source was 'Blue Star Line on the Web' (www. bluestarline.org), created by Fraser Darrah (an ex-long-serving Blue Star

Chief Engineer), with a vast volume of information. He curated histories, details (dimensions, tonnages, capacities) and photos of every ship. His collated copies of *Gangway* (the company's in-house quarterly magazine) and the crew lists were of immense help to me, as names triggered nostalgia and reminiscences – as well as making my reporting more accurate. Sadly, he 'crossed the bar' a few years ago but his website is ably maintained by Jim Blake.

It was through the Blue Star Facebook site that I regained contact with a handful of old shipmates. Since leaving the company, I'd had no contact with anyone at Blue Star. I was delighted to have email correspondence with Billy Doran, Mike Finney, and Neil McBride nearly 40 years later.

I'm grateful to Graham Durrant, another contact from the Blue Star Facebook page. I bought his recent book *The Sea, the 70s and the Passage* and thoroughly enjoyed it – another seafarer's book I can recommend. His perspective was that of a late-teenage chap running away to sea as a 'baby' seaman about a decade before I went to sea. I learnt quite a bit in our chat via Facebook messenger about his own experience of writing, reviewing and self-publishing his memoirs.

The brilliant cover photograph is courtesy of John Kennedy, another ex-Blue Star man. It perfectly illustrates the gigantic size of Blue Star ship funnels, like none other in the merchant navy. The ABs on 'stages' or in the 'bosun's chair' are dwarfed by it. The Vesteys didn't miss a trick in advertising their presence. I doubt that today's inflexible health and safety culture allows painting or 'soogeeing' (washing) the funnel in this traditional way. John's photo (*Auckland Star*, 1962) captures a bygone era, when Blue Star dominated the world of refrigerated cargo shipping and its importance in global general cargo, heavy lift and container trades.

The back cover photograph of *Avelona Star* floodlit at night is courtesy of Philip Parker, another exceedingly helpful Blue Star Facebook member. That big blue star shone across the expanse of any port and guided you 'home' on dark nights in dodgy foreign ports.

A note of thanks, too, to Noel Payne for permission to use his poem 'A Sailor You Be' in the final chapter. As Lynne will attest, I'm not a fan of poetry, but his words encapsulate everything about being a merchant seaman. I wonder just how much of it is as pertinent today.

The accuracy of periods on board my ships was drawn from my Discharge Book. Dates quoted during each of my trips were collated by my mother. I sent a letter and at least one postcard to my parents from every port I visited. My mother plotted each voyage and dates in port on a map of the world. She gave it to me some years ago. Hence, I'm extremely grateful to her for this detail. I'm so pleased I kept it, together with my Discharge Book, Seaman's ID Card, hard-earned Second Mate's Certificate of Competency (Foreign-Going) and sundry other stuff, safely stowed away in a box at home.

Last, but definitely not least, I owe a great debt of gratitude to my late parents. They gave me (and my brother) a fantastic, happy childhood. They always encouraged and supported me to do whatever I wanted to do with my life, even when that meant I didn't see them for months, even years. They were truly wonderful. I miss them dearly.

1 Morning Watch, Mid-Atlantic

The ship was steaming west at ten knots in the tropical latitudes of the Atlantic Ocean when I came on watch at 0340. It was completely dark as I climbed the ladder from the accommodation deck to the bridge. Taking over responsibility for the ship as Officer of the Watch (OOW) was as smooth as the Captain's Night Orders were simple. The survey systems were operational and there were no shipping contacts within umpteen miles. Our handover completed, I bid my predecessor good night after a brief chat. He left the bridge. I was enveloped in darkness with a soothing, rhythmic soundtrack: the gentle hum of equipment; the ping of the echo-sounder; the heavy clunking of the plotter.

The change in temperature and humidity between my cabin and the bridge was noticeable as both had increased significantly. HMS *Hecla's* accommodation was air-conditioned, but on the bridge we usually shut it off and opened the bridge doors for easy access to the bridge-wings. My tropical uniform of white short-sleeved shirt, white shorts and sandals were comfortable.

I sipped the mug of tea I'd brought up with me from the pantry. You can't start the watch without a 'brew' (or coffee if preferred). I'm a tea man and my mug accumulated a healthy brown staining inside. I never washed it throughout a deployment so it got a 'draft chit' when we returned to Devonport after a few months.

I was not alone on the bridge. My watch mates were the Quartermaster (QM) and the Survey Recorder of the Watch (SR of the Watch, or just plain SR). We chatted; all was well with them both. We're looking forward to our next run ashore in Brazil. The only other sailor up and around is the On-Watch Stoker (engineering sailor) in the engine room (or mechanical garden). Once per watch, he visited the bridge to sign for 'rounds', confirming all was well in his hot, sweaty, noisy world. We don't have other contact with him unless something untoward occurs down below. At hourly intervals, I send the QM to conduct 'rounds' of the ship to ensure fire hasn't broken out in the accommodation and all is secure.

I continually checked the survey systems on the bridge. The Precision Depth Recorder (PDR) pinged away quite happily. The Automatic Data Logger (ADL) busily marked our track across the plotting table. The Transit satellite navigation system was due to provide a fix in 22 minutes. SINS (Ship's Inertial Navigation System) appeared to be behaving itself. Unseen several decks below, at the waterline and amidships, the mysterious Bell Gravimeter (BGM) silently gathered its data. As Gravity Officer, I was responsible for this prime system, assisted by the maintainer, a Petty Officer Weapons Electrical Artificer.

Most importantly, I continuously monitored the radar and kept a good visual look out for any surface contacts. As our location was tens, if not hundreds, of miles from merchant shipping routes, I'd be unlikely to see anything. We're very much off the beaten track as we plodded onwards, gathering invaluable data for use by Britain's Ministry of Defence and its American equivalent, the Department of Defense.

The morning watch (0400 to 0800) was by far my favourite. Although it was dark, it's pleasantly warm and comfortably humid in the tropics. I loved standing on the bridge wing, slowly sipping my tea, looking up at the clear black sky littered with millions of stars, their lustre unaffected by the light pollution you find ashore. The throbbing rhythm of the engines and generators resonated from the funnel, a lullaby that, perhaps strangely, complemented the tropical maritime environment and the twinkling blanket of stars surrounding our beautiful white ship with its buff funnel, gliding through the calm, warm Atlantic.

The QM sought my permission to do rounds and, as it was nearing 0500, he'll shake the chef (duty cook), to ensure he got out of his bunk and flashed up the galley. Meanwhile, I continued to check that the survey and navigation systems function satisfactorily, scan the radar, and take a good 360° look around the horizon for contacts.

Air temperature and humidity increased, astern the eastern sky lightened, the first hint of the pink of dawn in the cycle of astronomical, nautical and civil twilights to sunrise. In tropical latitudes at this time of year, nautical twilight occurs an hour or so before sunrise, which I'd calculated to be 0528, using the trusty *Nautical Almanac*. Ahead, in the west, the sky remained black, untainted by the gradual onset of dawn.

The rise in air temperature and humidity released a vapour from *Hecla's* teak decks, a distinct and pleasant aroma. I didn't know what chemical and physical reactions caused it, but I loved it. It complemented my keen lookout while I rested my elbows on the bridge wing dodger, sipping another brew, enveloped in a blanket of pleasant comfort.

The next hour slowly followed. The QM went off to do rounds again, the SR and I chatted about something and nothing. We both knew what to expect. The QM's triumphant return to the bridge with a large plate of bacon sarnies, provided by the duty chef. The SR 'wetted' (made) the tea and then we tucked into freshly baked rolls filled with soft, greasy bacon. Without doubt, these were the most enjoyable few minutes of the best watch on the bridge. Standing on the bridge wing, I savoured every mouthful of this treat, sipped my tea, and looked out over the empty, calm ocean with its gentle long low swell. The sun emerged from the previously undefined horizon, lightening the sky from pink to orange, and became a shiny gold orb, the sea glistened with its brilliance. The warmth and aroma from the teak deck pervaded. Crikey, life was good!

Sadly, these luxurious minutes were soon over. It was the last stretch of the watch. Life will gradually get a little busier. The odd bloke will emerge for a gentle jog around the upper deck, carefully avoiding becoming a casualty by banging his head on the many sharp and solid protrusions of vents and pipework. A few may work out in the hangar or on the flight deck. The occasional curious individual may visit the bridge to see where we are – not much different from yesterday, as the chart covered almost the entire Atlantic Ocean.

I prepared my script for calling the Captain at 0630. It's a standard format laid out in the Captain's Standing Orders so I just have to fill in the blanks and ensure my report is clear, accurate and punctual. After which, the Executive Officer (XO) might pop up to the bridge before taking his breakfast in the Wardroom. We'll have a brief chat about the night and our progress. That won't take long.

The next big event was 'Call the Hands' at 0700. Although it's the QM's responsibility to perform this ritual, if his piping is poor, the OOW (me), will also cop any grief and ribbing. It's usually wise for the QM to practise his bosun's call on the bridge wing before it's due. On this occasion, the QM's piping was perfect, so no repercussions.

Finally, our reliefs turned up and we handed over, which didn't take too long. I vacated the bridge and headed to the Wardroom for a hearty fat-boy breakfast, my job done until my next watch. I've a day's work to do in the Chartroom from 0900.

During quiet night watches, there's plenty of time for introspection. I often pondered on how I came to be on board HMS *Hecla*, conducting a geophysical survey in the Atlantic Ocean as a qualified hydrographic survey officer of the Royal Navy – proud of my uniform, the cap badge, the traditions and glorious history of the 'Andrew', and my chosen sub-specialisation as a 'Droggy' (hydrographic specialist).

The answer lies within the following chapters. I hope you'll enjoy accompanying me as we navigate my tales and travels across the globe. We'll meet a motley crew of interesting, exciting, eccentric and odd personalities and characters, civilians and naval folk. Some became lifelong friends. Others were 'ships in the night' as we interacted and cohabited on board for varying periods of time. Many more were acquaintances with whom I spent only a limited time before the inevitable separation symptomatic of a seafarer's transient working life. Nevertheless, occasional and chance meetings thereafter were always joyful, with much reminiscing as we 'swung the lamp' or 'pulled up a bollard to spin a yarn or two'.

My travels were truly worldwide: all continents (except the frozen wastes of the polar regions – far too cold for me!); numerous crossings of the Atlantic, Indian and Pacific Oceans; several transits of the Suez and Panama Canals and the Kiel Canal – and one through the little-known Cape Cod Canal; nearly 60 countries and countless ports. I lived overseas in four countries and served in five navies. In recounting these memoirs, I realised that not only had I been extremely fortunate throughout, but also that I'd thoroughly enjoyed every moment of my life and career. Truly, I feel I'm a very lucky bloke.

So, 'let go for'ard, let go aft', full steam ahead into my seafaring life, which began in my childhood.

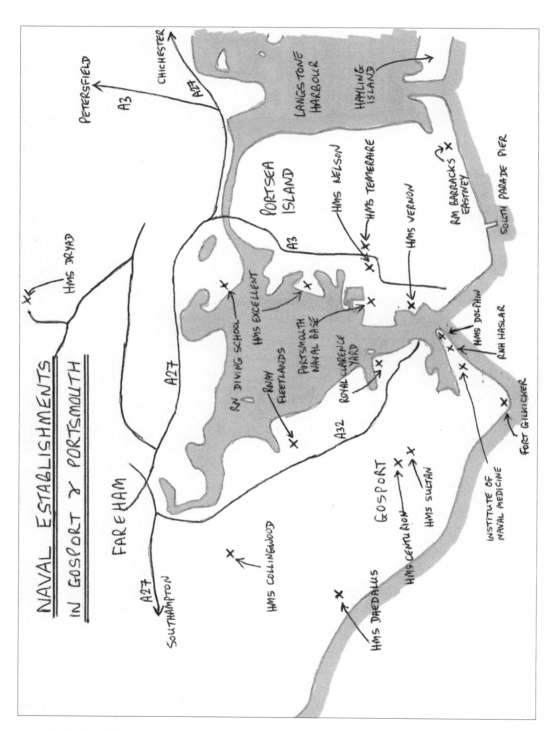

Fig 2.1 Naval establishments in Gosport and Portsmouth

2 Growing Up in Gosport
My First Taste of the Sea

Fig 2.2 *Vesta* (Photo © Alan Murray-Rust (cc-by-sa/2.0))

Fig 2.3 *Gosport Queen* (Photo © Peter Trimming (cc-by-sa/2.0))

Memoirs always begin with a few mundane facts. I was born on 27 November 1958 in Gosport, a quiet little borough across the harbour from Portsmouth, with an economy largely reliant on the Navy. A map of the time shows numerous Naval establishments in the Portsmouth/Gosport area. Some still exist, having evolved over the last 60-odd years of my life. Sadly, others have disappeared.

In Gosport were HMS Sultan (School of Marine Engineering), HMS Dolphin (home to submarines and its distinctive Submarine Escape Tower for training submariners), Royal Naval Hospital Haslar (adjacent to Dolphin), Institute of Naval Medicine (hidden along quiet Fort Road in Alverstoke – what do they do in there?), HMS Centurion (the Navy's drafting, pay and accounting centre from 1970 to 1994), and HMS Daedalus (naval air station along the coast at Lee-on-the-Solent).

On the A32, halfway to Fareham on the right-hand side, was Royal Naval Aircraft Yard Fleetlands ('proud to be the largest helicopter repair facility in Europe' for many years). Further along and to the left lay HMS Collingwood (School of Weapon Engineering at the time). Along the A27 near Portchester was the Defence Diving School on Horsea Island.

The A3 took us onto Portsea Island, with HMS Excellent on Whale Island on the right, home to HMS Phoenix (firefighting school) and several 'lodger units'. Portsmouth Naval Base and Dockyard dominated the east side of the harbour. HMS Nelson adjoined it and was the Naval Base's administrative and accommodation centre. Further along was HMS Temeraire (home of Navy physical training) on Pitt Street, before its move to swanky new premises at Burnaby Road in 1988. Down-harbour, past Portsmouth Harbour railway station, was HMS Vernon (mine clearance diving school), demolished and replaced by Gunwharf Shopping Centre in 1996.

Portsdown Hill, overlooking Portsmouth and Gosport, was occupied by a couple of Admiralty research establishments. In Southwick, on the backside of the hill, was HMS Dryad, the School of Maritime Operations where all warfare training was conducted, until 2004 when it moved to HMS Collingwood. Beyond, near Petersfield, was HMS Mercury, the Navy's Signals School.

My mother was born in Portsmouth and worked in a local timber merchant's office. After marriage, she continued working until her two sons came along: me first, followed by James in 1960. When James and I were old enough to get to school by ourselves, Mum returned to full-time employment as a clerical officer at the Royal Naval Armament Depot (RNAD) in Elson.

RNADs stored and supplied the Royal Navy with munitions. There were four in Gosport in those days: Bedenham, Elson, Frater and Priddy's Hard.

My father completed his apprenticeship as a fitter and turner in a small company in Portsmouth. He enjoyed his national service in the Royal Engineers in Malaya and Singapore in 1950 to 1952 (lucky fellow), busying himself in the workshops and playing a lot of football for his unit. He worked in Portsmouth Dockyard until moving to HMS Sultan in the 1960s to serve as a civilian instructional officer until he retired.

Dad was a keen racket sportsman and introduced us to badminton, tennis, and squash. My first contact with Navy sailors was playing with and against them in doubles at Sultan's badminton club, which Dad founded. James and I joined Brodrick Badminton Club and Alverstoke Lawn Tennis Club, where our racket-wielding skills were honed. When I started to play squash, Dad fixed up games for me with several of his sailors.

Dad spent a lot of time with Sultan's physical training instructors (PTIs) and involved himself in sport at the establishment. Annually, he officiated at Sultan's boxing competition. I enjoyed these great evenings. The entire 'ship's company' attended and vociferously voiced support for their classmate during his fight. It was a formal, well-organised and managed event. Sultan's officers were present, dressed in mess kit at ringside, sailors in Number 1 uniform sat behind. Everyone had a great evening except the poor novices: absolutely hopeless at boxing, punched to a bloody pulp and helped from the ring. The Medical Officer and his staff patched up the damaged amateurs, and carted them off to sick bay or Haslar Hospital depending on their injuries.

Like all armed forces establishments in this glorious era, Sultan annually held an Open Day in the summer and a Firework Display on or close to 5 November. These were always well attended by naval personnel, their families and the public. My father always manned a stall on Open Day. I helped out a bit, but wandered off to see the demonstrations and displays. In the workshops, the deck splattered with poo from the pigeons perched on the cross-girders supporting the roof, I was fascinated by the vast old hangar filled with rows of lathes. Sailors demonstrated their use, showed the skill required to create things from a chunk of metal. Dad's Tool Room was also open and I glimpsed what he did for a job. However, Sultan couldn't compete with the Dockyard's Navy Days or Daedalus' Air Day. Nevertheless, such vivid memories of Sultan impregnated my mind.

Every August Bank Holiday weekend, Navy Days were held. All RN and visiting foreign warships were open to visitors. Tours were confined to the upper deck, but guns and missile mountings impressed a boy like me. Stalls and exhibits were arrayed around the Dockyard, with all sorts of kit and demonstrations of various skills and specialisations. I went annually and collected hundreds of leaflets and souvenirs.

In July, HMS Daedalus held its Air Day. I enjoyed its focus on the Fleet Air Arm, including static displays of aircraft and helicopters. They fascinated me, as I was enthralled by NASA's Apollo space programme. There was always an air display or two, often the faultless Red Arrows. One year, a RAF Lightning turned up. Crikey, that certainly was off the scale for beauty, power and machismo. I stared in awe and wonder as this glistening silver beast took off and went vertical at max power. The magnificent roar of its jet engines at full throttle, afterburner flames issuing from its twin exhausts, it disappeared high into the wild blue yonder. Chapter 9 of James Hamilton-Paterson's *Empire of the Clouds* describes the Lightning's development and brilliantly evokes the thrill of seeing it perform at air shows.

My education started at St Mary's Roman Catholic Primary School, Gosport. I enjoyed school and passed entrance exams for St John's College, Southsea, an independent, fee-paying boy's school. I started there in September 1966

A vivid memory was morning break. The class milk monitor doled out to each classmate a glass bottle of milk – a third of a pint, supplied free by the government to all schoolchildren. The crate was left on the fire escape outside the classroom. In winter, the milk was too chilled; in summer, the milk was almost lukewarm, curdled and tasted foul. Sometimes the silver foil top had been pecked and pierced by birds. Yuk!

St John's was an excellent school and gave me my first regular taste of the sea. My mother dropped me and Anthony Walsh, who lived near us, at Gosport ferry pontoon. Anthony and I crossed Pompey harbour by ferry and walked to Lower School, situated outside the rear gate to 'main school'. We spent our bus money in a little sweet shop in Elm Grove on Black Jacks, Fruit Salads, Parma Violets, Refreshers, and those funny Flying Saucers of sherbet encased in rice paper.

I enjoyed the ferry. In those days, there were four identical ones – *Vadne, Vesta, Vita, Venus* – with an open bridge, open upper deck seating and a small seating area below the upper deck. The ferry was always full as Anthony and I travelled at the same time as the sailors and dockyard maties. Back then, working men wore trousers, shirts, ties and jackets, often topped with a cap. They stowed their bikes right up forward against the chains and stanchions on the forecastle. Health and Safety hadn't been 'invented', so there was risk in sending two eight-year-old boys on such dangerous voyages twice per day, five days per week.

Boarding and disembarking was dicey if there was a bit of a chop in the harbour. The ferries nestled against the pontoon with only the rake of the bow, with an increasing gap between ferry and pontoon the further aft you went. The independent movement of ferry and pontoon meant potential for accidents aplenty. Boarding was leisurely but disembarkation could be frantic as blokes wanted to get off as swiftly as possible to get to work or home. I loved standing as far for'ard as possible, bikes permitting. I was invigorated by the relative wind and sea spray in my face as the bow plunged into the waves. I rammed my school cap hard onto my head and kept a firm grip of my satchel. When my shoes dried, a telltale white wavy salt stain appeared on the toecaps.

During my second year at St John's, the four sisters were replaced by two swanky new ferries: *Gosport Queen* and *Portsmouth Queen*. In comparison, they were large, luxurious and innovative. The bow was rounded and enclosed and fitted with wooden bench seating. There were separate embarkation gates for pedestrians and cyclists. The port side was for bikes and riders, the starboard side was a foot-passenger saloon with another seating area a deck below. There was further seating on the top deck and aft. The crew occupied an enclosed bridge. A propeller each in bow and stern made the *Queens* highly manoeuvrable. But I sorely missed standing in the fo'c'sle chains getting weather-beaten and spray-soaked.

From the ferry, it was impossible to miss the Dockyard and its impressive length of wharf, which stretched north to the upper reaches of Pompey harbour. In those heady days of my schoolboy sea-time, the wharf was always filled with Royal Navy warships: destroyers, frigates, aircraft carriers. Britain had a Navy then, deployed worldwide on missions, tasks, commitments to NATO and other allies. Foreign warships frequently visited Pompey and usually berthed at this visible, exposed end of the wharf, easily seen by ferry passengers.

My time at St John's Lower School neared its end. I passed the eleven-plus (exams in maths, English and verbal reasoning) but chose to 'go comprehensive'. Harold Wilson's government was determined to convert all independent fee-paying schools, like St John's College, into comprehensives.

In September 1970, I started at Brune Park School. The Prideaux-Brune family donated land to the local education authority to establish the school, which was founded in 1965 and situated at the opposite end of Military Road to HMS Sultan. Before the school was built, it was a grass field. As we lived in nearby Elson, Dad, James and I occasionally went there to play football.

I had seven very happy years at Brune Park. It was an enormous campus with separate departmental blocks for music, metalwork/woodwork, domestic science, art and humanities. With over 2,000 pupils, it dwarfed St John's. The school's catchment area included the adjacent, large, naval married quarters estate. Perhaps another subliminal influence upon me was the turnover of pupils as their fathers posted into and then out of Naval establishments and Pompey-based ships. The transitory nature of a Royal Navy career.

By 1977, I was in the Upper VI form and A-levels loomed, with the utter tedium of revision a constant presence. I submitted my UCCA (Universities Central Council on Admissions, today's UCAS) form to study Geography. I attained B in Pure Maths and C in Geography and was delighted to be off to the University of Newcastle-Upon-Tyne. It was somewhere I'd never visited and knew nothing about except that it was 340 miles (550 km) 'up norf' and Newcastle United played at St James' Park. The university halls of residence were full, but they explained the process for finding accommodation and I secured university-approved lodgings in Whitley Bay.

I had an immensely happy, loving and stable childhood. I was subconsciously heavily influenced by the ever-present warships and submarines. The constant visibility and presence of the Navy engulfed Gosport, Fareham and Portsmouth. Frequent contact with sailors through badminton and squash at Sultan and daily interaction with 'Navy brats' at school further contributed to an intense subliminal effect on my childhood and shaped my future. It's a surprise, then, that I didn't join the Navy straight after school, like some of my peers. I did eventually join as a mature officer entrant after a somewhat circuitous route of several years. Why? I don't know!

I enjoyed the summer of 1977, much tennis at Alverstoke and squash at Sultan. I got my first 'real' job on a building site at RNAD Elson. Although, as a schoolboy, I'd earned money as a shelf filler at the local Spar. Wimpey was contracted to build two pairs of armament stores. These were monstrous buildings, with very thick, reinforced concrete walls, floors and roofs, plus a curved blast wall across the entrance in case of an accidental ordnance explosion inside the building.

I had a great summer on site as 'chain boy' – the building surveyor's assistant. I lugged Graham's tripod, theodolite, level and staff all over the site to where he was working. He directed me where to stand with the levelling staff to complete his measurements. I moved little wooden pegs slightly to left or right so the ground markings for excavations and foundations were precisely located via his theodolite. It was fascinating. Perhaps another subliminal influence towards eventually becoming a Navy hydrographic surveyor? It was a great summer, being paid for manual labour in fresh air and sunshine.

In early October 1977, I moved to Newcastle. I packed two large grips and a little rucksack from which my wellington boots protruded. My mother thought they'd be handy in wild, windy and wet northern England. Your mum knows best! It was an adventure as the rail route took me from Portsmouth Harbour to Waterloo, across London on the Underground to Kings Cross, then to Newcastle. On my own and without a safety net!

The journey went well. The trains were punctual, Underground travel was easy to follow but slow as I carted my luggage up and down large escalators and along endless tiled corridors. I arrived in Newcastle in darkness. I caught a local train to Whitley Bay and trekked to my lodgings in Beach Avenue, one of many streets of three-bedroom, terraced houses in the town.

I was welcomed by the landlady, Mrs Graham, and her husband. She was a housewife, he was a hairdresser and they had two small sons. I met the other two students sharing the digs: Clive Wilkinson from Halifax, and Eddie (with an unpronounceable Polish surname) from Scunthorpe. Eddie had arrived first and had chosen the single bedroom. Clive and I shared the twin bedroom. We three had our own sitting/dining room, with a television, downstairs at the back of the house. We were all freshers: Eddie was a geology student, Clive a fellow geographer.

Winters were harsh in Newcastle. In November and December, our bedroom was bitterly cold and without central heating. An electricity meter was connected to a small electric heater. Each morning, Clive and I took turns to leap from bed, feed 50p into the meter, switch on the heater and get back under the duvet until the room had lost its chill. Sometimes there was ice on the inside of our window.

Student life settled into a routine of commuting, lectures, study in the library, and occasional tutorials with our assigned tutors. Mine was Dr Hal Lister, an eminent glaciologist. Born in Keighley in 1921, he graduated from King's College, which later became Newcastle University. He led a pioneering expedition to Iceland in 1948 and was a glaciologist in the British North Greenland Expedition (1952–54) and a member of the Commonwealth Trans-Antarctic Expedition led by Sir Vivian Fuchs, the first overland crossing of Antarctica in 1955–58. Thereafter, he remained an academic, lecturer and tutor at the University of Newcastle-Upon-Tyne.

At the end of our first term, Eddie, Clive and I moved into Castle Leazes Halls of Residence, a complex of three towers of single rooms, each tower had its own refectory to provide meals. It was a significant improvement on Whitley Bay as we were now only a half mile (800 m) walk to university and the city centre, and a quarter of a mile (400 m) from St James' Park. Importantly, the rooms had central heating. It was easier to develop friendships with our classmates, make new friends among the Hall's residents, and attend student parties in flats in nearby Benton and Jesmond.

Keith Bothamley, Mike Douglass and I frequently stood at the Gallowgate End in St James' Park to watch Newcastle United's dismal performances. At the end of the 1977/78 season, the Magpies were relegated to the Second Division. We were part the smallest crowd ever at St James' Park (7,986) for the midweek clash with Norwich City on 26 April 1978. Conversely, we were three of the 42,167 crowd to witness Blyth Spartans' magnificent performance in a Fifth Round FA Cup replay against Wrexham. Non-league Blyth earned a draw at Wrexham, but sadly Spartans lost this replay. Their star player, Alan Shoulder, transferred to Newcastle the following season.

Clive and I remained in Leazes until the end of our second year. For our final year, he moved into a flat with his girlfriend and other friends from Leazes. I moved to a university flat in Gosforth. Kirkley Close was a three-storey quadrangle of flats, each accommodated six students – a bedroom each, a kitchen and two bathrooms. Kirkley Close was a short walk to the Great North Road to catch the bus to the university and city centre.

I knew most of my flatmates: Jim and Steve were fellow geographers; Ross was joint geography and surveying; John was general science and surveying. I didn't know Nigel (biology) as he was one of Ross' mates from Ethel Williams Hall (aka Brothel Bill's). We got on well together. A quartet of us played bridge (badly) and we occasionally cooked up a big Sunday roast together. Jim kept the chicken bones in a saucepan afterwards so he could make soup from them. Not once in our year together did he ever make that soup.

The flat above was occupied by six girls. We used to bump into one or two of them en route to the bus stop. One evening our television blew up so we went upstairs and gatecrashed the girls' TV. Luckily, they didn't seem to mind and I met Sue. Years later, we married.

It was the punk era, so there were many rowdy concerts to attend, with beer being swilled and spilt plus energetic pogo-ing. The Police appeared at the University Refectory, just prior to their making it big with British, then global, success. Like the majority of students, I listened to Annie Nightingale's Radio One show every Sunday afternoon. Great music, great times!

I joined the Officers' Training Corps (OTC), the Territorial Army for students. Despite my 'naval upbringing', I harboured an interest in joining the Army. The OTC was a good opportunity to get a taste of it, acknowledging it probably wasn't too accurate an experience of the 'real' Army. The OTC had three sections: Infantry, Royal Armoured Corps and Artillery. I chose the Infantry. I rather enjoyed the weekly drill nights with marching, stripping the self-loading rifle, Sterling submachine gun and Browning pistol, and so on. On selected weekends the OTC collectively headed off to deploy into the field at Otterburn Ranges. I'd never experienced such cold. I couldn't feel my fingers or toes, and was cold to the very core. Bloody miserable. Nevertheless, I continued to attend and enjoyed the summer camps.

Each summer, a fortnight was spent at camps and ranges elsewhere in UK. Our first one was near Arbroath, on the North Sea coast, east of Dundee. The barracks were reasonably good and food plentiful. Our OTC staff directed us in a variety of exercises, including fieldcraft and section attacks with blank rounds. A night attack exercise degenerated into a free-for-all fist-fight between the two sides.

Summer camp the following year was on Salisbury Plain. This proved rather different from Arbroath as a large NATO or British exercise was underway and our OTC was designated as 'enemy'. We spent the fortnight as partners-in-crime with the Infantry Demonstration Battalion. This was based at Warminster and designed to act as enemy for units at the nearby School of Infantry and Sandhurst and any other nefarious tasks. They were all rufty-tufty incomprehensible Scotsmen, riven with incessant foul language and permanent aggression. However, as we were on the same side, they sort of welcomed us into their fold. I enjoyed that fortnight as we were in the field, perpetually on the move, conducting section attacks, setting up defensive positions, digging shell-scrapes, building bivouacs. Salisbury Plain teemed with soldiers, tanks, and armoured personnel carriers, as helicopters and aircraft buzzed overhead. It helped that the weather was sunny, warm, and dry. My highlight was a helicopter assault. We clambered into a handful of Wessex helicopters, took off, hugged the ground at a very low level, whizzed through the countryside along contours and below hillcrests until we landed. We swiftly disembarked using the method we'd been taught and formed an all-round perimeter defence until the helicopters took off. Brilliant fun.

In June 1980, I graduated from the University of Newcastle-Upon-Tyne with BSc (Honours) Geography. It was a distinct end to an important phase of my life. Newcastle gave me an academic education, an education in life skills, and an experience in independence and self-reliance. I also met a wide spectrum of people from all parts of Britain and a sprinkling of foreign students. Overall, I had a brilliant time. My parents drove up to attend the graduation ceremony and were very proud of their eldest son.

GRADUATE ENTRY SCHEME

CURRENT TERMS AND CONDITIONS OF EMPLOYMENT

(Effective - 1st November 1977)

TITLE   Graduate Entrants will be known as Officer Trainees.

SALARY   Total consolidated salary for Officer Trainees will
be £3828

Examples of subsequent starting salaries are as
follows:-

3rd Officer holding a 2nd Mate's Certificate of
Competency £4524

2nd Officer holding a 1st Mate's Certificate of
Competency £6000

Chief Officer holding a Master's Certificate of
Competency   ..   ..   .. £7824 to £8928 on seniority.

Master holding a Master's Certificate of Competency
..   .. £9648 to £11652 on seniority.

LEAVE   Paid leave is earned at the rate of 183 days per year
served i.e. one day's leave for two days worked.   Leave
is not earned during shore College courses.

UNIFORM   Officer Trainees will be expected to provide themselves
with a full outfit of Merchant Navy Uniform.   Their
uniform will carry no insignia of rank.

**UNIFORM
ALLOWANCE**   An allowance of £60 will be paid to Officer Trainees
on entry to assist them in the purchase of uniform.
Subsequently this allowance will be paid annually in
January but a second payment will not be made until new
entrants have served for at least 12 months.

M.N.A.O.A.   All Graduate Entrants will be required to become
members of the Merchant Navy and Airline Officers
Association.

MEDICAL   All entrants will be required to pass a medical
examination to be arranged conveniently with the
Merchant Navy Establishment Administration.

PENSION   Officer Trainees will be obliged to join the Company's
Contributory Pension Fund in which the Employer's
contributions match those of the Employee.

JAN.78/ALT

Fig 3.1 My terms and conditions of employment

3 Off to Sea with Blue Star Ship Management Ltd

In about February and March in my final year at university, the Milk Round occurred. National and multinational companies and conglomerates toured Britain's universities to explain what they do and to attract students to apply for their respective graduate entry schemes.

I still didn't know what I wanted to do for a career so I spent time in the Careers Office thumbing through brochures and lists of companies programmed to visit Newcastle. After a while, they all seemed the same and not very interesting graduate entry, trainee manager programmes. I sort of went through the motions. My parents never pestered me with endless questions about 'what are you going to do?', 'have you been looking for a career?'. Thankfully, they just let me get on with it in my own prevaricating, obfuscating, indecisive way.

The upshot was I lost interest in becoming an infantry officer, no longer attracted to spending my life grubbing around in mud and discomfort for a living, at risk of being shot or blown up.

Somehow, somewhere, I came across an advertisement for Blue Star Ship Management (BSSM) and going to sea in the Merchant Navy. Now that looked pretty exciting: sail the world, visit all sorts of interesting places, and get paid for it. I submitted my application form and was invited for interview at Albion House, BSSM's headquarters in James Street, Liverpool, within sight of the famous Liver Building and Pierhead.

The interview was with a selection board of the Cadet Training Manager, a serving Master, a serving Chief Officer, and a lecturer from Liverpool Polytechnic (whose relevance became clear later). I must have impressed as I was offered a job as Officer Trainee (O/T), commencing September 1980. I was to be paid the princely sum of £3,828 per annum.

Albion House was an impressive building. Its red and white brick and granite exterior were of such architectural merit that it was eventually listed as Grade II* in 1952. Completed in late 1897, it was named Oceanic House and served as the head office of Oceanic Steam

Navigation Company Ltd. Better known as the White Star Line, the
company was almost at its peak and, by 1912, included *Titanic* in its
fleet. Thereafter, White Star Line fell into decline particularly in the
recession and slump of 1927, and passed to Royal Mail Steam Packet
Co. which crashed in 1932. Oceanic House was largely unused until
post-World War II when, renamed Pacific Building, it became the joint
head office of Pacific Steam Navigation Company and Royal Mail
Lines. Under the umbrella of Furness, Withy & Company, another
famous British shipping line, it was empty by 1973 as companies moved
to alternative offices. Fortunately, the Vestey Group decided to base its
ship management operations as BSSM Ltd in Liverpool and acquired
the building in 1975, renaming it Albion House.

Fig 3.2 Albion House (Bill Houghton Boreham)

Few non-Blue Star veterans will have ever heard of either BSSM or Blue Star Line (BSL). Older readers will doubtless remember Dewhurst the Master Butcher, a branch of which was found in almost every British high street at the time. Blue Star Line and Dewhurst were directly linked through the very wealthy Vestey family.

In 1876, the founder, William Vestey, was sent to work in Chicago stockyards to scout for business opportunities. Surprised at the quantities of 'wasted' meat, he teamed up with his brother Edmund in the UK and established a factory to can this surplus as corned beef and export it to Britain. William and Edmund quickly realised that imported meat could be even more valuable if it were fresh rather than canned and tapped into the vast supplies of beef in the Americas to meet demand in the UK. The invention of the ammonia compression plant made refrigerated shipments possible and the Vestey fortunes took a great leap forward.

By the early 20th century, the Vesteys had cold storage businesses in Liverpool, Manchester, London, Hull, and an outpost in pre-revolutionary Russia. They imported eggs from China (40,000 tonnes annually at the outbreak of World War II), and meat from New Zealand, Venezuela, and Brazil. In Britain, they founded JH Dewhurst, which became the UK's largest chain of retail butchers by the early 1990s.

In 1911, they expanded into meat production, processing and distribution, with pastoral properties and meat-works in Venezuela, Brazil, Argentina, Australia, and New Zealand. In London, they bought stalls in Smithfield Market. Three years later, they established the North Australia Meat Company in Darwin and acquired Wave Hill Station (1,200 square miles) in Australia's Northern Territory.

When Prime Minister David Lloyd George refused the Vesteys' request for income tax exemption, the brothers decamped to Buenos Aires in 1915 to avoid paying UK income tax. This enabled the family to legally avoid an estimated total of £88 million in UK tax, until the loophole was closed in 1991.

By the 1920s, Union Cold Storage was the largest cold storage company in the world with 30,000 employees, 450,000 cattle on ranches in Australia, South America, and South Africa, 20% of Britain's frozen meat imports, and a third of the country's cold storage capacity. The Vesteys were the second wealthiest family in the UK after the Royal Family.

A Sunday Times investigation revealed that, in 1978, the Dewhurst chain paid £10 tax on a profit of more than £2.3 million. In my era at BSSM, Edmund's grandson, also Edmund, and his cousin, Lord Samuel, were at the helm.

In the early 1900s, a range of possibilities for food refrigeration became increasingly apparent. Edmund and William Vestey founded BSL in 1909 to transport their foodstuffs from source to market and cut out the middleman. A decade or so later, it was the largest refrigerated fleet in the world. With their distinctive outsized funnels, Blue Star ships were instantly recognisable throughout the world. Initially, BSL vessel names were prefixed with *Brod*. By 1912–13, the fleet's eight vessels were also trading with China and Singapore. Like other British shipping companies, BSL operated throughout World War I and its casualty list included *Brodmead* and *Brodholme*.

In 1916, the South American service commenced. The fleet grew to 15 ships by 1918, when *star* suffixes were adopted, exemplified by *Albionstar, Royalstar,* and *Doricstar*. In the early 1920s the BSL fleet was composed entirely of refrigerated ships (reefers), trading between the UK and Continental ports, South America, China, and North America's Pacific coast.

The first phase of new-build vessels focused on significantly increasing BSL's services to and from the River Plate. In 1926–27 four new 15-knot, 11,000 gross ton reefers were launched for this 'chilled meat service' (*Africstar, Napierstar, Rodneystar,* and *Stuartstar*). In 1929 the star suffix became a separate word and the seven ships were renamed *Albion Star, Royal Star, Doric Star, Afric Star, Napier Star, Rodney Star,* and *Stuart Star*.

Simultaneously, BSL entered the passenger-liner trade, and opened a first-class, luxury passenger service between London, Lisbon, the Canary Islands, Brazil, Uruguay and Argentina with five new twin-screw, 16-knot vessels of 14,000 to 15,000 gross tons. These 'A'-boats (*Almeda Star, Avila Star, Avelona Star, Andalucia Star,* and *Arandora Star*) were soon recognised as the very essence of luxury travel and became firm favourites with the travelling public. They also carried chilled and frozen meat. By the mid-1920s, BSL had an excellent reputation for its passenger comfort and enhanced its well-established name for skilled transportation of refrigerated goods and other cargo.

In 1930, *Arandora Star* had her cargo spaces refitted to focus on cruising and trebled her passenger-carrying capacity. Throughout the 1930s, she was renowned worldwide for her outstanding accommodation and service. Celebrities enjoyed the luxury and relaxation of cruises to the Northern Capitals and the Land of the Midnight Sun in summer, to the Mediterranean in spring and autumn, and to the West Indies or Honolulu in winter.

During this period, BSL's second phase of expansion occurred by opening services to New Zealand, Australia, South Africa, and the West Indies. This necessitated an extensive new-build programme from 1930 to the outbreak of war in 1939. BSL regularly took delivery of new vessels, built to their own specification and embodying the most up-to-date shipbuilding techniques of the famous yards that constructed them. Cammell Laird at Birkenhead built *Sultan Star, Dunedin Star*, and *Brisbane Star*; Belfast's Harland & Wolff delivered *Sydney Star, Australia Star, Imperial Star, Auckland Star, Wellington Star, Melbourne Star, New Zealand Star*, and *Empire Star*. Their names indicated BSL's new sphere of operations and its contribution to the world of commerce in general and to Britain's wealth in particular. In the late-1930s, the West Indian and North Pacific Coast trade was strengthened with three more ships built by Bartrams of Sunderland (*California Star, Canadian Star*, and *Columbia Star*).

During World War II, most Blue Star vessels were commandeered by the British Government to deliver much-needed food to the UK. The ships were fast and sailed unaccompanied, but casualties inevitably happened. Of the new tonnage constructed in the fleet expansion of 1926–29, every passenger and cargo vessel built in 1926–27 was sunk. *Brisbane Star* was the sole surviving Cammell Laird ship. All but three of those built at Harland & Wolff were lost, and two of the Pacific Coast vessels were sunk. Famously, *Doric Star* was sunk by Germany's *Graf Spee*, while *Arandora Star* was lost to a U-boat off the west coast of Ireland. Tragically, *Dunedin Star* went aground on Namibia's Skeleton Coast in 1942. Her dramatic story was retold in Simon Winchester's excellent book *Atlantic. Blue Star Line at War 1939–45* by Captain Taprell Dorling, RN (aka Taffrail) is a cracking account of Blue Star's service during the War.

Melbourne Star and *Brisbane Star* participated in the famous Malta convoy in mid-August 1942, which included the tanker *Ohio*. The convoy survived relentless attacks from Axis aircraft and limped into Valetta with vital general cargo and *Ohio's* oil. As a boy, I read *Malta Convoy*, a thrilling account by Peter Shankland and Anthony Hunter (Max Hastings' *Operation Pedestal*, is a 2021 account of the same convoy). *Melbourne Star* and *Brisbane Star* were damaged by enemy bombs, but survived. The former was sunk by a U-boat in April 1943, the latter survived the war and was broken up in 1963.

Blue Star Line served with distinction, losing 29 ships from an initial fleet of 38, and 646 Blue Star crew were killed in action. It was only in recent years that the Merchant Navy's invaluable contribution to Britain's war effort was recognised. Long overdue, in my opinion.

Post-1945, with less than a third of its pre-war fleet as a nucleus, Blue Star Line began to rebuild. To replace the lost luxurious passenger liners, the South American passenger service resumed with four vessels built in 1947–48 (*Argentina Star, Brasil Star, Uruguay Star*, and *Paraguay Star*). They carried 68 passengers and a cargo of chilled beef on a seven-week round trip between the UK and South America and maintained Blue Star's high standard of luxury service and cuisine. This traditional passenger service ceased in 1972. The company continued to replace war-time losses and its fleet eventually exceeded 40 ships.

To meet the challenges of changing patterns of world trade, four new vessels (*America Star, Halifax Star, Montreal Star*, and *New York Star*) entered service between 1962 and 1965. They traded between Australia and North America's east coast on a strict schedule, and normally didn't return to the UK.

In 1965, a new *Australia Star* joined the fleet, equipped with a Stülcken derrick to ship very heavy cargo. Capable of lifting 300 tons, it was the largest ship-mounted derrick in the world at the time.

Two years later, three more new vessels were delivered. Two bore names from Blue Star's earlier years (*New Zealand Star and Timaru Star*), plus *Southland Star*, emphasising the important trade links between the UK and New Zealand.

The Austasia Line was formed in 1952 to operate services between Singapore, Indonesia, Malaysia, and Australia. Blue Star acquired the Lamport & Holt Line (L&H) and the Booth Line in the 1960s. This allowed ships from one company to be re-badged to another in the group, depending on evolving trade routes – for example, Booth Line's new ship *Hubert* was renamed *Malaysia* to join the Austasia Line service.

In the 1950s, *Adelaide Star, Wellington Star, Tasmania Star*, and *Auckland Star* were a new class of four large refrigerated cargo liners carrying 12 passengers. For many years, *Adelaide Star* was the largest refrigerated cargo ship in the world, with seven hatches totalling 602,991 cubic feet (17,075 cubic metres) of reefer space. When *English Star* and *Scottish Star* joined the fleet, they made this half dozen vessels the last of Blue Star's 12-passenger reefers. Blue Star's long-renowned luxurious passenger service sadly ended in the mid-1970s.

Containerisation loomed. In 1969, Blue Star, with Ellerman Lines and Port Line, formed Associated Container Transportation (ACT) and, in 1971, inaugurated a new service between Tilbury and Australian ports. This offered a weekly service to meet the actual and anticipated demand for containerisation. When I joined, Blue Star managed and crewed four of these ships. Capable of carrying 1,334 TEUs (20-foot equivalent unit containers), the first three were inspiringly named *ACT 1*, *ACT 4*, *ACT 5*. In 1977, they were joined by *ACT 7*, a much larger container ship of 2,485 TEU capacity.

In 1971, *California Star* and *Columbia Star* were purpose-built as container ships to supersede the 'conventional' ships that previously operated the service between Europe and North America's west coast.

This unwieldy conglomeration of shipping lines led to the creation of Blue Star Ship Management (BSSM) in 1975. All ships, regardless of their house flag, were now under one umbrella organisation.

Six new-generation 'A'-boats, built at Smith's Dock, Middlesbrough, entered service in 1976 (*Afric Star*, *Almeda Star*, *Andalucia Star*, *Avelona Star*, *Almeria Star*, and *Avila Star*). They were refrigerated fruit carriers, primarily for bananas, and fitted with side (banana) doors for loading in Central American ports. Initially, they had successful long-term contracts to carry bananas from Costa Rica, Honduras, and Columbia to the US East Coast and European ports. Later, refrigerated cargoes included deciduous and citrus fruits and frozen meat.

BSSM entered the heavy-lift environment via Starman Shipping, a joint venture with Sloman Shipping (Germany) with the acquisition of two Blue Star-manned vessels in 1977: *Starman America* and *Starman Anglia*.

I was fortunate to make trips on all types of BSSM vessel and sail under every house flag, except L&H (nicknamed Lean & Hungry). When I joined BSSM, the fleet had over thirty ships operating worldwide.

Having succeeded at interview, I had to pass the medical examination and the eyesight test. Only Department of Trade approved doctors could be used so I took a trip to the one in South Shields, where there was a merchant navy training college at that time. The ENG1 Medical was a routine examination of medical history, blood pressure, heart rate, reflexes, and a urine test. The eyesight test was more stringent and was conducted without visual aids, as the wearing and use of spectacles by deck officers on a ship's bridge was illegal. Reading the standard Snellen chart had to be passed at the 20/20 level.

For a deck officer, colour perception was absolutely critical, so the next stage was passing the Ishihara test, a colour perception test for red-green colour deficiencies. If you can't discern red, green, or white lights correctly at long range, then you are useless as a bridge watchkeeping officer. Ships 'drive' around at night showing red and green sidelights and white masthead lights. A number of coloured plates (Ishihara plates), each contained a circle of dots in random colours and sizes, within which a pattern of dots formed a number or shape that was clearly visible to those with normal colour vision, and invisible, or difficult to see, to those with red-green colour blindness.

The final part of the eyesight test was the Holmes Wright Colour Perception Lantern. This reproduced night-time visual conditions to test whether the applicant correctly identified a series of red, green, and white pinpricks of light emitted from the lantern. The candidate was seated about 20 feet (6 m) from the light source, which represented viewing these lights at a range of five miles (8 km). A 100% correct result was required. My eyesight proved perfect. Phew!

My merchant navy career sorted, I relaxed during summer 1980. Back in Gosport, I resumed work for a removal firm. Joe Picken was one of Sultan's PTIs who Dad had known for years. Joe had completed his service and established a small removal business. He was a larger-than-life character in every way and was built like a brick outhouse. As a PTI, Joe played rugby, was heavily involved in Pompey's field gun crew, and had a sailor's wicked sense of humour. His business assets were a large lorry and a Luton van, which he parked in the lay-by outside Bay House School overnight, and one full-time employee, Norman, a short, middle-aged bloke with jet-black hair. My father had mentioned me to Joe in case he needed the odd extra hand. Joe 'interviewed' me by asking me to come along to one of his jobs and do some fetching and carrying. Joe was surprised and impressed with both my stamina and strength, despite my lean, wiry frame. As a result, he welcomed me on board and I enjoyed working with and for him during all my university vacations. He and I became firm friends.

Typically, I cycled to Joe's house to arrive at 0730, as Joe aimed to arrive at the loading address by 0800. After assessing the job, he always requested a mug of tea for us and we cracked on with the job, pausing briefly to sip our tea. Norm and I emptied the house and Joe packed the van. Having loaded the wagon by mid-morning (we certainly didn't hang around), we invariably went for brunch, as unloading usually occurred in mid-afternoon. Most of Joe's jobs were local and predominantly naval married quarter moves. We did, however, frequently move sailors to Plymouth. Those were very long days, due to loading, unloading, and an almost 400-mile (650-km) round trip to get home that same evening. I got very familiar with the A303, passing Wincanton, Ilchester, Ilminster, and seeing the Naval Air Station at Yeovilton in the distance. We always stopped at The Frying Pan, a quality transport café on Camel Hill, just outside Sparkford, to enjoy a cooked breakfast and a mug of tea.

Even when in BSSM's employ, I always managed to do a few jobs with Joe and Norm when between ships. It was an extra bit of cash-in-hand, occasional intercity travel and, crucially, great fun and loads of laughs, as they were good company. It was a brilliant and thoroughly enjoyable experience.

BSSM sent me a kit list. My mother and I trotted around naval outfitters in Pompey for the required items of uniform. Other purchases included a pair of Doc Marten boots and boiler suits, essential for work on deck.

Waterproof trousers and a jacket for stormy weather. My mother bought me my formal uniform and made an appointment at a portrait photographer for photos of me (in uniform) and my brother James in jacket and tie. She proudly hung both single portraits at home thereafter. James and I looked rather good.

Fig 3.3 Blue Star Officer Trainee (O/T), September 1980

In September 1980, I set off from Gosport to drive 280 miles (450 km) to New Brighton on The Wirral in my Morris Marina 1.3 Coupé, loaded with all my kit and suitable 'civvies'. The journey took about five hours and I arrived at dusk. The company habitually accommodated its O/Ts in the Belgravia Hotel. I parked outside and noted the Bel (as it was known to O/Ts) was a typical British seaside hotel, built in the 1930s and with a licensed bar. I checked in and struggled up the stairs with my luggage. En-suite facilities were unheard of in such establishments in the 1970s and 1980s but at least there was a washbasin in my room.

That evening, Mr Burke, BSSM's Cadet Training Manager and specifically responsible for the company's O/Ts, had arranged a meet-and-greet in the bar. There were thirteen of us in this intake. We chatted among ourselves until Mr Burke joined us. Introductions were made, welcomes proffered on behalf of the company, and then a briefing about the next few weeks.

Traditionally, the British merchant navy recruited A-level entrants to deck cadet and engineering cadet training programmes. So, lads like my old schoolmate 'Fred' Kemp joined straight from school, completed a cadetship of about four years and then started their career in earnest. 'Fred' was a tanker man for some years. BSSM noted that the industry wasn't attracting enough of such young blokes to meet their shortfall in junior deck officer numbers, so were the only British company to recruit graduates to train. Flighty graduates were unlikely to remain in sea-going roles, patiently doing the time required to qualify as a Master and then waiting umpteen years to fill what was usually a dead-man's shoes. BSSM expected many of us to leave after a few years but, meantime, we held the junior deck officer posts they were having trouble filling with 'normal' school leavers.

To distinguish graduates from standard deck cadets, we were designated as Officer Trainees, with a training programme shortened to reflect our graduate status. After completing an introductory six weeks, we'd be sent to sea to accumulate as much sea-time as possible, and return for the first college phase about 18 months later. More sea-time followed until the final college phase, which culminated in exams for the Certificate of Competency (Deck Officer) Class 3. This used to be called the Second Mate's ticket, the first qualification en route to becoming a Master Mariner. Provided we passed all the exams, we earned our ticket on completion of 24 months sea-time and then go to sea as Third Mate. You always served at one rank below the ticket you held. So, the theory was that we'd gain our ticket by spring 1984, in three and a half years rather than a deck cadet's minimum of four years.

Mr Burke explained all the above, plus the content of the introduction and subsequent college phases. We'd be issued with a Merchant Navy Training Board (MNTB) task book to complete and the college's self-study modules while away at sea. He said that the scheme had been running for several years, had proved successful, and that our intake had been selected from about 1,200 applicants.

After questions and general conversation, he departed and we carried on socialising in the bar. It was a bit of a late night. I quickly struck up an acquaintance with four colleagues: Nigel Lawrence (a Bristolian); Tom Moffatt (a Scotsman); Simon 'Sam' Davies (a Yorkshireman from Doncaster); and Mick Swann (a Londoner). During each college phase, we commuted to college and socialised together.

Next day, we travelled on MerseyRail from Wallasey, under the Mersey, and alighted at Moorfields to walk a few hundred yards to Liverpool Polytechnic. We found the Department of Maritime Studies on the sixth floor of the main teaching building. The college emerged from a movement in the 1960s that offered a vocational approach to higher education, concentrating on science and technology. Over time, its composition and identity evolved and Liverpool Polytechnic was established on 1 April 1970. In the Blair government's shake-up of tertiary education, 'polys' disappeared and morphed into universities. Hence, Liverpool Polytechnic is now Liverpool John Moores University.

In what became our classroom, our academic staff introduced themselves. They were all experienced Merchant Navy Masters and had commanded a variety of cargo ships during their sea-going careers. Having retired from the sea, they seemed to enjoy being lecturers at Liverpool Polytechnic. Head of Department was Captain Holder, who we saw occasionally, but the bulk of our lessons were conducted by Captain Moore and Captain Watson. In the two main college phases, Captain Bole was also on the scene to teach us about electronic navigation systems and the principles and practice of radar, gyros, and other 'wiggly-amp' stuff.

The purpose of the initial phase was to prepare us to go to sea so we'd have some idea of how a ship operated (at sea and in port), of day-to-day routines, and of on-board organisation. In addition, we were introduced to the subjects in which we would be examined in three years' time. Chartwork, navigation, mathematics, physics, and meteorology were the basic building blocks. Chartwork and navigation were obvious topics in which you must gain proficiency to be a deck officer. Mathematics focused on spherical trigonometry and familiarisation with *Norie's Nautical Tables*, a thick book of mathematical tables used to calculate position from observing celestial bodies (sun, moon, stars, planets) using a sextant. Such tables as haversines were, initially, incomprehensible. I still have my old copy of *Nories* on a bookshelf. I couldn't bear to part with it as it was an integral part of my life in the Merchant Navy. Physics encompassed the basics as applied to the maritime environment.

One other academic subject was quite nebulous: General Ship Knowledge (GSK) consisted of anything to do with ships that wasn't covered in the aforementioned syllabus, among the multitude of topics were: stability, cargo work and equipment, ship construction, and seamanship.

Two subjects could prove to be your downfall in the final examinations: Morse code and Rule of the Road (ROR). The standard required in Morse code was to read a flashing light at six words per minute. ROR or, to give its correct title, 'International Regulations for Preventing Collisions at Sea 1972', was definitely a hazardous subject. Part of the final examination series was an oral exam with the Principal Examiner of Masters and Mates, and you had to be 100% correct in answering questions on the contents of a very slim booklet of 38 rules and four annexes. This doesn't sound like much in terms of quantity, however the content was extremely detailed, specific, and laden with pitfalls. Captain Moore, our prime ROR instructor, encouraged us to learn its contents by heart. His oral quizzing of us in class brought their meaning and application into focus.

We completed a two-day firefighting course at Liverpool Speke Airport (Liverpool John Lennon Airport since 2001). The airport fire service training centre instructed us in dealing with shipboard fires with handheld fire extinguishers and foam- and water-pressurised hoses. The training ground included a gas-fired ship firefighting module, a large steel cube to represent the interior of a ship: a couple of decks, hatches, doorways, ladders, compartments. We took part in several practical exercises fully dressed in a fireman's suit and breathing apparatus, clambering around inside the unit in intense heat while manhandling heavy, charged hoses. Movement and mobility were hampered by the suit, by the weight of the breathing apparatus strapped to your back, and by hefting the high-pressure water hoses. Everything was made a little more difficult because the decks and bulkheads of the unit had buckled after years if use. The deck, particularly, was pitted with puddles and mounds to produce an uneven and unpredictable surface when viewed through a facemask. It was an exciting and novel experience but frightening if translated into real life on a large ship pitching and rolling at sea, probably at night, and with no means of escape except over the side and into a life raft or lifeboat, hundreds of miles from land.

Finally, we completed a two-day sea survival course. This introduced us to life rafts, their hydrostatic release mechanism, distress radio beacons, correct donning of a standard Department of Trade lifejacket, and how to enter the sea wearing it by stepping off a 16-foot (5 m) diving platform into a swimming pool.

I enjoyed this initial training phase, learning new subjects relevant to my chosen career at sea. Armed with my new-found knowledge and limited expertise, we bomb-burst to our respective homes. We were on leave until Mr Burke notified us of our first ship and details of where and when to join her. With my Discharge Book and British Seaman's Card at the ready, my globe-trotting odyssey was about to begin!

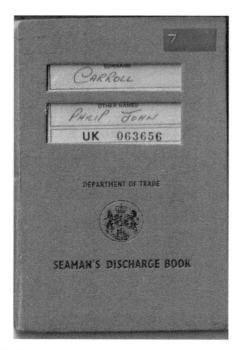

Fig 3.4 Discharge Book, front cover

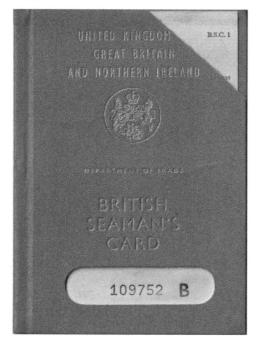

Fig 3.5 Seaman's ID Card, front cover

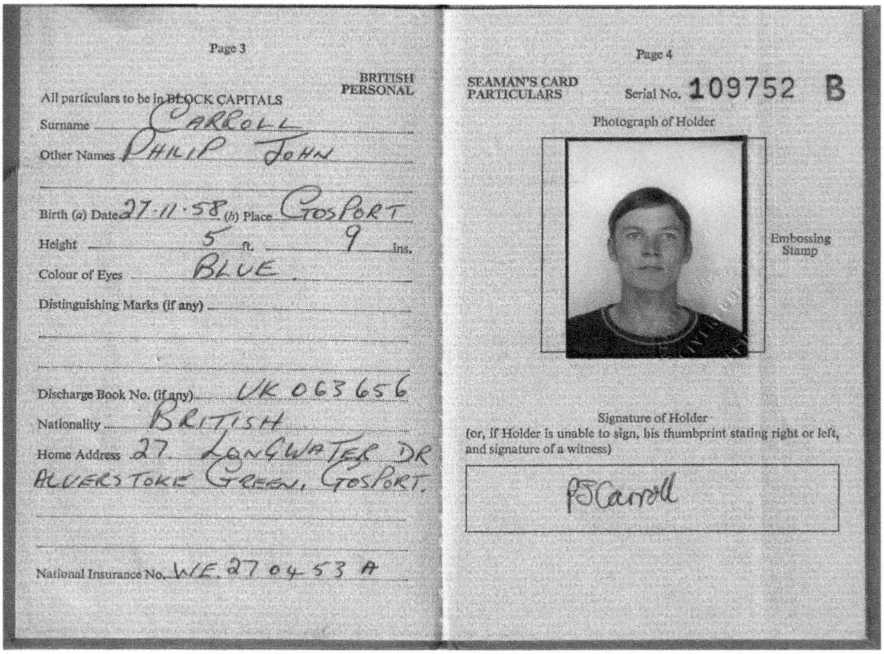

Page 3

BRITISH PERSONAL

All particulars to be in BLOCK CAPITALS

Surname CARROLL

Other Names PHILIP JOHN

Birth (a) Date 27.11.58 (b) Place GOSPORT

Height 5 ft. 9 ins.

Colour of Eyes BLUE

Distinguishing Marks (if any)

Discharge Book No. (if any) UK 063656

Nationality BRITISH

Home Address 27. LONGWATER DR ALVERSTOKE GREEN, GOSPORT.

National Insurance No. WE 27 04 53 A

Page 4

SEAMAN'S CARD PARTICULARS

Serial No. 109752 B

Photograph of Holder

Embossing Stamp

Signature of Holder (or, if Holder is unable to sign, his thumbprint stating right or left, and signature of a witness)

PJCarroll

Fig 3.6 Seaman's ID Card, inside pages

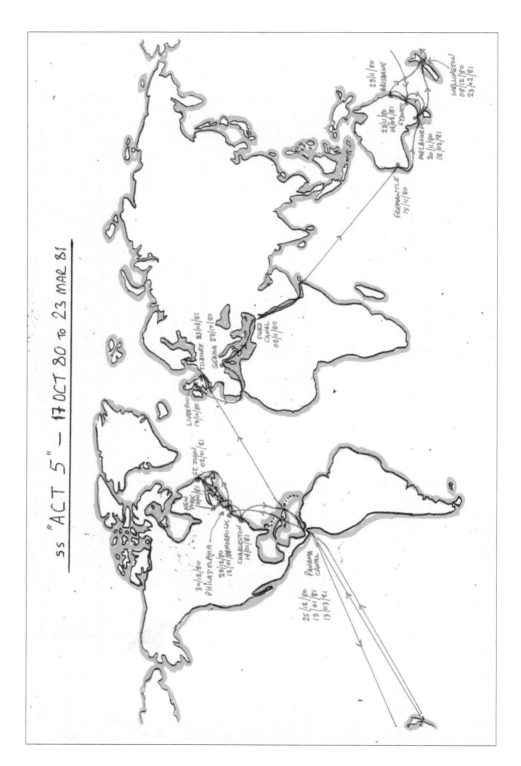

Fig 4.1 *ACT 5* voyage

4 First Trip to Sea
Around the World on *ACT 5*

Fig 4.2 *ACT 5* (Fotoflite)

In October 1980, Mr Burke phoned to say that a ship was available to join in a week or so. It was *Mandama*, an Austasia Line reefer (refrigerated cargo ship), but that joining it in Bandar Abbas would be rather awkward due to the situation in Iran. During the Iranian Revolution, demonstrators forced access into the US Embassy in Tehran, occupied the premises, and took 52 American diplomats and citizens hostage on 4 November 1979. In December 1979, the Shah of Iran was overthrown and scuttled off to exile in the United States. After prolonged negotiations, the hostages were eventually released on 20 January 1981, some 444 days after their capture. Unsurprisingly, it proved impracticable to join *Mandama* in Iran.

A few days later, Mr Burke called me again. This time, there wouldn't be any difficulties as my ship was in Liverpool. On 17 October 1980, I excitedly packed my kit and set off by train to Liverpool, via Waterloo and Euston stations in London. A short taxi ride from Liverpool Lime Street Station delivered me to the gates of Royal Seaforth Container Terminal at the north end of the vast dockland area occupied by the Port of Liverpool.

> The docks had a long history. The Dock Committee of 1709 was superseded by the Liverpool Dock Trustees in 1750. About a century later, the Mersey Docks and Harbour Board took over the management of the docks and morphed into the Mersey Docks and Harbour Company in 1972 in order to raise money for new building initiatives and projects, including the new container terminal at Seaforth.
>
> The Port of Liverpool was an enclosed dock system of some seven and a half miles (12 km) from Brunswick Dock (just north of the Kingsway road tunnel) to Seaforth Dock (adjoining Crosby) on the east side of the River Mersey. It also included Birkenhead Docks between Birkenhead and Wallasey on the west side of the river. White Star Line and Cunard Line were based at the port and it was the home port of many great ships, including RMS (Royal Mail Ships) *Baltic, Lusitania,* and *Titanic.* Royal Seaforth Dock was opened in 1972 as a purpose-built dock and container terminal at the northern end of the dock system. It connected to Gladstone Dock to the south that, via its lock entrance, provided access to Royal Seaforth Dock from the Mersey.

The British Transport policeman allowed the taxi to transit via a safety road. This ensured that the constant activity of straddle-carriers and trucks around the containers stacked four-high, close to the wharves, wasn't interrupted by taxis or delivery trucks. Nor was the movement of portainer-cranes impeded by non-port authority traffic immediately adjacent to the berthed ships being loaded and unloaded.

Dusk approached as I clambered out of the taxi and retrieved my kit. I was dwarfed by the sheer, vertical, grey, slab-side of my ship. A long, rather spindly-looking, galvanised gangway ladder at a frighteningly steep gradient rose from the wharf to access the upper deck at the base of the ship's accommodation block. I glanced to my right and saw her name: *ACT*

5. Hardly the most romantic or even maritime name, but I was elated that I had finally joined my first ship.

I climbed the gangway clutching one of my bags. It took a bit of doing as the gangway was quite narrow, making it difficult to carry it at my side. So I adjusted my grip and held it ahead of me with one hand, using my other hand to steady myself on the handrail. The gangway wobbled as I clambered up. I reached the top and stepped on board. The gangway watchman, one of the Able Seamen (AB) welcomed me in West Indian patois and confirmed the ship was expecting me – quite a relief! I dropped my bag on deck and returned to the wharf to fetch my second bag.

The watchman used an internal phone to contact the Officers' Mess. Soon after, Roger Odell, the other O/T, appeared and bid me welcome. He helped cart my bags to my cabin, which was two decks up within the accommodation block and to the aft end. Roger told me that it was nearly dinner but there was just enough time to go to the bar first for a drink and to meet some of my new shipmates. We went down a deck and entered the bar, located at the starboard aft end. I was introduced to a number of blokes, whose names soon eluded me and, after a swift beer, Roger and I went to the dining room at the forward starboard side of the same deck. The three-course dinner was rather good, with steward service. Afterwards, Roger and I retired to the bar for a few more sherbets (beers) and a good conversation about each other and the ship. This was my introduction to Victoria Bitter (VB) – the bar's preference. It wasn't generally available in UK in those days as Foster's had taken the UK by storm. It was the same brewer and same can design, but Foster's was blue, VB was green.

Eventually, the combination of a long train journey, excitement at joining my first ship, getting on board, meeting my new shipmates, plus a few sherbets, meant it was definitely time for my bunk! I needed to unpack some basic stuff and get a good night's sleep before commencing my sea-going training in earnest. Roger and I arranged to meet at breakfast.

ACT 5 **was one of seven ships owned and operated by Associated Container Transportation (ACT), all unimaginatively named** *ACT 1* **through to** *ACT 7*. **ACT was created in January 1966 by five British shipping companies (Ben Line, Blue Star Line, Cunard (Port Line), Ellerman Lines, and Harrison Line) to rival Overseas Containers Limited (OCL), itself formed in 1965 by four British companies: British and Commonwealth Shipping, Furness Withy, P&O, and**

Ocean Steamship Company. ACT partners participated in newly containerised trades where they already had conventional liner services.

In August 1967, Blue Star, Ellerman, and Port Line joined together to form Associated Container Transport (Australia) or ACT(A) to containerise the Europe-Australia trade. Two containerships of 1,334 container capacity were ordered (*ACT 1, ACT 2*). The Europe-Australia container service was launched in partnership with OCL in March 1969, ACT/ANL (Australian National Line) provided three ships and OCL five ships.

Another ACT subsidiary, Pacific America Container Express (PACE) Line was formed in March 1971 for the Australia-New Zealand-East Coast North America trade. ACT/ANL operated four ships of 1,334 container capacity on this service: *ACT 3, ACT 4, ACT 5*, and *Australian Explorer*. When I joined, BSSM operated four of the ACT fleet: *ACT 1, ACT 4, ACT 5*, and *ACT 7*. Despite her being on the PACE service, I joined *ACT 5* in Liverpool because she had just completed a dry docking in Bremerhaven.

I never have a problem settling into a different bed, regardless of its location. Thus, I enjoyed a blissful sleep and arose punctually for breakfast. I dressed in uniform: black trousers, white shirt, black tie, black shoes and a woolly pully – it was autumn 'up norf' after all! My first time dressed 'in anger'. It was quite a thrill to be finally starting my job proper.

After breakfast, we changed into boilersuit and boots. Pete the passage-worker joined us. He was a very pleasant, bespectacled chap, about the same age as us and, through some family connection, he'd signed on to work his passage to Australia, where he'd get off to enjoy a post-university gap year. Passage-workers were increasingly rare on merchantmen. In those days, they were blokes who paid for their journey on a ship with work instead of money.

Roger gave us a guided tour of the ship. *ACT 5* had been built at the Bremer Vulkan Schiffbau & Machinenfabrik in Vegesack, Germany in 1971. Unusually for this era, she was a steam ship, whereas the vast majority of modern merchant ships were motor ships. She was 712 feet 9 inches (217 m) in length, a beam (width) of 95 feet 3 inches (29 m), with a draught of 34 feet 6 inches (10.5 m). Gross tonnage was 24,212 and net tonnage 14,234.

Tonnages are obtained by measuring the ship's volume and then applying a mathematical formula. Gross tonnage is 'the moulded volume of all enclosed spaces of the ship'. Net tonnage is 'the moulded volume of all cargo spaces of the ship' and constrained to be no less than 30% of her gross tonnage. The definitions of tonnages are specified by the International Convention on Tonnage Measurement of Ships (1969) and adopted by the International Maritime Organisation (IMO). Gross tonnage is used to determine a ship's manning regulations, safety rules, registration fees, and port dues.

ACT 5 was a refrigerated modular containership with nine holds, of which eight were designed to carry standard TEU containers. Each hold was divided into port and starboard halves, further divided within each into forward and aft halves, and fitted with cell guides to retain the containers in position when loaded. No additional lashings or other fixings were required. There was capacity for eight containers across the width of each hold and six containers high. Several holds had fitments to maintain the correct temperature of a refrigerated container. The hatch covers were removed by the dockside portainer-cranes in port to allow access to unload and load the below-deck containers.

The hatch covers were strengthened to allow them to carry on-deck containers, stacked eleven across the breadth of the ship and up to four high. They required lashing with specially designed rods, turnbuckles, and twist-locks to ensure they didn't fall overboard. Refrigerated containers were carried on deck, each fitted with a special fridge unit. Overall, *ACT 5's* capacity was 1,334 TEUs.

The forward hatch (No. 1 hold), situated on the forecastle (fo'c'sle), was used for break-bulk general cargo. Its hatch opened and closed hydraulically, folding upwards in two parts and guided along tracks atop the hatch coaming. The only craneage on board was a small crane to serve the forward hatch, otherwise the upper deck was completely clear of obstructions for clean access by dockside portainer-crane operations.

The six-deck accommodation block was right aft and the topmost was the bridge deck. The deck below held the two lifeboats plus, between the enormous engine-room fan trunkings and abaft the funnel, a small swimming pool.

Roger guided me all around the accommodation block and introduced me to the Old Man, George Stubbings. A short, stumpy bloke, he was one of Blue Star's senior Masters. As *ACT 5's* continuity Master, he was the ship's permanent Captain and when he was on leave a relief Master took over. We also met George Henderson, the Mate (Chief Officer) and second-in-command of the ship. He seemed a rather dour, serious, pipe-smoking, old Scotsman. Roger, Pete and I had most dealings with him as he allocated our daily work each morning.

We toured the bridge. It was immense, spacious, and fitted with the bridge-watchkeeper's standard tools. The view from the bridge windows and from the extremes of the bridge wings was impressive. We were some 70 feet (21.5 m) above the weather deck, which stretched into the distance ahead of us. Our view was interrupted by the stacks of containers atop the hatch covers; the fo'c'sle crane indicated the ship's bow. The view astern included the lifeboats and the poop deck at the stern.

The ship was working cargo when we strolled along the weather deck. On both sides, outboard of the hatches, an uninterrupted walkway allowed easy access along the length of the weather deck. You walked beneath the first layer of on-deck containers as they straddled the gap between the hatch cover and the guardrails, supported by steel pillars. I was fascinated to observe for the first time a container ship being loaded and unloaded by portainer-cranes. The laden 20-foot metal boxes were suspended by wires from the crane cab as it moved along the portainer boom from the dockside to the correct position on the ship, then lowered either below deck within the cell guides or atop the hatch cover. The rhythm and routine seemed almost balletic and, to me, a bit of a marvel.

The crew was made up of British officers and a Barbadian (or Bajan) crew. We met the Bosun, Chippy (carpenter) and some of the ABs. Mr Best was Bosun, of stocky, muscular stature. He habitually wore a small, paint-streaked, peaked cap and sleeves half-rolled up to reveal his powerful forearms. He had a meaty pair of hands and his fingers were like Mars bars. He was most welcoming and his ABs were friendly although I knew it would take a little time to get used to their Bajan patois. As the voyage wore on, I thoroughly enjoyed working with Mr Best and his crowd on deck, chipping and painting, maintaining and cleaning kit, emptying lockers, scrubbing them out, and re-stowing them.

On the fo'c'sle we viewed the crane, the forward hatch, and the anchor windlasses. Four self-tensioning mooring winches maintained the ship's position alongside using sisal mooring ropes as well as wire ropes secured to bollards. The mooring rope was always secured to a self-tensioning winch's barrel, which used an automatic self-tensioning device via a special pressure-relief valve that automatically operated the winch until a set tension was achieved. The valve then closed and the winch stopped. Thereafter, if the tension eased, the winch automatically took in the rope until tension was restored. The opposite occurred when tension increased. Hence, self-tensioning winches automatically allowed for variations in tide and draught while alongside. When cargo operations ceased, the eerie silence of the fo'c'sle was broken by the constant whirr of the winch fans and intermittent clicks as the self-tensioning winches adapted to any change in rope tension.

From the fo'c'sle, we climbed down a couple of internal ladders and proceeded aft along the Burma Road, a passageway on each side of the ship to allow below-deck access between the fo'c'sle and the accommodation and engine compartments aft. The Burma Road also had a hatch into each of the holds, which permitted the Chief Refrigeration Engineer (CRE or Fridgie) to conduct daily inspections of the refrigerated containers. I noted the gentle curve of the ship's side when looking from one end of the Burma Road to the other and that, midships, the horizontal curvature was more pronounced as the doors at each end were obscured.

At the aft end of the Burma Road, we entered the engine room compartments, situated directly below the accommodation block. This space was enormous and extremely noisy as the generators, pumps, and a multitude of miscellaneous but important machinery clanked and clunked away, each to its own rhythm. *ACT 5* was powered by two Stal Laval steam turbines of 32,000 brake horsepower double reduction geared to a single shaft driving a six-bladed propellor, yielding a service speed of 22 knots. The steam was derived from two gigantic Foster-Wheeler ESD III boilers, which dominated the space. The ship's electricity was supplied by three Brotherhood turbo-alternators of 1,360 kilowatts and two Paxman diesel generators.

Roger, Pete and I wandered around this vast space, up and down narrow steel ladders, along grated walkways, and ended up in the machinery control room (MCR) where *ACT 5's* engineering empire was controlled and managed. We met a couple of the engineers and had a brief chat.

Our last stop on the tour was a wide platform overlooking the engine room, where the ship's most important bit of kit was situated: the boiler suit washing machine! *ACT 5* was equipped with a laundry for uniform and civvies, but as deck and engineering personnel habitually wore boiler suits for work on board, they inevitably got grubby, filthy, and greasy. So, it was absolutely forbidden to dhoby (wash) your boiler suit in the laundry. Instead, we used the dedicated washing machine in the engine room. With powerful detergent that would probably disintegrate your civvies, a boiler suit was renewed and sparkling clean after its wash. Drying wasn't a problem as freshly dhobied boiler suits were draped over adjacent guardrails and were dry in hours due to the ambient heat of the engine room. So even after dhobying my 'boilie' at the end of a day's work, it was always stiff, clean, and dry long before breakfast.

The tour completed, we emerged from the engine room access and had a cup of tea in the duty mess, a room dedicated to grubby crew for refreshment during the working day. Boiler suits were absolutely forbidden in the accommodation itself and in the bar and dining room particularly.

The rest of my day passed in a state of heightened excitement as we were sailing at dusk. I unpacked my bags, stowed my kit, and had lunch. My cabin wasn't quite the aft-most one but I didn't care as it was large and equipped with an en-suite bathroom and shower, a decent-sized bunk, a day bed, and ample wardrobe and drawer space for all my stuff.

Prior to sailing, it was the cadet's job to run around the ship with the *All on Board* book. Roger and I strolled around the accommodation, catching all those listed in the book to prove they were on board and to confirm that no one was missing, or was still ashore, or had done a runner.

Dressed in my smart uniform, I arrived on the bridge at dusk to see what was going on. I didn't really know what I was supposed to be doing but took a keen interest in observing the scene. The fo'c'sle and poop deck were manned by the Mate and Third Mate respectively, each with three or four ABs. On the bridge, the Master and Second Mate, together with the helmsman (one of the ABs), were making final preparations. The Radio Officer (Sparky) was in his shack behind the bridge. The MCR was manned by the Chief and Second Engineers, one or two junior engineer officers, the Engine Room Storekeeper (the engineer's equivalent of the deck department's Bosun), and a greaser and a donkeyman (equivalent to ABs), both Bajans.

Tugs appeared off the bow and stern and were secured to the ship. The pilot arrived on the bridge and was greeted by Captain Stubbings. I was detailed off to make tea and/or coffee for them. I stood beside Roger, whose role was to monitor and note engine movements and when ropes and wires were let go, tugs secured and let go, and *ACT 5*'s departure from the berth, passage through the lock and out into the Mersey and the Irish Sea beyond.

Royal Seaforth Dock was quite a large basin so there was plenty of room in which to manoeuvre the ship and line up, with the tugs pushing and pulling under the pilot's command. Once entry into Gladstone Lock was achieved, *ACT 5* was secured alongside as the water-level was matched to that of the River Mersey. Then the lock gates were opened and the ship manoeuvred out. Gladstone Lock was orientated almost north-south, with the seaward access upriver, whereas the channel out to sea was to the north, hence the ship turned sharply to starboard, through almost 180°, into the buoyed channel that took us downriver.

The tugs were released and *ACT 5* settled on an outbound course between the red and green buoys that marked the channel, maintaining the 10 knot speed limit. It was now dark. Astern the lights of Liverpool were to starboard and of The Wirral to port. The buoys' red and green flashing lights were clearly visible, as were the rotating white beams of lighthouses ashore. I popped out to the bridge wing to look astern and noted a small boat quickly approaching us. It settled and took station on our port quarter. This was the pilot boat, recognisable as, in addition to its port and starboard sidelights (red and green) and white sternlight, it showed white over red, all-round lights. Roger told me it was easy to remember as pilots were always old blokes with white hair and red faces!

The pilot boat waited for the pilot to call him alongside for his disembarkation. Roger called me inside as our next job, as cadets, was to escort the pilot down the external ladders of the accommodation, onto the upper deck and to the pilot ladder the AB had rigged. The pilot boat manoeuvred alongside and the pilot clambered down the vertical precipice of the ship's side and stepped onto the pilot boat. With a cursory wave, the pilot boat increased speed, turned away from *ACT 5* and returned to Liverpool.

We steamed on to the end of the buoyed channel and noted the bar light vessel. Using the VHF radio on the bridge, we reported our exit from Port of Liverpool jurisdiction. The poop deck and fo'c'sle were secured, the ABs returned to their accommodation. Stand-by (as the process of entering and leaving port was known) complete, the crew settled into its watch routine. The bar light vessel was on our starboard quarter, and then on our stern, its flashing white light faded under the night sky and eventually disappeared. Neither Roger nor I had any further work that night. I mooched about the bar for a short while before retiring to my cabin for my first night's sleep at sea.

Overnight, *ACT 5* steamed down the Irish Sea on passage to Genoa. In the morning, Roger and I started early as the first job each day was to take soundings of the bilges. The bilge was the rounded part at the bottom of the hull where the ship's side curves round towards the keel. It's the place in the hold that collects any loose water and must be periodically pumped out to prevent it from becoming too full. Our route involved collecting the log book from the deck office, following an efficient route around the ship, along both Burma Roads. Each hold had a sounding pipe topped with a screw-lid, down which a metal measuring stick on a length of cord was lowered to the bottom of the bilge, hauled up, and the level of 'wet' inches on the measure was noted in the book. Forward of No. 1 hold, the forepeak bilge was the turning point to return along the starboard Burma Road to the aft peak tank's bilge. The route and measurements were completed and we changed out of our boiler suits and went to breakfast at 0700.

Roger, Pete, and I reported to the Mate on watch on the bridge at 0740 to get our jobs for the day. This was our routine start unless the Mate had other tasks for us. Roger (being a year senior to me) either joined me and Pete with the deck crowd or did some bridge time. It was traditional for deck cadets to spend the majority of their time between ports on deck with the Bosun and his boys. This work was mostly chipping and painting on deck, around hatches and hatch coamings, on the fo'c'sle and poop deck. Occasionally, you were assigned to chip and paint an item of deck equipment, such as a winch or windlass. These tasks were quite prolonged as they were large bits of kit with a huge number of nooks and crannies to tend to.

Chipping was the process for removing rust patches using a variety of tools: chipping hammers; wire brushes; and scaling hammers, which were electrically-powered for chipping large areas, usually great swathes of deck surface. Painting, using brushes and/or rollers, entailed applying an undercoat of red lead (lead tetroxide/calcium plumbate) as an anti-corrosive primer coating over exterior steelwork. It was known to be a major cause of lead poisoning. A top coat of an appropriate colour completed the task. It was quite satisfying to note the extent of the day's work as a focused team of ABs (and cadets) were capable of covering wide expanses of deck.

We progressed past Land's End, crossed a benign Bay of Biscay (despite its notoriety for rough seas), around the north-west tip of Spain and south off the Spanish and Portuguese coasts. *ACT 5* rounded the south-west tip of Portugal, crossed the Gulf of Cadiz, and transited the Strait of Gibraltar to enter the Mediterranean Sea. Despite it being October, the sea and swell were rather gentle and the weather was good and dry.

In the Mediterranean late one afternoon, the junior engineer officers played a prank on Pete. We expected a mail delivery by helicopter so Pete was privileged to be designated Flight Deck Officer to control its approach and the winching down of our mail-bag. They dressed him in a pristine white boiler suit, goggles, hard hat, rubber-gloves, and a pair of table-tennis bats to wave in and control the helicopter. The rest of the day-workers, including

Roger and me, observed proceedings as Pete waited for the helicopter to enlarge from a speck on the horizon to a giant noisy whirly thing above the deck. After a while, Pete realised all wasn't quite right. We fell about laughing. He was a good sport and had free beer all evening.

After nine days at sea, *ACT 5* berthed in Genoa, my first foreign port, the capital of the Liguria region of Italy and historically one of the most important ports in the Mediterranean. It had been the capital of one of the most powerful maritime republics from the 11th to the end of the 18th centuries. Today, it's at the southern corner of the Milan-Turin-Genoa industrial triangle.

The approach and pilotage into the port were unremarkable. We berthed at one of the container wharves and cargo work started. As cadets, we were assigned to one of the cargo watches with either the Mate or the Second Mate, while the Third Mate was on watch solo. This allowed the senior Mates to take a back seat so they could attend to their other duties in port. The Mate was responsible for the loading and unloading of cargo and the cargo plan, while the Second Mate was the navigator.

Container ports operated 24/7, so there was no relaxation for watchkeeping deck officers. On joining a ship, a deck officer picked up his predecessor's watch and remained in it until he was paid off several months later. The Master commanded the ship and ultimately carried all responsibility for the safety of the vessel and its crew. He was a 'day-worker' and was on-call at a moment's notice to deal with crises. The other three qualified deck officers carried the six four-hour watches in each 24-hour period. The Mate had the 4–8 watches and was the Master's right-hand man. The Second Mate did the 12–4 watches and his navigation duties. His responsibilities included keeping the charts and publications up to date, as and when the latest editions of the Admiralty's Weekly Notices to Mariners, Lists of Lights and Radio Signals were received on arrival at a port. He also applied any corrections to the navigation charts held on board. The Third Mate occupied the 8–12 watches and was responsible for the ship's lifeboats, life rafts and safety/distress equipment. As you gained seniority as a deck cadet, you spent more time doubled-up in bridge watchkeeping, particularly 'on the coast', until the great day that Master and Mate deemed you competent to go solo on watch. This released the Mate to day-work, while the Second and Third Mates moved up a watch as the cadet took over the 8–12 watches.

All deck officers were required for stand-by: the Master and Second Mate on the bridge; the Mate on the fo'c'sle; the Third Mate on the poop.

Deck cadets were usually on the bridge. For the short duration in a container port (typically from four to 24 hours), all deck officers endured some very long days. After stand-by on arrival, the deck watch system resumed as cargo operations immediately started and continued until complete. Then preparations for departure began, culminating in the departure stand-by. If you were unlucky, you picked up your standing watch after the pilot disembarked at the fairway buoy.

What about the engineering department? The Chief Engineer was the Master's equivalent in the engine room. For stand-by in and out of port, he sat in *ACT 5* MCR's comfy chair, habitually smoking his pipe. Unfortunately, this was directly beneath the smoke alarm, which of course perpetually went off. Despite the other engineers politely telling him that it was his pipe smoke that set it off, he remained in situ, oblivious. Strange behaviour. The Second Engineer had equivalence to the Mate. Below these two, there were any number of combinations of Third, Fourth, Fifth, Sixth and Junior Engineer officers, plus engineer cadets. During my time on board, we didn't have any cadets. The Third Engineer was a Kiwi, Dolf van Asbeck, noted for going barefoot around the accommodation. Marty Griffith was Fourth Engineer, a big-hearted, brawny, bearded Welshman who rather took me under his wing. Scouser Billy Doran was   Fifth Engineer, cheerful, quick witted, and with a wicked sense of humour. Others in the engineering department were the Fridgie and Electrical Officers (Lecky), of which *ACT 5* had two: Chief Lecky and Second Lecky (for my time on board, Dave Wilson and Norm Cowley respectively). Billy and Norm were great chums who constantly exchanged a lively banter. They were always great fun to be around.

Two others completed a merchant ship's officer complement: a Purser/Catering Officer (Bert Pearson, a moustachioed, middle-aged Liverpudlian), responsible for catering, stewards and stores; and a Radio Officer.

We were due to sail later that night, so I went 'up the road' (ashore) alone for a stroll around Genoa. My only experiences of going abroad had been a school trip to Normandy and a university field trip to Denmark. It was both novel and exciting to be solo in a foreign city. Genoa wasn't very attractive from what little I saw, although I didn't stray too far beyond the docks. I enjoyed a lovely fresh pizza at a nearby trattoria. Apart from constant rain, Genoa was quite an unremarkable, disappointing, and dull place for my first foreign port. I hoped things would pick up.

It was a quiet passage direct to Port Said, where *ACT 5* anchored on the afternoon of 10 November. Uniform had changed from black trousers and woolly pully, to tropical whites: a short-sleeved shirt, white shorts, long socks and canvas deck shoes. Preparations were made for our Suez Canal transit as we were rostered for the night's southbound convoy.

> Constructed by the Suez Canal Company between 1859 and 1869, the Suez Canal is an artificial, sea-level waterway in Egypt that connects the Mediterranean Sea to the Red Sea, through the Isthmus of Suez. Numerous dynasties, from the ancient Pharoahs, through the Ottomans, to Napoleon had wanted to build such a canal, but it was Ferdinand de Lesseps who led the project to its completion. An excellent history of its construction is in Zachary Karabell's *Parting the Desert: The Creation of the Suez Canal*. It has a troubled history, including the 1956 Suez Crisis, precipitated by Nasser nationalising the canal, and its strategic importance in the Arab–Israeli Wars of 1967 and 1973. The subsequent mine-clearance operation by the Royal Navy in 1973–74 led to its reopening.
>
> The Canal offers a direct route between the North Atlantic and the northern Indian Ocean that avoids the South Atlantic and the southern Indian Ocean. It reduces the distance from the Arabian Sea to London by about 5,500 miles (8,900 km). It extends from Port Said in the north for 120 miles (193 km) to its southern exit at Suez. The single shipping lane has passing areas in Ballah Bypass near El Qantara and in the Great Bitter Lake. On a typical day, three convoys transit the canal, two southbound and one northbound, taking 11 to 16 hours at about 8 knots, a speed calculated to prevent ships' wakes eroding the banks.

While at anchor that evening, a Suez Canal Authority gang came on board to fit the special searchlight required by the Authority for all vessels transiting the Canal. They installed it on the ship's centre line, right at the very point of the bow. Its specifications had to fulfil Authority requirements, so most shipping companies paid the Authority to provide and fit the searchlight, instead of retaining one on board. Security was uppermost. We locked our cabin doors and the doors that opened on the weather deck. A feature of the Canal was the constant presence of small boats touting a variety of goods, leather grips and shoes of dubious quality were common. Gully-gully men attempted to clamber on board. They weren't members of the Magic Circle, but if one was allowed on board, he gave a good magic show.

The southbound convoy commenced at 0330. The ship was prepared and the pilot embarked in good time. Captain Stubbings remained on the bridge for the first few hours, until relieved by the Mate for the middle section of

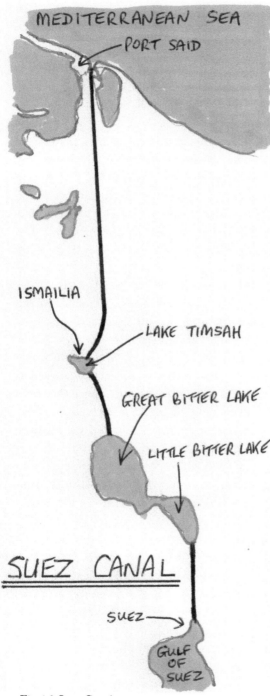

MEDITERRANEAN SEA

PORT SAID

ISMAILIA

LAKE TIMSAH

GREAT BITTER LAKE

LITTLE BITTER LAKE

SUEZ CANAL

SUEZ

GULF
OF
SUEZ

Fig 4.3 Suez Canal

the transit, then he came back on the bridge for the last couple of hours as the exit approached. The on-watch AB manned the helm and followed the orders given by the pilot. Meanwhile, on the fo'c'sle for the duration, the Bosun was on stand-by to drop the anchor in case of emergency. Roger and I split the time equally, as one of us was required on the bridge throughout, while the Mates rotated through their watches. Our role was to monitor and record progress in the *Bridge Movement Book*, particularly as we passed a numbered fixed beacon on either side of the channel. Of course, we were also the tea/coffee wallahs for the on-watch Mate and the pilot.

The night's weather was good, the temperature warm. The canal cut through the city of Port Said, street lights visible to port and starboard, but not much life was evident. The eastern sky reddened with the onset of dawn to port as *ACT 5* left Port Said astern. The expanse of desert sand seemed endless to east and west, the narrowness of the canal became apparent as its blue line stretched ahead to the horizon. The temperature increased gradually and the humidity slightly, although it was predominantly a dry heat.

A wide band of green, cultivated land abutted the west bank, but beyond it the desert occupied the distant vista. Crops were interspersed with clumps of palm trees and hamlets of mud-brick houses. People were increasingly out-and-about on their daily business – and not remotely interested in the convoy of merchant ships cutting through the sand. Intermittently on both banks were Egyptian military installations: gun emplacements; small garrisons; radar and communication masts and aerials. Occasionally, I spotted the odd dead tank, a remnant from the Arab–Israeli wars.

The day wore on, the ships immediately ahead and astern maintained their statutory distance from *ACT 5*. Roger relieved me, but I was so immersed in the novelty of my first Suez Canal transit that I didn't feel the least bit tired. I mooched about the bridge wings and up on the monkey island (the deck above the bridge) to take photos. I was enthralled, especially not knowing when, if ever, I would pass this way again.

The southbound convoy anchored in Great Bitter Lake about lunchtime to allow the northbound convoy to pass by unimpeded. The Bajan cooks laid on a lovely curry buffet with poppadoms, naan bread, and a selection of condiments. I grazed for a while, as I'd missed breakfast and was ravenous. When the last ship of the northbound convoy had passed by, the southbounders weighed anchor, resumed correct relative positions and continued towards Suez.

Dusk began to fall as *ACT 5* approached Suez and Port Tawfik. The Authority searchlight gang dismounted the light from the bow and prepared to disembark, their job done – although they hadn't done anything during the transit. As each ship emerged into the Gulf of Suez, a pilot boat came alongside to collect the pilot. I escorted ours down to the pilot ladder and witnessed his safe descent into the pilot boat. We were alone again, despite all the maritime traffic in the vicinity. Roger and I were released from our duties on the bridge and *ACT 5* settled into her overnight passage down the Red Sea and beyond.

Daily life on board resumed the next day for an unremarkable passage across the Indian Ocean. The only notable event was Crossing the Line, about halfway to Fremantle, Western Australia. As first trippers, Pete and I were subjected to a Crossing the Line Ceremony planned by the day-work engineer officers. It was a weekend afternoon and I was sunbathing by the pool. At about 1600, Fourth Engineer Marty Griffith (big as a whale, so we used to pretend to harpoon him when his back was turned – silly, even childish, but it gave us a chuckle) and a couple of others appeared and grabbed me. I was 'escorted' to the poop deck where Pete and I were lashed to the guardrails clad only in skiddies (underpants).

Fig 4.4 Crossing the Line, me (left), Peter (right), Indian Ocean, October 1980

We were drenched by a fire hose at full jet pressure and covered in the contents of several buckets. I'm not sure exactly what they contained but it was certainly an interesting cocktail of galley slops, bilge oil, general waste, and anything else of a suitably revolting nature! Photos were taken, laughs were had by all. We were then released from our bonds, given detergent and a tin of Swarfega, and directed back to our cabins for a shower.

Crikey, that was undoubtedly the longest shower I've ever had. Eventually, the combination of detergent and Swarfega (a brand of heavy-duty, dark green, gelatinous, thixotropic hand cleanser used in engineering, construction and other manual trades to clean grease, oil, or general persistent, hydrophobic dirt from the skin), followed by soap, scrubbed me clean. Washing my hair with Swarfega was an interesting experience but it did the trick, with a dose of shampoo to finish. Alas, my skiddies and two towels were beyond economical repair and went over the side.

Marty checked on me and Pete, and invited us to join him, Roger, and others (Dave and Norm, the Leckies, and Fifth Engineer Billy Doran) on the port (engineers) side of our cabin deck for a beer or three. I survived unscathed a definitive rite of passage for any seaman and we enjoyed our VBs, sat in the alleyway until dinner time.

At last, we reached the Australian coast! What excitement – arrival at a vast continent that I'd studied in school, and seen on *Mad Max* at the cinema and *Boney* on television. *ACT 5* berthed at Fremantle's Inner Harbour on 15 November. Crew and watchkeepers swung into cargo mode as portainer operations started.

Fremantle (or Freo, as shortened by the locals) was at the mouth of the Swan River, in the metropolitan area of Perth, Western Australia's capital. Freo was the first area settled by colonists in 1829. It struggled in its first decades, but the advent of penal transportation to the colony in 1850 meant Fremantle became Australia's primary destination for convicts. The convict-built Fremantle Prison operated long after transportation ended in 1868. During World War II, Fremantle was home to the largest base for Allied submarines in the southern hemisphere. Today, it's home to the Royal Australian Navy's submarine service at HMAS Stirling. In 1987, Freo was firmly put on the map when it hosted the America's Cup.

I worked 8–12 cargo watch on deck with Mike Finney, on his first trip as Third Mate. He instructed me in our role on watch: to constantly monitor the movement of containers on and from the ship. The wharf manager provided the ship with pages of stapled A4 sheets on which every container movement was listed, where those being loaded were to be positioned, together with each container's serial number. There was no indication as to their contents, except if the cargo was certified as hazardous. I enjoyed strolling perpetually up and down the length of the weather deck and along the walkways between the holds, ticking off each movement. Thus, we always knew how the cargo operation was progressing, the rate of movement in containers-per-hour, and so on. At the end of our watch, we handed over to the Second Mate, Pete Fawcett, and to Roger to continue the vigil on deck that afternoon.

The container wharves were on the opposite side of the Inner Harbour to the city. So, when I went up the road after my watch, I walked rather than wait for a taxi, as I had no idea how long I'd have to wait for one. It was a lovely, bright, sunny, warm day, perfect for shorts, sandals, and polo shirt.

Freo seemed a rather quaint town, with many old and substantial buildings from the 19th century. I got a bite to eat at a café and spent all my time wandering around. Luckily, I've always had a reasonable sense of direction and relative position so I rarely get lost. Eventually, I retraced my steps back to the container wharves, followed the 'yellow brick road', as the pedestrian path through the container park was known and from which you strayed at your own peril. Straddle-carriers sped around the park, lifting and shifting containers. You had to remain alert at all times, until you reached the foot of *ACT 5's* gangway and got back on board for dinner.

Fremantle was a much better experience than Genoa, including the weather. I thoroughly enjoyed wandering solo around new places, at my own pace, and we still had a few more Antipodean ports to visit. In merchant navy parlance, we were now 'on the coast'.

We sailed that evening, turning south on clearing the harbour limits and keeping the coast on our port side to round the south-west tip of this vast continent. *ACT 5* steamed across the Great Australian Bight, a reasonably calm experience, in contrast to the considerably rougher passage I experienced a couple of years later on *Mandama*.

On 20 November, *ACT 5* embarked the Port Phillip Sea Pilot and proceeded between the heads of Point Lonsdale and Point Nepean, via The Rip, a narrow and dangerous channel. It was infamous for strong turbulent tidal streams of up to eight knots, due to the seabed's uneven contours and dependent on the range of tide and prevailing environmental conditions. Once through, we were in Port Phillip Bay, a large horsehead-shaped bay on the central coastline of southern Victoria. Although mostly navigable, it was extremely shallow for its size, at its deepest only 79 feet (24 m) and half the bay was shallower than 26 feet (8 m). At the head of the bay was the state capital of Victoria, Melbourne, on the River Yarra. Its suburbs occupied the northern and eastern coasts of Port Phillip Bay. There were many beaches, most of which were flat, shallow, and long, with very small breaks, which made swimming relatively safe.

> This area had a long history of aboriginal occupation until Europeans arrived, the first was Captain Murray in HMS *Lady Nelson* in 1802. The more famous Matthew Flinders, Captain of HMS *Investigator* entered the bay some ten weeks later. To thwart French claims on the region, the Governor of New South Wales decided to establish a convict colony. Melbourne and its rival Geelong gradually developed, with the former taking precedence during the Gold Rush of 1851 over the latter's role as the main port for the wool trade.

The Port of Melbourne was the largest for containerised and general cargo in Australia. At the mouth of the Yarra River, it was downstream from Melbourne city centre. The berthing pilot took over from the sea pilot and

ACT 5 berthed at Swanson Dock container terminal and cargo operations soon started. Mike and I kicked off the cargo watch.

That afternoon, I took a taxi to the city as Swanson Dock was just too far from civilisation to go on foot. Melbourne city centre was beautifully situated astride both banks of the Yarra. The main streets of Collins and Bourke were wide boulevards with tram tracks along the centre. Flinders Street Station, at the corner of Flinders and Swanston Streets in the city centre, was a distinctive and eclectic Edwardian building. Its prominent dome, arched entrance, tower, and clocks, made it one of the city's most recognisable landmarks and the hub for Melbourne's suburban and regional rail services.

I wandered around and ended up on the Yarra's south bank, in the picturesque Royal Botanic Gardens, which led me to the Shrine of Remembrance. This was an impressive memorial to the dead of World War I and all subsequent wars and conflicts in which Australia participated. From a lofty position on the balcony of the Shrine, I espied, across the river, Melbourne Cricket Ground, universally known as the MCG, and Melbourne Park, venue for the Australian Open Tennis tournament.

My meanderings led me back across to the north bank to St Paul's Cathedral, the Treasury Gardens, and Parliament House. It was a glorious afternoon, bathed in sun and warmth. The Yarra was busy with small boats and numerous rowing eights from the riverside rowing clubs and folks jogging along the promenades.

I ended up at the GPO Building on a mission: I wanted to telephone my mother. Communication in those far-off days was just about non-existent, there was neither email nor internet, personal mail was difficult to organise, satellite phone calls from the ship were prohibitively expensive. I routinely wrote long letters and postcards to my folks and to my girlfriend Sue. Getting anything back was almost impossible. In the GPO Building, I booked an international call at the counter and was directed to one of several telephone booths along the wall. Inside, I dialled the number and enjoyed a nice chat with my mother. Afterwards, I returned to the counter where the charge was calculated and I paid up in cash. I didn't own a credit card.

Pete the passage-worker left the ship at Melbourne. He'd been great company and, with Roger, we'd had some laughs on deck, working with the Bajans. I have no idea what happened to him.

I returned on board via taxi, had dinner and then out on deck for cargo watch. It was a long night, as I think we sailed after midnight and stand-by didn't end until *ACT 5* had crossed Port Phillip Bay outbound and dropped the sea pilot outside the heads. When we were clear, the ship steamed eastwards through the Bass Strait and up the coast to Sydney, where we arrived on 23 November.

Naturally, I was very excited at the prospect of going to Sydney. Imagine my shock when I discovered that 'Sydney' was actually Botany Bay Container Port. I had no idea where Botany Bay was until we got there.

> Eight miles south of Sydney city centre, Botany Bay was, surprisingly perhaps, a distinguished footnote in history. On 29 April 1770, Captain James Cook made his first landing in Australia here from his ship HMS *Endeavour*. Although a convict colony was initially founded there, it didn't last long and was quickly moved to Sydney Cove. The area ultimately developed into an industrial zone: the container port itself, Sydney International Airport, numerous industrial businesses, and not much else that was of interest or pleasing to the eye.

After the initial disappointment, I took a taxi into Sydney after my morning watch and had another thoroughly brilliant afternoon. I walked to The Rocks (below the Harbour Bridge and site of Sydney's founding), and strolled round Circular Quay, the major terminus for the ferries that criss-cross Sydney Harbour and go to destinations upriver, as far as Parramatta. I ended up at the Opera House, an architectural marvel. From the surrounding promenade, the scene upriver was framed by the dominant Sydney Harbour Bridge, at the foot of the tower on the opposite side was the famed Luna Park. Through 180°, the view towards North and South Heads, the vertical cliffs which mark the entrance to the harbour, captured the extent of one of the world's largest, busiest, most expensive and beautiful natural harbours with its myriad inlets, bays, and beaches. So, this was what going to sea was all about!, Blimey, how lucky did I feel to be here?

I retreated from the Opera House and found myself in Sydney's Royal Botanic Garden – a beautiful haven of peace and greenery. I walked along Macquarie Street, skirted St Mary's Cathedral, and wended my way to the ANZAC Memorial at the south end of Hyde Park. This was another impressive memorial to Australia's war dead since World War I. I meandered back to the Town Hall and the Queen Victoria Building, noted the Sydney Tower dominating the immediate skyline of office buildings. Alas, it was time to return to the ship. I easily found a taxi outside the Town Hall and, in the fading light, arrived back on board.

I don't recall the time of day we departed Botany Bay, but it was undoubtedly another long day for all. *ACT 5* continued her progress northward along the coast, leaving North and South Heads to port, en route to Brisbane, where *ACT 5* berthed in Hamilton Reach during the evening of 29 November.

> Brisbane was the state capital of Queensland, the third most populated city in Australia, and one of the oldest. Flinders initially explored the Moreton Bay area – he certainly got about with his prolonged voyages of exploration! On 17 July 1799, he landed at present-day Woody Point, which he named Red Cliff Point after the coloured cliffs visible from the bay. The Brisbane River flowed through the city and out, via Moreton Bay, to the Coral Sea. After a short period as a penal colony, Brisbane was opened for free settlement in 1842, and became state capital when Queensland was proclaimed a separate colony from New South Wales in 1859. During World War II, the city played a central role in the Allied campaign and served as the South West Pacific headquarters for General Douglas MacArthur.
>
> The Port of Brisbane was located in the lower reaches of the Brisbane River on Fisherman Island, an artificial island reclaimed from the smaller Fisherman Islands group at the mouth of the river, adjacent to Brisbane Airport. It was Australia's third busiest port and its fastest growing container port, and the endpoint of the shipping channel across Moreton Bay. Logging and timber formed the base of Brisbane's economy until the latter half of the 19th century when coal and agricultural products were exported and manufactured goods imported. By 1888, the frozen beef trade was introduced, quickly followed by the processing of sugar, meat, and oil and mining output. In 1969, the first container terminal was built in Hamilton Reach.

There was no opportunity for me to go ashore as I worked cargo that night and then picked up the watch the next morning. We sailed that afternoon. It was a long stand-by as *ACT 5* navigated along the 56-mile (90 km) buoyed channel of Moreton Bay. We were still in pilotage waters when an emergency occurred. Ray the Fridgie had fallen down one of the hatches in the Burma Road while on his rounds of below-deck fridge containers. He'd broken his thigh bone. We about-turned and headed back up the channel towards Brisbane as medical assistance was mobilised ashore. After a couple of hours, Ray was safely landed, hospitalised and repatriated to the UK.

Meanwhile, *ACT 5* resumed her exit from Brisbane. At the Fairway Buoy, I escorted the pilot to the ladder. I was getting used to meeting-and-greeting pilots and escorting them away. I was also responsible for hoisting the courtesy flag of the nation we were visiting and the 'H' flag, which has a white left half and a red right half and means, in the International Code of Signals, 'I have a pilot on board'.

We turned to starboard on leaving Moreton Bay and set off south-east across the Tasman Sea to New Zealand. This sea can be quite punishing but, fortunately, both sea and swell were kind as we closed on the 'Land of the Long White Cloud'. After landfall at Mount Taranaki, *ACT 5* traversed South Taranaki Bight and entered Cook Strait, which separates North Island from South Island. The Strait gradually orientated north-south and narrowed appreciably between Arapawa Island off South Island to the west of us and Wellington on North Island to our east. The ship eased a turn to port and slipped into Wellington Bay, between Pencarrow Head and Palmer Head, a gap of about a mile (1.6 km). Ferries criss-crossed the harbour and also went to Picton on South Island.

> Wellington Harbour is a large natural harbour on the southern tip of New Zealand's North Island. Surrounded by hills nearly 1,000 feet (300 m) high, it provides sheltered anchorage in a region vulnerable to strong gales. The capital city, Wellington, and its port are located on the harbour's western side and took its name from Arthur Wellesley, the first Duke of Wellington and victor at Waterloo in 1815. His title originated from the town of Wellington in Somerset.
>
> The area was first inhabited by Maoris in the 10th century. The British arrived in 1839 and Wellington was declared a city the following year and designated the capital in 1865, replacing Auckland to assuage concerns about the possibility that the more populous South Island with its goldfields could declare itself a separate colony. Wellington is the southernmost and remotest capital city in the world. 'Windy Welly' is also the world's windiest city.

ACT 5 was alongside for a couple of days so, on both afternoons, I explored solo as, being unable to drink my own body weight, sitting in bars all day, held no appeal. Besides, I was on the opposite side of the world to home and there were so many places to visit.

Wellington was a neat little place although, save for the impressive Victorian public buildings, it was hardly the prettiest of cities. I took the funicular from Lambton Quay, the main shopping street, up to Wellington Botanic Garden in Kelburn, a hill-top suburb about 400 feet (120 m) above the city. The reader will note a theme, as I enjoyed wandering around the peaceful, relaxed environment of botanic gardens. These were locations that complemented visits to the notable (and usually densely crowded) tourist sights of whatever port we were in.

On departure from Wellington, *ACT 5* began an uneventful transpacific passage of about a fortnight. We saw few other merchant ships. The weather was good: warm sunshine, no rain, slight sea and low swell all the way. We crossed the Equator northbound and the International Date Line (IDL).

> The IDL was established in 1884 and passes through the mid-Pacific Ocean. It roughly follows a 180° longitude north-south line – although it zigzags around political borders such as eastern Russia and Alaska's Aleutian Islands. It is located exactly halfway round the world from the prime meridian, that is 0° longitude, which was established in Greenwich in 1852. The IDL's numerical designation is 180° East … or West. It functions as a 'line of demarcation', separating two consecutive calendar dates. When you cross it, you become a time-traveller of sorts! Cross to the west and it is one day later; cross to the east and you've 'gone back in time'.

We gained a calendar day. Lord Sam Vestey ensured he got his money's worth from his crews, as it was always deemed a week day, so we never got an 'extra' day off. On Christmas Eve, *ACT 5* anchored in the Gulf of Panama before transiting the Panama Canal.

> Since the early 16th century, there'd been a desire to build a canal across the isthmus to connect the Atlantic to the Pacific. Nothing much happened until the French got involved, under the enthusiastic conqueror of the Suez Canal, Ferdinand de Lesseps. Although excavations began in 1881, the project was mired in workers' deaths due to tropical disease, the company's bankruptcy, and political corruption in France. It was abandoned in 1889 but reinvigorated by President Theodore Roosevelt, who viewed it as of vital strategic interest to the US. Construction resumed in 1904 and the 48-mile-long (77 km) canal opened on 10 October 1913.
>
> After construction, the canal and the Canal Zone surrounding it were administered by the US. In 1977, President Jimmy Carter signed

the Treaty to transfer control to Panama. It gave Panama a 20-year grace period to gain increased responsibility for canal operations before complete US withdrawal on 31 December 1999. Since then, the canal has been administered by the Panama Canal Authority. Among the many engineering feats in its construction were the creation of two artificial lakes (Gatun and Miraflores) and three sets of locks.

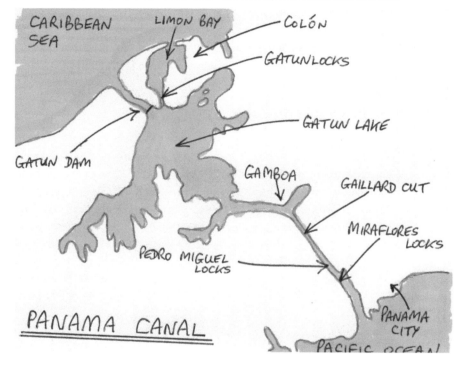

Fig 4.5 Panama Canal

On Christmas Day 1980 I made my first transit of the Panama Canal. As in Suez, there was a convoy system. The northbound convoy anchored in Gatun Lake to await the passage of the southbound convoy. Yes, the Panama Canal's orientation was generally north-south rather than the expected east-west. In addition, and equally surprising perhaps, the Pacific access at Balboa is east of the Atlantic access at Colon.

ACT 5 made her sedate way into the two-flight Miraflores Locks. The lock gates closed astern, the water level slowly rose and she exited into Miraflores Lake. The second set of locks (Pedro Miguel) were then negotiated. From the bridge and the monkey island it was really noticeable how the array of three- and four-high containers on deck severely restricted visibility to the bow and immediately beyond. I saw each side of the lock but the crane at No. 1 Hold was the only visible reference to the bow's location.

Fig 4.6 View from the bridge roof (monkey island), Panama Canal, Christmas Day 1980

Thereafter came a slow transit of the Gaillard or Culebra Cut. Great care was required as the Cut was very narrow before it eventually opened out into Gatun Lake. The early afternoon was spent at anchor waiting for the southbound convoy, which steamed slowly past. The triple-flight Gatun Locks were the final obstacle. Each set of locks was paired so there were two parallel flights of locks at each of the three sets. In principle, this allowed ships to pass in opposite directions simultaneously; however, large ships couldn't pass safely through the Culebra Cut at speed. So, in practice, ships passed in one direction for a time, then in the other, using both 'lanes'.

One important safety feature was that ships were guided through the lock chambers by electric locomotives (mules) running along the lock walls. The mules were used to control ships' side-to-side and braking in the narrow locks. Forward motion into and through the locks was by the ship's engine. A ship approached the locks, pulled up to the guide wall (an extension of the centre wall of the locks) where it was taken under control by the mules before proceeding into the lock. As it moved forward, additional lines were taken to mules on the other wall. Large ships had two mules on each side at the bow, and two on each side at the stern (eight in total), for precise control.

The mules ran on rail tracks with traction by electric power. Each mule had a powerful winch, operated by the driver, to control two cables to keep the ship centred in the lock while moving it from chamber to chamber. With a clearance of as little as two feet (60 cm) on each side of a ship, the drivers had to have considerable skill and coordination.

Fig 4.7 'Mule' at Miraflores Locks, Panama Canal, Christmas Day 1980

A good trick to play on first-trippers was, a few days before arrival, to encourage them to collect and save carrots from the galley to feed the mules at Panama. I was very wary of such suggestions from Marty and the other junior engineers and, fortunately, didn't fall for this jolly jape.

We exited at Colon that evening and set off through the Caribbean to our scheduled ports along the east coast of North America (ECNA in ACT parlance). For me, it was an extraordinary Christmas Day and, not for the first time, I thought: crikey, what a lucky bloke to have experienced both Suez and Panama Canals on my very first trip to sea.

ACT 5 steamed north-east, passing through the Windward Passage, between Cuba to port and Hispaniola to starboard, which was the most direct route between Panama and ECNA. The next few days were quite hectic navigating as the coast was busy with all sorts of vessels and there were short stops of only a few hours in Norfolk (29 December) and Philadelphia (30 December).

We were also in a northern hemisphere winter, so the air temperature decreased to single figures and then to sub-zero. Luckily, I was solo on cargo watch so there was plenty of walking around the weather deck, monitoring container movements to and from the ship. I didn't get ashore in either port, due to the limited time and because they were a fair old hike from town. The freezing weather didn't encourage me to make the effort.

New Year's Eve and New Year's Day were spent en route to St John, New Brunswick, with a limited celebration of the incoming 1981: a few sherbets in the bar with the day-work engineers. We berthed in St John on 2 January 1981.

It was bloody freezing on deck for cargo watch with an air temperature of about -20°C. There was always quite a breeze, so windchill reduced the temperature to under -30°C. Thankfully, there was not a howling gale. The Bajans wore rather natty, all-in-one thermal suits. Unlike me. I resorted to a couple of pairs of jeans and T-shirts and pullovers beneath my boilersuit and 'oilskins'. Fortunately, I had gloves and a bobble hat, but my fingers and toes were particularly numbed and the intense cold gradually penetrated to my very core. I went to the bar after my cargo watch and had a few sherbets to belatedly celebrate New Year with Marty, Dave, Norm, Billy, and George. Billy and Norm engaged in the habitual banter in their heavy regional accents (Scouse and Geordie respectively). There was no appeal whatsoever in going ashore.

> St John was a small town with zero attractions. In 1785, it was the first incorporated city in what eventually became Canada. Situated in the south-central portion of New Brunswick, along the north shore of the Bay of Fundy, it is a deep-water port that is ice-free all year. Its economy was dominated by maritime industries: shipping, fishing and shipbuilding. It also had one of Canada's largest oil refineries and a thriving pulp and paper mill industry.
>
> The Bay of Fundy has the greatest tidal range in the world (up to 52½ feet/16 m) due to a combination of the bay's funnel shape and the water's natural resonance. This rocking motion, called seiche, is similar to the movement of water in a bathtub, which sloshes from one end to the other and back again in a few seconds. But it takes about 13 hours for the water in Fundy to rock from the mouth to the head of the bay and back again. As the ocean tide rises and floods into the bay every 12 hours and 25 minutes, this rocking motion is reinforced.

Arctic sea smoke was ever-present for the duration of our time in St John. This fog forms when a light wind of very cold air mixes with a shallow layer of saturated warm air immediately above the warmer water. The warmer air is cooled beyond the dew point and no longer holds as much water vapour, so the excess condenses out. It was both quite eerie and rather graceful to witness a white veil covering the wharves and ships, with only the dock cranes and masts clearly visible.

Fig 4.8 Cape Cod Canal

After St John, *ACT 5's* next port was New York, via the Cape Cod Canal, part of the Atlantic Intracoastal Waterway, an artificial waterway connecting Cape Cod Bay in the north to Buzzards Bay in the south.

A transit of the Cape Cod Canal, avoided rounding Cape Cod and passing near Nantucket Island and Martha's Vineyard – a worthwhile shortening of the voyage. This shortcut between New York and Boston had been considered since the mid-17th century. After numerous surveys during the early 19th century, construction began in 1909 and was completed in 1914. It was widened and deepened just prior to World War II.

It was a brief visit to New York on 11 January 1981. So brief, that I saw the Statue of Liberty on the way in at dawn and on the way out at dusk. In between, I was on cargo watch and caught some sleep. We were too far from civilisation to step ashore and it was still bloody freezing. There was a part-crew change: Captain Stubbings was relieved by Captain Ian MacKillop; George the Mate was replaced by Colin Munday; a couple of other officers also changed out. Roger was paid off, relieved by Gregor McKenzie, an amiable deck cadet from Scotland. He was senior to me so I was still the 'junior joe'. The Bajan crew remained intact.

The rest of my first trip to sea became rather routine. Brief stops in Norfolk and Charleston (12 and 14 January respectively), back through the Panama Canal on 19 January, and across the Pacific. A quick whizz to Botany Bay (14 February), Melbourne (18 February) and Wellington (23 February), was followed by another transpacific voyage to transit the Panama Canal on 13 March. *ACT 5* crossed the Caribbean and entered the Atlantic via the Mona Passage between the Dominican Republic and Puerto Rico, the most direct route from Panama to Europe. We were homeward-bound! When we were clear of the tropics, we had more temperate weather as we steamed north-east. Sea and swell increased a little but nothing dramatic.

Our total average speed was an impressive 22½ knots for the transpacific voyage from Wellington to the Panama Canal, a day for the transit, then transatlantic to Tilbury. At last, we docked at Tilbury in the eastern reaches of the Thames, just upriver from and on the opposite bank to Northfleet and Gravesend.

I paid off from *ACT 5* in Tilbury. 'Suitcase trials' (packing my bags) were successful. My parents came to collect me as they were interested in seeing 'my' ship and I wanted to show them around. I introduced them to Mr Best and the Bajan ABs. I shook Mr Best's hand and was very sad to say cheerio. I learnt a lot from him and his boys and very much enjoyed working for him and with them on deck. I'd grown fond of them all and hoped to sail with some again in the near future.

I bade farewell to the officers and, finally, to Colin the Mate and Captain MacKillop, who filled in my Discharge Book and paid me off. With that final bureaucratic formality, I was now free and my folks and I went down the gangway, packed into their car, and drove home to Gosport.

It had certainly been an extremely enjoyable and exciting first trip: transits of the Suez and Panama Canals; crossing the Indian, Pacific and Atlantic Oceans; crossing the Equator and the International Date Line several times; and steaming one-and-half times around the world. I'd settled comfortably into the work on deck; qualified for my steering ticket (12 hours on the helm, following the Mate's orders to alter course and maintaining that course); witnessing the Second Mate observing the sun with his sextant and following his calculations to attain our astronomical position at noon; completing some of my task book; learning much of the *Rule of the Road* off by heart, signed off in my task book; and experiencing doubling up on watch with one of the Mates; navigating the east coast of North America and the coasts of Australia and New Zealand. I certainly felt I'd learnt a lot in five months.

Home at last for what I considered some well-earned leave. I wondered when Mr Burke would phone me with details of my next trip.

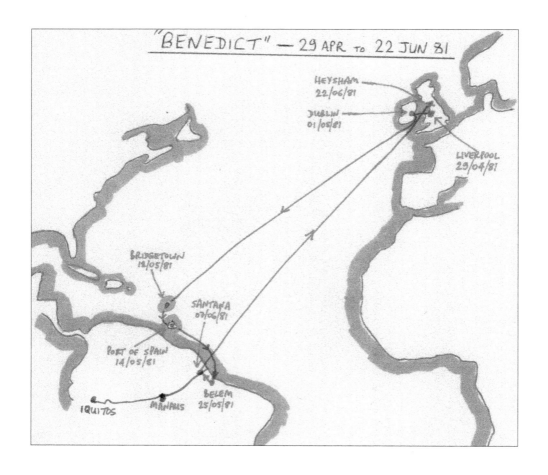

"BENEDICT" — 29 APR to 22 JUN 81

HEYSHAM
22/06/81

DUBLIN
01/05/81

LIVERPOOL
29/04/81

BRIDGETOWN
12/05/81

SANTANA
07/06/81

PORT OF SPAIN
14/05/81

BELEM
25/05/81

IQUITOS

MANAUS

Fig 5.1 *Benedict* voyage

5 To the Amazon with Booth Line

Fig 5.2 *Benedict* (Fotoflite)

In April 1981, Mr Burke informed me of my next trip. Alas, I wasn't destined to jet off somewhere glamorous, exotic, or at least foreign, to join a ship. It was back to Liverpool by train to join *Benedict* at Canada Branch Dock on 29 April.

Benedict was built at Engenharia e Maquinas S.A. in Rio de Janeiro and entered service in February 1979. She was 380 feet (115 m) long, 57 feet (17 m) in the beam, with a draught of 21 feet (6.5 m). She was a much smaller vessel than *ACT 5*, at 3,636 gross tonnage and 1,967 net tonnage. *Benedict* and her sister-ship, *Boniface*, were three-hold, general cargo vessels equipped with four Velle 'hammer-head' derricks, each with a safe working load (SWL) of 22 tons and designed to slew like a crane.

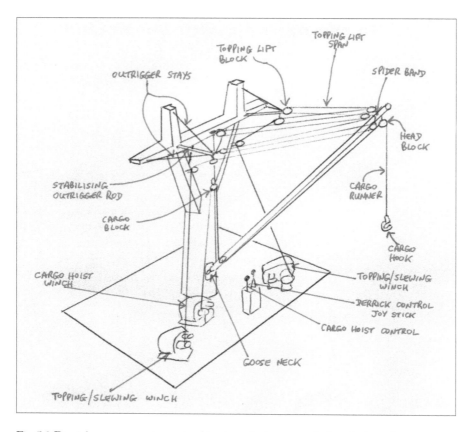

Fig 5.3 Derrick arrangement: topping/slewing winches, cargo hoist winch, and one-man operated control column

What's the difference between a derrick and a crane, both a bit of kit for lifting cargo between ship and dockside? A crane uses a hoist rope, a wire rope, or a chain with a sheave (pulley system) to lift and move heavy objects. A derrick makes use of at least one guyed mast and a boom or jib, and the guy wires are adjusted to lift objects. Cranes often replace derricks to lift lighter loads. The crane-driver slews his crane and simultaneously raises and lowers the jib so the cargo is more easily and exactly placed on board or on the wharf. Derricks are used for heavier lifts.

There is more to a derrick than simply a boom (jib), a mast and a couple of winches and guy wires. The purchase (a wire rove through two or more blocks) reduces the weight of the total load at the point where power is supplied to lift that load. On ships, a block (comprising a pulley wheel or wheels), is fixed within a frame. Basic physics, particularly mechanical advantage, velocity ratio, friction, and efficiency, are integral factors in the design and operation of a merchantman's lifting gear. Clear but simple explanations to these principles are found in texts such as CH Wright's *The Efficient Deck Hand* and Danton's *Theory and Practice of Seamanship* – both indispensable reference books for a deck cadet.

A ship's lifting gear is subject to mandatory periodic testing and inspection. All blocks (single or multi-sheave), wires, guys, shackles, swivels, chains, rings, hooks, and derrick booms are tested and stamped to a certified SWL, which is not to be exceeded under any circumstance. It's incumbent on the ship's staff to examine ropes and wires regularly for chafing, cutting, internal wear, deterioration of fibres, dryness in a wire rope, and opening of the lay of a rope. All of which could cause them to part and result in serious injury or death to crew or stevedores.

Benedict's prime lifting-gear was the Velle derrick – a boom with a T-shaped head and several sheaves and blocks through which steel wires roved. The boom was controlled by winches, whose wires were heaved in or eased out in harmony to swing the derrick between the hold being worked and the dockside. Guys added stability and rigidity to the rig. It was critical that winch operators worked in synchronicity to ensure a safe, controlled, and smooth loading or unloading operation.

Benedict's derricks and associated winches were sited on two masthouses, one forward of, and the second aft of, Number 2 hold. With an extra accommodation deck to meet European manning levels, ship stability was extremely poor. Both ships were especially designed with a shallow draught to operate up the Amazon. Propulsion was by a MAN 4,375 brake horsepower, seven-cylinder, four-stroke engine to a single screw via a reversing gearbox. But that's enough 'clanky' stuff!

Benedict and *Boniface* were the latest additions to Booth Line, founded in Liverpool in 1866 by Alfred and Charles Booth. The company traditionally named ships after notable bishops and other historic figures: Saint Benedict (480–547 AD) is the venerated patron saint of Europe and founder of western Christian monasticism; Saint Boniface (675–754 AD) is celebrated as a missionary and unifier of Europe, particularly by German Catholics. He was a native of Crediton (where, by sheer coincidence, I now live), and in 2019 he was officially recognised as Devon's patron saint.

Like many British shipping lines, Booth repeatedly used the same name. The first *Benedict* was built in 1894, and my *Benedict* was the fourth iteration. *Boniface* was also the fourth, the first was built in 1904 and then torpedoed and sunk in 1917 off the Aran Islands, near Galway Bay.

Originally, Booth Line carried English leather to the USA and subsequently started a regular steamship service between Liverpool and northern Brazil and along the Amazon River. The patenting of the pneumatic tyre in 1888 opened up a significant trade in natural rubber from Brazil. By 1914, Booth Line had a fleet of 14 ships and operated passenger liners from Liverpool to Lisbon, Madeira, and the Amazon.

Booth's *Hildebrand* was a magnificent passenger liner, built in 1911 at the peak of the Brazilian rubber bonanza. At 6,995 gross tons, 440 feet (134 m) long, 54 feet (16.5 m) in breadth, and 27 feet (8.2 m) draught, she carried 218 first-class and 406 third-class passengers. In World War I, she was commissioned as HMS *Hildebrand*, an armed merchant cruiser, and returned to Booth Line in late 1917. From 1922 to 1930, she was Booth's only first-class passenger ship on the regular service to Oporto, Lisbon, Madeira, and Belém.

An obscure fact is that Sir Edward Elgar, composer of such famous works as *Pomp and Circumstance* and *Enigma Variations*, was an inveterate traveller and keen amateur chemist. He never fully recovered from his wife's death in 1920 and spent much of the last 14 years of his life in a virtual creative silence. He took a round trip on *Hildebrand* in 1923 and was apparently impressed by Manaus' opera house (Teatro Amazonas). But no records have survived about Elgar's activities or experiences during his voyage. Interestingly, James Hamilton-Paterson won the 1989 Whitbread Award for first novel, *Gerontius*, an enjoyable, poetic, dreamy, fictional account of Elgar's voyage on *Hildebrand*. Elgar's *The Dream of Gerontius* interprets Cardinal John Henry Newman's text in which the central character, Gerontius (a derivation of 'old man' in Ancient Greek), prays for assistance to the Blessed Virgin Mary and other saints. After his soul-searing first sight of God, Gerontius doesn't go straight to Heaven, but is committed to Purgatory for purification.

As with other British shipping companies, Booth suffered losses of ships and crews during both World Wars. In 1946, Booth Steamship Company was bought by the Vestey Group. Booth Line ceased to exist as a separate entity when BSSM was established in 1975.

When I joined BSSM, Booth Line operated a scheduled service between Heysham, Liverpool, and Dublin across to Barbados, Trinidad, and Belém in Brazil. Several times a year, there were 1,000-mile trips up the Amazon to Manaus to load Brazil nuts and, occasionally, nearly another 1,000 miles to Iquitos in Peru.

In, the 1960s Booth boats (*Cuthbert* and *Clement*) spent up to two months in the Amazon on every voyage, usually a fortnight in Manaus, a week or so in Iquitos, and stops at small lumber camps to load timber. As labour was significantly cheaper in Brazil, the felled timber was cut into planks at these camps prior to loading on a Booth boat.

An excellent Snowbow Productions DVD captures the essence of Booth Line's extended Amazon trips, using the Radio Officer's 1970s cinecamera footage. *Cuthbert* steamed upriver to Manaus and Iquitos, secured to trees at isolated timber and logging camps in minor Amazon tributaries, overtook ferry boats, and waved at sister ship *Clement* heading downriver. A brilliant piece of maritime history and heritage. Those certainly were the good old days of the merchant navy.

I was the only cadet on board, so the Mate (Alan Brown, a young, rather brash, Yorkshireman) gave me a ship's tour. It was distinctly different being on a cargo ship with deckhouses, masts, derricks, and associated winches and rigging, compared to my container ship experience on *ACT 5*. Further, *Benedict* had no refrigerated cargo capacity. When the hatch covers were opened, the hold was a deep, gaping, regular rectangle within which a couple of tween-decks were visible. In the uppermost tween-deck a hatch was folded back to reveal the vast lower hold below.

Like ACT 5, the compact accommodation block was at the stern and surmounted the engine room. The cosy, rather cramped officers' bar and dining room were on the starboard side, the crew's on the port side. The galley, internal ladders, and casing for funnel exhaust pipework and engine room fans straddled the ship's centre line. As *Benedict* was significantly smaller than *ACT 5*, the tour didn't take long. I met several of the Bajan crew and, later, the British officers (Master, three Mates, Chief Engineer, three Engineers, Electrician, Purser and Radio Officer). I was allocated the pilot's cabin as there was no designated cadet's cabin. It was considerably smaller than my luxurious *ACT 5* cabin, but equipped with two bunk beds, a small wardrobe and desk, and a tiny en-suite bathroom. It didn't take me long to feel at home. After cargo operations were complete the following day, *Benedict* sailed on 30 April.

I briefly met Captain John 'Flash' Harris the day I joined. He was a prim, proper officer and *Benedict*'s continuity Master. His tropical white uniform was always immaculate and beautifully ironed, with sharp creases. As the sole cadet, I was always stationed on the bridge for stand-by, and my role expanded from that on *ACT 5*.

Although an AB acted as helmsman, I was responsible for operating the telegraph. A cute little handle was used to communicate orders to the engine room by setting it to 'stop', 'dead slow ahead', 'half ahead', 'full ahead', and the equivalent astern movements. In the engine room, a similar telegraph was used to acknowledge the Captain's orders. When a ship was securely berthed, the Captain's final engine order, 'finished with main engine', was 'rung' on the telegraph.

I used the *Bridge Movements Book* to note our passing of navigation marks and buoys, and to record all engine movements. In parallel, I maintained a concise summary in the *Deck Log* (a legal document) of times for our entry into and departure from each port and included 'POB' (pilot on board), 'pilot away' when he disembarked, when mooring lines (head ropes, stern ropes, breast ropes) were passed to the quay, when the anchor was 'let go' and 'aweigh', and FWME (finished with main engine). It was a bit of an art to decide the level of detail to insert in the Deck Log. But my *ACT 5* experience had shown me the typical content required.

I hoisted and lowered all flags (courtesy ensign, plus 'H' flag when the pilot was embarked). My pilot escorting duties were reprised. I made tea or coffee at the behest of 'Flash' Harris and the pilot; and any other miscellaneous tasks the Old Man thought of. Crikey, I was like a one-armed wallpaper-hanger.

During one port entry, 'Flash' Harris disappeared without warning, leaving me and the AB alone on the bridge. Then I heard his radio crackle as Alan Brown called him up on the walkie-talkie. The Captain's reply echoed behind me. He was having a pee in the bridge heads (toilet) with his walkie-talkie slung over his shoulder. 'Flash' Harris confidently re-emerged as if nothing had happened. Overall, my responsibilities on the bridge were excellent experience. I learnt much not only from my tasks but also by monitoring the walkie-talkie chatter between the bridge, for'ard and aft, VHF communications between the ship and shore authorities, and observing the working relationship between Master and pilot.

Departing the berth, *Benedict* manoeuvred into Langton Lock. The lock gates closed astern of us, the water level adjusted to that of the Mersey, the gates opened and off we went via a sharpish turn to starboard. The Wirral on our port side, the lengthy extent of Liverpool Docks to starboard, while Pierhead and the Liver Building gradually fell astern as *Benedict* proceeded down the River Mersey's buoyed channel. I escorted the pilot down the external ladders to the pilot ladder and waved him off as the pilot boat turned away from *Benedict* and sped back to the safe haven of Liverpool. It was a short, overnight, virtually east-west passage, skirting round Holyhead, to Dublin, Ireland's capital city, where we berthed mid-morning.

Dublin Bay and the approach to the port were hardly scenic. We left the Howth peninsular to starboard as we closed the mouth of the River Liffey, which flowed in an east-west direction, splitting Dublin in two. With the pilot embarked, *Benedict* glided along the Great South Wall, which extended some 1,300 yards (1,200 m) into the Bay and berthed at the wharf on the south bank. It was a rather flat, grubby, industrial zone and seemed a bit of a wasteland when I viewed it from my lofty perch on the bridge wing. I saw the city skyline in the distance and made out a couple of bridges across the Liffey. At this range, it didn't appear to be very attractive.

I didn't have an opportunity to go up the road to disprove my initial impression of Dublin. I was fully engaged in observing cargo operations. This was quite a contrast from working containers. For a start, our derricks were in use and stevedores were down the holds, either preparing cargo for discharge or stowing and securing newly loaded cargo.

Another job for a deck cadet in port was the hoisting of flags and switching off deck floodlighting in the morning and the reverse (flag lowering and lights on) at sunset each evening. There were usually three flags: red ensign, the company's house flag, and the host country's national flag.

In general cargo ships, there was more work for a deck officer to do as the cargo plan had to be closely monitored to ensure not only that hold space was efficiently occupied, but that cargo was loaded in the correct position. This was essential for two reasons: ship stability and ease of access for unloading to avoid unnecessarily moving other cargo out of the way. Time is money! A cargo plan was both of an art and a science, for which the Mate was primarily responsible. It showed the distribution and location of all cargo parcels stowed in the holds for the voyage. Each entry on the plan detailed a commodity's quantity, weight, and ports of loading and discharge. It included special loads, such as heavy-lifts, hazardous, and valuable cargo.

The Mate's hand-drawn cargo plan was extraordinarily annotated and detailed. It required updating in each port as cargo was discharged and other cargo was loaded. Sometimes this necessitated a complete redraw. Today, software (such as stowage planning software) creates a cargo plan in a fraction of the time and allows real-time monitoring of the parameters of ship's

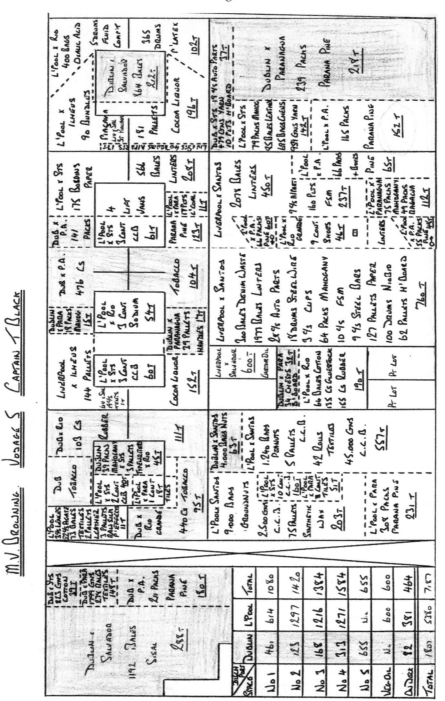

Fig 5.4 Example of a cargo plan, showing detail required. *Browning* was one of four Lamport & Holt general cargo ships trading between Liverpool and South America. Her sister ships were *Belloc, Bronte, and Boswell*. (Stephen Pridmore)

stability and floating status when stowing and moving cargo. The distribution of weight within each hold has to be carefully planned and managed so as to not adversely affect stability and endanger the ship.

The central open 'square' of the hold was used to receive and dispatch cargo. The wings of the hold were packed first and then cargo encroached into the square until the lower hold was full and the tween deck hatch closed. The tween deck was then loaded. Depending on the volume of cargo to be moved, it was possible to work all three hatches simultaneously. This meant the mate on deck had to be constantly mobile to properly monitor and supervise the whole operation. Not only from the upper deck, looking over the hatch coaming, but also by climbing down and up ladders within each hold. A deck watch was therefore pretty exhausting physically and mentally, as you had to remain continuously alert to cargo movements in and out of a hold, as well as within it.

Benedict was reasonably well loaded. Among a variety of general palletised and break bulk cargo were old buses from Liverpool. The Dublin cargo added Guinness concentrate in tanks and Irish malt whisky. Break bulk describes goods loaded individually in bags, boxes, crates, drums, or barrels. Unit loads of these were secured to a pallet or skid. Items such as sacks or bags were loaded in batches using a sling or cargo net, while cartons and boxes were placed on trays and then lifted on board.

Once in the hold, each item was stowed separately. Hence, break bulk cargo operations were labour-intensive. Stevedores were highly skilled workmen, as loading and unloading ships meant knowing how to operate loading equipment (lifting gear), proper techniques for lifting and stowing cargo, and correct handling of hazardous materials. They were responsible for ensuring that all cargo was sufficiently and correctly secured in the hold, usually with rope lashings.

Stevedores use dunnage, timber boards that are laid in single or double patterns under cargo to keep the bottom clear of the steel deck plate. The air space created prevents 'cargo sweat'. Dunnage was also used as shims between cargo crates for load securing. It was the Mate's responsibility to physically check the secured cargo when the stevedores claimed they had completed this task.

Prior to loading, the deck crew ensured that: debris from the previous cargo was removed; holds were swept and washed down if necessary; any damage was repaired; the bilges were emptied; dunnage was laid ready for the cargo or left in bundles for the stevedores to lay out during loading. These tasks required swift, efficient activity as time was critical and costly in merchant shipping. As deck cadets, we were inevitably part of the Bosun's hold-cleaning team. One of the dirtier tasks was emptying the bilges, not just of muck but also of liquid of dubious origin. Stevedores often had a pee in the hold rather than have to go ashore to answer the call of nature. When in port, we always locked our cabins and all but one point of entry from deck to the inside of the accommodation block.

On departure from Dublin, *Benedict* turned to starboard and headed south in the Irish Sea, leaving Wicklow and Arklow to starboard. Navigating close to the Irish coast, we steamed through St George's Channel between Rosslare and an unseen Fishguard in Pembrokeshire, far over the horizon. The Irish coast fell away astern as we encountered the South West Approaches – an area of water with which I would become very familiar some five or so years later as a Royal Navy hydrographic surveyor. Eventually, Ireland disappeared from view and *Benedict* set off across the Atlantic. When completely clear of land both visually and by radar, it was Captain Harris' practice to switch off the radar to ensure that his bridge watchkeeping officers kept a particularly acute visual watch rather than breezily relying on radar while crossing the vast expanse of empty ocean.

We settled into a daily routine as *Benedict* slowly progressed through the Atlantic. I was on day-work with the Bajans for most of the time. They were another jolly bunch of sailors and I was used to their work practices and pace. The morning and afternoon periods were interrupted at 1000 and 1430 for smoko (tea/coffee break) – a great merchant navy tradition. If you were lucky, the galley might provide cakes, which made it occasionally rather more special and known as 'tea and tabnabs'. Meanwhile, as the mates and engineers were all watchkeepers, life in the mess in the evenings was pretty quiet. This afforded me no excuse not to get on top of my correspondence courses and became more au fait with the ROR. My *Task Book* was slowly filling with signatures, with a focus on parrot-fashion recitals of the RORs to Captain Harris or Alan the Mate.

I visited the bridge some evenings to keep the 3rd Mate company for a while. During day watches, although alone on the bridge, there was always crew to observe working on deck as well as the Old Man (as the Master is traditionally called) popping up at times. Night watches were rather lonely as the bridge team was just the mate and a watchman. The former worked primarily inside the bridge, the latter acted as lookout from the bridge-wing and, for half an hour, was legally permitted to go below for smoko, which left the on-watch mate completely alone.

I learnt much from my short visits to the bridge: navigation, chartwork (although not much in mid-ocean using a chart that covered the entire Atlantic), and various electronic navigation systems. Importantly, I also became more familiar with many of the standard publications that a deck officer habitually uses; such as Admiralty publications like the *List of Lights*, *List of Radio Signals* and the *Nautical Almanac*. I discovered one of my favourite publications, *The Mariner's Handbook*, a UK Hydrographic Office product which I found simply enthralling and full of interesting 'stuff'. Its chapters covered: charts and books and their terms, symbols, and orthography; use of charts and other navigational aids; navigational hazards; and natural conditions like meteorology and bioluminescence. There was a fascinating chapter on ice, complete with definitions and photographs of ice features, and the principles of navigation in ice. It described the Beaufort wind scale and included a few useful conversion tables. I never expected to need most of the content but all this miscellaneous information was good to know and helped broaden my nautical education. Call me sad, if you wish.

Weather and sea conditions for our transatlantic voyage were good, particularly as we reached the lower latitudes. The sun shone warmly and made it very pleasant to work on deck every day, all day. There was always a multitude of tasks aside from chipping and painting.

I cleared out the lockers in the fo'c'sle. These were compartments for storing particular bits of kit. The rope store had new mooring ropes and wires in case any of those in use parted or became irreparable. The bosun's locker held heaving lines, shackles, blocks, rope stoppers, chain stoppers, bosun's chairs, stages, and a miscellany of seamanship items. In the days of sail, it must have been a larger compartment, as the store for sails, ropes, canvas, and associated items of rigging. I made an inventory of the contents of the bosun's locker for the Mate and then cleaned and greased all items before re-stowing everything neatly.

I also helped the painter sort out his paint locker. The painter was the AB responsible for the ship's paint shop, located right up forward in the fo'c'sle. Paint brushes and rollers and empty paint tins were fine, but the aromatic blend of paint (red lead, primer, top coat), thinners, spirit, and turpentine was quite heady. If there was anything more than a slight sea, you felt yourself slowly edging towards a headache and possible vomiting. Ships gave off a distinct combination of smells – steel, rust, damp, chemicals, oil, and grease – and a general grubbiness when you looked beneath the surface.

One day, the Mate gave me the job of greasing the lifting gear. This was quite a big job as it included the winches, masts, derrick booms, swivels, and blocks. I reported to the Bosun. He furnished me with a grease gun and a rag, instructed me on using a grease gun (including how to reload it and where to find the grease when my gun was empty).

Fig 5.5 *Benedict's* masts and masthouses: I lubricated every grease nipple with my grease gun

A grease gun was a common workshop tool used for lubrication, similar to the filler guns used in domestic DIY. Its purpose was to apply lubricant through an aperture to a specific point via a grease fitting. The grease gun's aperture fitted closely on a receiving aperture or 'nipple' on the item of machinery. The snug fit of these apertures ensured that lubricant was applied only where it was needed. A grease gun was a metal barrel filled with grease, with a short rubber hose with an attachment at its end, and a hand-operated lever to pump grease into the machinery. I took several rags as I expected it to be a grubby job. I wasn't wrong on that score! A merchant ship's engine room was always well-stocked with large bundles of 'engine room rags' and 'cotton-waste', bundles of scraps of waste cotton yarn used to clean machinery. A ship's engineer was never seen without his rag and, equally importantly, his torch!

The Bosun showed me where to find grease nipples and how to attach the grease gun to them. At several places on a winch, grease nipples were visible. He left me to it, so I began the task by slowly inspecting every nook and cranny of the winch. Attaching my hose end to the grease nipple was easy as it just slid into place. Once I got the hang of it, the pace increased. There were about a dozen winches on *Benedict*'s two deckhouses. I then moved on to the other items of lifting gear. I was in my own little world and no one bothered me.

Eventually, I finished all the grease nipples on the deckhouses. Next were those on the blocks on the cross-members of each mast. I clambered up the first mast clutching my grease gun, rag hanging out of my shorts pocket. It was awkward accessing each block as I had to get flat on my belly some 50 feet above the deck, lean out, attach the end of the hose to the nipple, then pump in the grease until the lubricant had filled the block. Fortunately, sea state and swell were low and gentle during this period. *Benedict* wasn't subject to heavy rolling, so the mast (with me belly-flat on the cross-tree) wasn't swinging through a lengthy arc.

One morning I was up the mast, focused on grease gun and grease nipples, no idea of the time, when suddenly the ship's horn blew. I almost jumped out of my skin and nearly fell off the mast with shock. I looked towards the bridge and saw the 3rd and 2nd Mates on the bridge wing chuckling furiously at my expense. Luckily, I was wearing my safety harness attached to the railing. But it wasn't some cruel joke being played on me, it was standard practice (in Blue Star, anyway) to sound one short blast on the horn at noon daily. I knew it was a 'short blast of about one second's duration' as defined in Rule 32 of the *International Regulations for Preventing Collisions at Sea* having learnt it and had it signed off in my *Task Book*. In Blue Star, at least, this daily 'honk' alerted the deck crew that it was lunchtime.

As I was now the ace grease gun expert, the Mate gave me the task of continuing with the windlass on the fo'c'sle and the capstan on the poop deck. Another good couple of days' work outside on deck in the sunshine. Wonderful.

On 12 May 1981, *Benedict* rounded the northern tip of Barbados and steamed down the west coast to Bridgetown harbour on the south-west coast. Entry to the port was a simple easterly course, to pass between the breakwaters, a turn to starboard and *Benedict* soon nestled alongside Berth 2, right beside the cruise ship berth. It was quite a hive of activity, even before the present-day popularity for cruising began. A P&O Princess-class cruise liner was in port, so there was constant pedestrian traffic of, predominantly, American 'wrinklies' going ashore or returning on board. We deep-sea, foreign-going cargo seamen sniffed at the crews of 'fanny freighters', cruising around on floating hotels, never getting their hands dirty. We held a similar opinion on the dull, mind-numbingly tedious life of cross-channel ferry crews. A sort of inverted snobbery, I suppose, as we were obviously the merchant navy workhorses, moving mass volumes of all sorts of goods worldwide day in, day out, keeping global trade ticking over. I had no inkling that a dozen years hence I'd return as part of a Royal Navy survey team to conduct a hydrographic survey of Bridgetown harbour.

Fig 5.6 *Benedict* in Bridgetown, 12 May 1981

Barbados is the most easterly of the Caribbean Islands, initially claimed by Spain in 1511, then Portugal in 1532, and ultimately Britain in 1625. It developed into a wealthy sugar colony. On 30 November 1966, Barbados became an independent state and a Commonwealth nation. Historically, the economy depended on sugarcane cultivation and related activities, but by the late 1970s and early 1980s it had diversified into manufacturing and tourism.

The capital, Bridgetown, was established by English settlers in 1628, and eventually became a major West Indies tourist destination, particularly as a cruise ship port of call in the Caribbean. Bridgetown Port (also known as Deep Water Harbour) was the major port of entry for cruise and cargo ships visiting Barbados and one of the major shipping and transhipment hubs from international locations for the entire Eastern Caribbean.

Alas, it was only a short stop in Bridgetown, as only a few tons of cargo were unloaded: whisky and Guinness. I got no further than the passenger terminal shop to buy, write, and post a couple of postcards to my folks and girlfriend. It was then a short passage to Port of Spain, the capital of Trinidad and Tobago. *Benedict* steamed south-south-west and passed through the Bocas del Dragon, the strait separating Venezuela on mainland South America from the island of Trinidad. We turned to port into the Gulf of Paria, navigated along the coast and into the port.

Trinidad is the largest of the two islands of Trinidad and Tobago. Lying 6.8 miles (11 km) off the north-east coast of Venezuela, it is the southernmost island in the Caribbean. Christopher Columbus discovered the islands on his third voyage in 1498. From 1889 Trinidad and Tobago was a British Crown colony, but gained independence from the UK in 1962. Among the top five exporters of liquefied natural gas, it was one of the wealthiest Caribbean nations.

Port of Spain's port was a natural harbour on the sheltered south coast of Trinidad's north-western peninsular, so the approach was straightforward as there were no breakwaters or other man-made sea defences for *Benedict* to negotiate. We simply picked up the pilot and 'drove' straight to the berth. Port of Spain's location was ideal for servicing major sea lanes between the Americas, the Caribbean islands and trading links between the Atlantic and Pacific Oceans via the Panama Canal.

As *Benedict* had a couple of days working cargo, I went up the road, as it wasn't far to walk into town. I'd been warned that Port of Spain was quite a dangerous place, so I kept my wits about me throughout my rather limited solo wanderings. My overall impression was of a rather shabby town, with sadly neglected, colonial buildings from a grander age. The streets were unkempt and scattered with litter. The whole place needed a jolly good clean-up and a lick of paint to perk it up. Superficially, the citizens seemed friendly, but I detected a slight undercurrent of threat and felt a little uncomfortable as dusk approached. I didn't hang around to get mugged and scuttled back on board for dinner. I wasn't sorry to leave and Port of Spain is not on my holiday bucket list.

On departure, *Benedict* steamed direct to Belém in Brazil, a five-day voyage of 1,372 nautical miles (2,540 km). The coasts of Venezuela, Guyana, Suriname, and French Guiana were on our starboard side, the vast emptiness of the Atlantic stretched beyond the horizon to port. As *Benedict* closed Belém, the sea gradually changed from its usual blue/green to a grubby discolouration, due to the enormous plume of the Amazon's outflow.

> Research has revealed the Amazon as the largest single source of terrestrial freshwater to the ocean, contributing about 30% of total river discharge into the Atlantic. Amazon plume water was traced offshore and north-westward along the north Brazilian coast, into the Caribbean and over 620 miles (1,000 km) eastward into the North Atlantic.

Benedict entered Baja de Marajó, some 12 miles (20 km) wide, and penetrated the River Pará to berth at Belém on 25 May. The port of Belém was situated about 62 miles (100 km) up the River Pará, on its east bank, and was the most important commercial port on Brazil's north coast.

> Belém is the capital and largest city of the state of Pará, gateway to the Amazon, and a busy transport hub. The city eventually became the main exporting centre for the Amazon rubber industry. Its importance was enhanced by the opening up to navigation of the Amazon, Tocantins, and Tapajós rivers from 1866. The River Pará itself was part of the greater Amazon River system, separated from the larger part of the Amazon delta by Ilha de Marajó (Marajo Island), opposite Belém.
>
> Captain Sandy Kinghorn's excellent autobiography, *Before the Box Boats*, includes a description of his first trip as 2nd Mate on Booth Line's *Dominic*. She was a compact general cargo ship of some 4,000 gross tons, 338 feet (103 m) long, a beam of 50 feet (15.2 m) and a 23 feet (7 m) draught. Built in Wilmington, California, in 1945 as *Hickory Stream*, Booth acquired her in 1947. Captain Kinghorn described arrival at Belém, the home port of *Dominic's* Brazilian crew. They disappeared ashore to home and family until the ship sailed.

In 1955, the eclectic mix of cargo loaded into *Dominic* included bales of jacaranda leaves, sacks of gum, bags of wax, drums of balsam and rosewood oil, Brazil nuts, cocoa, skins of otter, deer, alligator, jaguar, and wild boar. Guided by two embarked pilots, *Dominic* then set off 1,000 miles (1,610 km) up the Amazon to Manaus where she loaded kapok logs. Kapok fibres were used as filling for mattresses, pillows, swimming belts, lifejackets, and insulating material. Our bulky, cumbersome UK Department of Trade approved lifejackets were of kapok encased in orange nylon covers.

Captain Kinghorn also noted Booth Line's important influence in the Amazon delta since 1866. Special Booth Line charts were used, the company's tugs assisted in berthing their ships, and towed Booth Line barges. What a wonderful experience his *Dominic* trip must have been. Sadly, by the time I was involved, that was all consigned to history, lost forever, as Booth Line's influence gradually declined.

With *Benedict* in a riverine fresh water environment, it's an opportune moment to describe the Plimsoll line (or international load line).

Samuel Plimsoll, MP, was concerned with the loss of ships and crews due to vessel overloading. In 1876, he persuaded Parliament to pass the Unseaworthy Ships Bill, which mandated marking a ship's sides with a line that, if submerged below the waterline, showed the ship was overloaded. This Plimsoll line is found amidships on the port and starboard sides of merchant ships. It indicates the draught of the ship and the legal limit to which a ship may be loaded for specific water types and climates to safely maintain buoyancy.

Water temperature affects a ship's draught: warm water is less dense than cold water, yielding less buoyancy. A similar reduction in buoyancy is found in fresh water, as its density is lower than sea water's. The exact location of the load line is calculated and verified by a classification society (such as Lloyd's Register), which issues the relevant certificates. International Load Line Rules (1968) specify the exact dimensions and relative positions of each load line mark:

- Deck line: horizontal line marking the freeboard deck, which is the uppermost complete deck with a permanent means of closing all openings and hatches
- Load line disc (Plimsoll line): a circle with its centre amidships and below the deck line; the disc is bisected by a horizontal line

that marks the summer salt waterline and letters that indicate the classification society (in Figure 5.7 LR is Lloyds Register)

- Summer load line (S): is the basic computed load line and is level with the Plimsoll line
- Winter load line (W): a line 1/48th of the summer draught below the summer load line
- Tropical load line (T): a line 1/48th of the summer draught above the summer load line
- Winter North Atlantic load line (WNA): marked 50 mm below the winter load line on all vessels 100 m or less in length and applies to voyages in the Atlantic north of latitude 36° north during winter months
- A ship's draught increases when it passes from salt water to fresh water, because fresh water is less dense than salt water. This sinkage is calculated using a formula which defines the Fresh Water Allowance (FWA), measured in millimetres. It means that a ship can be loaded to its fresh water load line (F) because when she returns to salt water, her draught will reduce to the summer load line (S).
- Fresh water load line (F): a line marked by the distance calculated for FWA above the summer load line (S)
- Tropical fresh water load line (TF): a line marked a distance of FWA above the tropical load line
- In addition, timber-carrying ships engaged in the timber deck-cargo trade must have a second set of load lines, each prefixed with L (lumber).

I was on deck as an extra pair of eyes and hands to assist the deck officers during cargo operations.

In Belém, *Benedict*'s deep tanks were filled with vegetable oil and we loaded bags of fish maw, Brazil nuts, and coffee, as well as hardwood veneer and sawn hardwood. Fish maw was the commercial term for the dried swim bladders of large fish, like sturgeon. It did not have a fishy taste and it absorbed the flavours of other ingredients. It was a good source of collagen, proteins, and nutrients. Apparently, the Chinese considered fish maw a traditional delicacy representing fortune and health. It sounded pretty disgusting to me, though. Yuk!

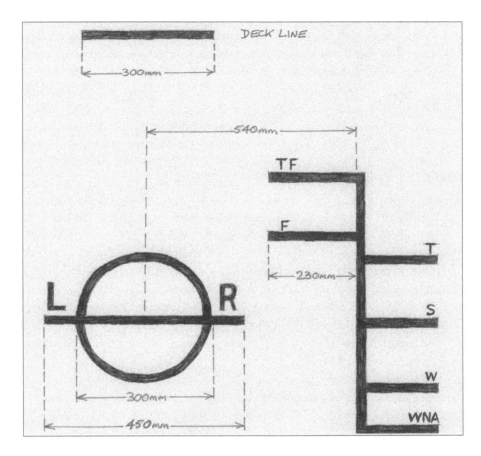

Fig 5.7 Load line markings and dimensions on a merchant ship

I managed to get up the road for a couple of afternoons. From *Benedict* to the dock gates was a short walk and I was then almost in town. Solo, I meandered around, stretched my legs and took photos. I visited the Cathedral da Sé, an impressive white church founded in 1917. Its frontage was topped by three towers, the outer two held bells with a clockface beneath, while the centre tower had an alcove in which a lovely statue of Our Lady of Grace (the Virgin Mary) clutched Jesus to her chest. Inside, the cathedral was equally impressive with its arched, pure white ceiling with gold crests and bosses. The internal walls were filled with glorious paintings visible between arched porticos. At the far end, the altar area focused on a painting of the Madonna in a typical blue dress.

There were numerous squares in the city centre and most of the architecture was colonial Portuguese-style, but interspersed with more modern office and apartment blocks. I noticed that in all the parks, squares and wide, tree-lined boulevards, tree trunks were painted white to a height of about four feet. Insects climbed trunks and caused damage to the trees. A repellent (lime) or a sticky substance (oil) was added to white latex non-oil-based paint to trap them and prevent them from reaching unprotected parts of the tree. The insects were also more easily seen and picked off by birds.

My evenings were free, so I was up the road again after dinner on board. The Radio Officer and I teamed up for mutual security to enjoy a few Antarcticas (Brazilian-brewed beer in large bottles) in a bar or two. Inevitably, as we didn't stray too far from the docks, there was a selection of local girls 'available' if you dared. This was my first experience of 'ladies of the night'. They all looked young and were smartly dressed in tight-fitting outfits, with decent make-up. Most spoke a smattering of English. Of course, their objective was to entice a merchant seaman to become a fee-paying punter. It would undoubtedly have been the safest option to take them back on board, but apparently that was extremely difficult because of the security guards at the dock gates. The standard option was to 'tap off' with one of the girls and accompany her to a nearby hotel, known in the merchant navy as a 'bag-off hotel' – bag-off being merchant seaman parlance for sexual intercourse.

The whole thing seemed incredibly high risk. Not just because you might get mugged or even murdered in some grubby hotel room, but also because of the painful and embarrassing 'souvenir' that might appear in your nether regions a few days later. The cure was a penicillin jab in the buttocks. As a good Catholic boy (well, I was at that time), I easily resisted their charms, as did the Radio Officer (young and recently married).

You also had to be wary when popping to a bar's toilet as there were always rather unsavoury, dodgy-looking characters loitering around. The risk of getting mugged was ever-present but, nothing untoward happened to either of us on these forays and we were usually back on board by 2300 at the latest.

At last, *Benedict* departed Belém. It was about a day and a half and 310 nautical miles (575 km) to our next port. I spent most of it on the bridge on my usual tasks, as well as assisting the Mates and wetting the tea or coffee. I knew my place! With a pilot embarked, we steamed further upriver before altering course to starboard. We rounded Ilha de Marajó on our starboard side and entered the distributary that cut across the Amazon delta to the Amazon itself. The waterway narrowed to a couple of hundred yards (200 m) and on each side was a dense mass of impenetrable rain forest. The water was smooth as glass, disrupted only by *Benedict* scything through, her bow wave gently rumbled outwards in a chevron until it lightly disturbed the shoreside vegetation and foliage.

At irregular intervals, I saw tiny settlements of wooden huts clinging to the shore, with only a limited horizontal extent into the jungle and short, small, fragile jetties of wooden piles and timber deck protruding into the waterway. Occasionally, one or two dugout canoes paddled out to investigate as *Benedict* steamed past and to pick up anything dropped over the side – which we didn't, being ever mindful to avoid pollution.

Fig 5.8 Amazon transit: Belém to Santana

The sun shone, the sky was blue, the air temperature was comfortably hot and not overly humid. Barely a sound interrupted our peaceful progress, save for the steady, low, rhythmic throb of the engine. It all looked serene and idyllic until you considered what dangers were hidden in the dense jungle and the river itself. It was a different story as dusk fell. The jungle came alive with the sounds of wildlife, mostly birds screeching and squawking. Loud thunderclaps dominated, the sky lit up with bright daggers of lightning, and an intense soft patter of rain on the jungle canopy.

In late afternoon on 7 June *Benedict* arrived at Santana, a suburb of Macapá, the capital and commercial hub of the state of Amapá. Gold, iron, lumber, manganese, oil, timber, and tin ore from Amapá's interior passed through Macapá to Port Santana, but we loaded a rather less glamorous cargo: palletised plywood sheets and planks. Santana was on the north bank of the Amazon, almost slap bang astride the Equator. The wharf looked primitive and rickety, but *Benedict* sat comfortably alongside as late afternoon turned to dusk and then into darkness. Our derricks were in use and the deck, holds, and wharf were illuminated by the floodlights fitted to our masts.

Fig 5.9 Loading palletised plywood sheets and planks at Santana on the Amazon at dusk on the Equator

We sailed late that night, as soon as the cargo was loaded. It was a relatively easy stand-by as the Amazon was quite wide in the vicinity of Santana, with no shoals to restrict our exit to the Atlantic. It was a 5,495 nautical mile (10,177 km) voyage back to dear old Blighty, during which nothing much happened. We steamed north-east at 15 knots through the Atlantic, the climate gradually changed from equatorial to a northern hemisphere summer en route. It was very pleasant working on deck in sunshine, with tasks from the Mate or chipping and painting with the Bosun and his ABs.

Our final port on Booth Line's trade route was Heysham, a small coastal town overlooking Morecambe Bay. It had a ferry port with services to the Isle of Man and Ireland and a nuclear power station, which hardly made it an attractive destination for tourists. The Saxons and Vikings influenced its history, but nothing particularly noteworthy happened. So, it was here, in an unglamorous, little-known, Lancastrian port on 22 June 1981 that I paid off from *Benedict* and trundled home on the train for a spot of leave.

This trip had been something of a contrast to my first: a smaller vessel and crew; general cargo rather than containers; derricks fitted and used instead of the uncluttered hatch covers of *ACT 5*. I was fortunate to have gone to the West Indies and Brazil, but I was disappointed that the voyage hadn't included a run up the Amazon to Manaus. Maybe I'd be fortunate enough to do so if I had another trip on Booth Line? It was obviously a question of timing. Nevertheless, my nautical experience and education continued to expand, my sea-time was accumulating towards the 24-month target. Overall, I was a happy chap and looked forward to some time at home before my next trip.

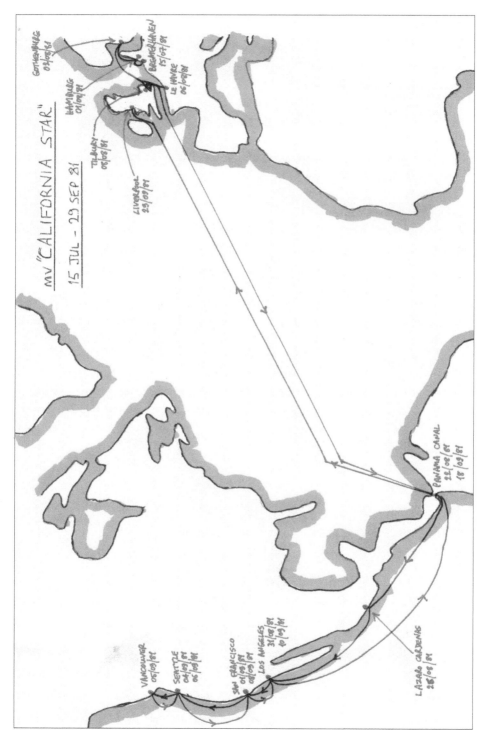

Fig 6.1 *California Star* voyage

6 Go West, Young Man!

Fig 6.2 *California Star* (Fotoflite)

After less than a month's leave, I was informed of my next trip. For a change, I wasn't signing on in Liverpool, but was to take a flight to the exotic city of Bremen in northern Germany. An arranged taxi from the airport delivered me to the shipyard at Bremerhaven, where *California Star* was in dry dock. Carrying my luggage, I strode across the horizontal gangway connecting the edge of the dock to the ship. The watchman welcomed me on board. I learnt that both crew and officers were all British – a first for me. 'Spike' Milligan, the Mate, came down from his cabin to meet me and show me to my cabin. It was also good to sail with Bert Pearson again. This affable, moustachioed Scouser had been Purser throughout my time on *ACT 5*.

I was back on familiar territory as *California Star* was a cellular refrigerated container ship, just like *ACT 5*, but slightly smaller. She weighed in at 19,095 gross tons and 10,730 net tons, had a capacity of 871 containers, and with a length of 620 feet (188.86 m), a beam of 85 feet (26 m), and a draught of 33 feet (10 m). Like *ACT 5*, she'd been built at Bremer Vulkan Schiffbau & Machinenfabrik, in Bremerhaven. Unlike *ACT 5*, she was a motor ship rather than a steam ship, with a service speed of 21½ knots. She and her sister-ship, *Columbia Star*, entered service in 1971. They were the first purpose-built container ships built by Blue Star Line for the Europe to West Coast of America service, superseding their conventional cargo ships that had previously operated the service.

Other notable design differences from *ACT 5* were her clutter-free weather deck and hatches, and no crane on the fo'c'sle, which was longer and had two holds before the break of the fo'c'sle where it dropped to the weather deck. There were a further six holds on the weather deck, with hatches strengthened to carry ten containers athwartships and stacked up to three- or four-high.

Further aft, the accommodation block surmounted the machinery spaces, and abaft (behind) was a ninth hold, also capable of carrying containers on deck. It was great to note that the funnel displayed the distinctive Blue Star logo: a blue, five-pointed star in a white disc on a bright-red background. Marvellous! I was told that as Blue Star funnels were so much larger than any other shipping line's and because they were floodlit at night in port, it was easy to find your way back to your ship after a few sherbets ashore.

I didn't have anything to do immediately except unpack my bags and settle into my new cabin, which was of a similar size and had the same amenities as on *ACT 5*. After breakfast the following morning, Spike and I had a chat in his cabin. I was the only cadet on board at present but others were to join when *California Star* berthed in Tilbury next month. Spike left me to familiarise myself with the ship. I wandered all over her, which wasn't too difficult as she had broadly similar features to *ACT 5*'s. My familiarisation with a new ship was always aided by studying the comprehensive general arrangement plans showcased on bulkheads in the main deck passageway. They showed the ship's layout deck by deck and included the locations of all firefighting equipment and useful miscellaneous information.

After smoko, Captain Newlin invited me for a chat. He was a thoroughly good, cheerful chap, of average stature. He stated what he expected of me during my time on board, signed me on the Ship's Articles and stamped my Discharge Book.

> Ship's Articles was the formal legal document in which the crew and supernumeraries (such as passage-workers) were listed when they 'signed on' (joined) a merchant ship. The Discharge Book was a full record of a seaman's career experience and certification. When you signed on and paid off a ship, the Master dated, signed and stamped an entry in it. A further document carried by merchant seamen was the British Seaman's Card. Recognised internationally, it permitted British

seamen to land at foreign ports to join or leave a ship without needing a visa. I still have both of my original documents. Couldn't bear to get rid of them!

Throughout the dry docking, the crew continued to live on board as all amenities functioned and the ship was connected to shore power. There were a couple of occasions when mains water supply and discharge ceased for a few hours due to the work package. Generally, there was no significant difference to being berthed at a wharf, except for the industrial sounds of a shipyard.

Spike had a few tasks for me. Under the Bosun's direction, I was occupied with rooting through lockers and stowages in the fo'c'sle, emptying them, sorting out their contents and cleaning the items before re-stowing them in an ordered arrangement and writing an inventory. It always took a bit of a time to do the initial rummage as, over a period of months, it was inevitable that shackles, hooks, blocks, and the variety of miscellaneous gear would become a disorganised mess. My days were full, at a gentle pace.

I also busied myself with walks around the top of the dry dock. I was fascinated to see my ship in her full naked glory, exposed from bulbous bow to the massive six-bladed propeller and the rudder at the stern. The rudder was removed for maintenance and rested on the dock floor supported in a vertical position by an enormous pair of block-and-tackles. I noticed a section of the ship's port side had been cut out, revealing the Burma Road. The original dented and damaged plates were replaced and the hull was shot-blasted and then completely repainted.

Hull painting involved washing, shot-blasting and painting and was one of the main reasons for dry docking, as it ensured efficient vessel operations for the next five years or so. After extended periods of sailing and service, marine growth (algae or slime) accrued on a ship's hull and above, on, and below the waterline. This accumulation directly impacted the efficiency of her movement and speed through the water and ultimately increased fuel consumption.

First, fresh water, high-pressure washers removed the marine growth and chlorides from her sides and hull.

Second, shot-blasting used compressed air to fire high-velocity steel abrasive. This removed rust or defective paint on localised patches, or in our case the entire ship's hull, to expose bare steel. It yielded a huge quantity of debris, from the used shot itself (a fine, black, dust-like substance, resembling soot) to the blasted off rust and old paint, which lightly covered the weather deck and the dock bottom. The noise during shot-blasting was deafening, even in the open air, accompanied by dust-clouds of abrasive shot, old paint and rust.

Fig 6.3 Shot-blasting, then red lead applied

Finally, *California Star* was cleaned and painted to protect the integrity of the steel and to prevent future corrosion. The hull at and below the waterline was painted with anti-fouling paint to prevent marine growth and to ensure that she operated close to her original design speed and fuel consumption.

I was even more fascinated to descend to the bottom of the dock via the steep steps built into the side of the dry dock. There, I appreciated the size and scale of *California Star*. Her keel rested on a line of huge cube-shaped blocks of timber. There were several parallel rows of these timbers each side of the central row that supported the hull's shape as it widened and curved upwards to become the ship's sides. The height of these blocks was sufficient to walk erect along the ship's length below her keel. Standing clear of the hull's curvature, the ship's sides towered over me.

The bulbous bow was an impressive protuberance that extended horizontally below the waterline, from the sharp cutting edge of the bow. This shape modified the water flow around the hull, reduced drag and increased speed, range, fuel efficiency, and stability. It also increased the buoyancy of the forward part, which helped reduce a ship's pitching. I noticed a series of black scratches around the bulbous bow and on the flare of the bow itself. These were a result of the anchor cable scraping against and around the bow when the ship was at anchor.

Fig 6.4 Bow marks caused by anchor cable during weighing anchor

The ship's paint scheme was evident. Below the waterline was red anti-fouling, straddling the waterline was blue boot-topping, above was the pale beige/cream of the hull with a narrow white band around the top. The superstructure was white. In the old days, Blue Star ships used to have black hulls, replaced during the 1970s by the now-familiar beige/cream, although sometimes a shade of lavender was used.

As I made my way aft, I observed vents and inlets covered by gratings. These recesses in the hull were the sea chests, which allowed the intake of sea water for cooling systems in the engine room. They were also used to discharge water. During dry docking, sea chests were accessed for cleaning, inspection, and painting.

At the stern, I was dwarfed by both rudder and propeller. The removal of the rudder gave the dry-dock engineers unfettered access to the bronze six-bladed propeller. I noticed that every blade had several small chips which, in sum, adversely affected the efficiency of the propeller and hence the ship's speed and fuel consumption.

Fig 6.5 Propeller and rudder removed for inspection

A very important element of a merchant ship's dry docking was ranging the anchor cable – a series of interlocked lengths of chain or shackles, each 90 feet long (15 fathoms or 27.5 m). The anchor and cable were slowly eased out, lowered and ranged (or laid out neatly on the dock floor), to be measured and inspected on the dock bottom. The cable could be 'broken' at the end of each shackle so damaged shackles or links could be replaced. The anchor was the most visible end, while the rarely seen 'bitter end' was fixed to the ship, inside the cable locker beneath the fo'c'sle. A merchant ship's anchor cable was typically eight or nine shackles in length (720 or 810 feet/220 m or 247.5 m).

Back on board, as the cable locker was empty, I took the opportunity to clamber down and poke my head through the opening usually covered by the access plate. I noted how the bitter end of each cable was clearly secured to the ship. Unless I did another dry docking, I was unlikely to witness the bitter end again.

All in all, I was captivated and in awe at the opportunity to get up close to not just any ship, but my ship, *California Star*. Not knowing when, if ever, I would be involved in another dry docking, I took every opportunity to wander around the dock bottom.

Fig 6.6 Port side hatch covers removed to show cell guides in holds

One Saturday, I went up the road to Bremen by S-Bahn, a typically efficient and punctual German local railway system. The Free Hanseatic City of Bremen, to give it its correct title, bestrode the River Weser in north-west Germany. Its port was second only to Hamburg in importance. I got off the S-Bahn at Bremen Hauptbahnhof (main railway station) and made my way to the Schlachte, Bremen's medieval harbour. It was a riverside boulevard with pubs and bars and also something of a maritime museum, with several old barques, barges, the former *Elbe 3* lightship, a tall ship, and a Kriegsmarine E-Boat. E-boat was the Western Allies' designation for these fast attack craft, where 'E' meant Enemy, but, strictly speaking, it was a German Schnellboot (S-Boot) meaning 'fast boat', usually a torpedo boat from World War II.

I strolled around the older part of the city centre and admired the mix of Gothic and Renaissance architecture, particularly that of the Marktplatz, which was dominated by the opulent façade of the Town Hall. It was a lovely day out, away from the industrial noise and activity of the shipyard. I enjoyed eating out on typical German food: currywurst mit pommes (yes, sausage in a curry sauce with chips – delicious and filling).

After about ten days on board, the dry-docking work package was complete. Preparations were made to flood the dry dock and re-float *California Star*. Both anchor cables were slowly and carefully heaved in by the windlass on the fo'c'sle until the anchors were home, their shafts in the hawse pipes and the anchor flukes resting against the specially thickened pads on each side of the flare of the bow. Ropes and wires were secured between ship and dockside. Our crew were stationed on the fo'c'sle, poop deck and bridge. The docking pilot embarked and tugs waited in the river.

When all was ready, the sluices were eased open and the dock slowly filled with water from the Weser. It was a gradual process of several hours duration but eventually I detected that *California Star* had floated gently off the blocks. When the dock water level equalled that of the river, the dock gates opened and the tugs manoeuvred the ship stern-first out of the dry dock and around to an adjacent berth on the river.

There were still some elements of the work package to be completed, not least the refitting of the length of plates that exposed the port side Burma Road.

On Saturday 29 July 1981, Prince Charles and Lady Diana were wed. To mark the occasion, *California Star* was dressed with just about our entire stock of signal flags. A necklace of flags from the stern to the top of the mast and down to the front of No. 7 Hold, a second necklace from the fo'c'sle break to the top of the foremast and down to the very tip of the bow. This was our entire contribution to this day of national celebration.

At last, the dry docking was complete and we sailed from Bremerhaven, steamed a short distance along the coast and rounded Cuxhaven. *California Star* embarked the river pilot and entered the River Elbe for the 68 mile (110 km) transit upriver to reach Hamburg's port. Who would have thought that in 2003, as Royal Navy Exchange Officer at the German Naval Academy, Flensburg, I'd be living in the quiet, up-market suburb of Blankenese, on the north bank of the Elbe?

Fig 6.7 Dress ship for Charles and Diana's wedding day

It was a delightful trip. The river's sandy beaches were backed with trees, parks, and suburbs as the skyline of Hamburg gradually came into focus. Many riverside houses were large and expensive, with great views along and across the Elbe. The port and shipyards were located on the south bank, opposite the city centre. It was a brief visit on 1 August to start filling *California Star* with containers. Despite the city's immediate vicinity, I didn't have any time to go up the road. This was becoming symptomatic of coasting on a container ship (or box boat).

We departed that evening, bound for Gothenburg. We hugged first the German, then the Danish coasts rounded the northern tip of Denmark at Skagen, and arrived in Gothenburg the next day. Although we loaded containers for a couple of days, I didn't go up the road, so have no impressions of the city. The exit from Gothenburg was via a decent-sized channel through an offshore archipelago, but we had to be wary of ferry traffic from Fredrikshavn and Kiel. We went through The Skaggerak, the strait that separates Denmark and Norway, and steered south-south-west across the North Sea.

Le Havre was our next port of call and entailed passing through the challenging Dover Strait. To gain experience, Spike doubled me up on the bridge with him. As the width of navigable water in the vicinity of Dover slowly narrowed, shipping traffic in both directions increased in volume as we saw the coast of the Netherlands wherein lay Rotterdam, Europe's busiest port. There was also southbound traffic from England's east coast ports and, of course, vessels exiting the Thames estuary. Spike and I spotted and tracked these vessels visually and by radar, cognisant of the myriad navigation buoys and oil and gas platforms that littered this confined sea area. We maintained constant awareness of own ship's position relative to charted hazards, while regularly fixing our position and keeping to the planned track. All this made for an extremely busy and mentally exhausting watch.

We entered the south-west bound lane of the traffic separation scheme, with North Foreland, Deal, and then Dover to starboard. In the distance to port, traffic was in the north-east bound lane and beyond was the French coast.

> The Dover Strait is one of the busiest channels in the world, with an enormous volume of shipping passing through and a multitude of ferries crossing the English Channel between Dover and France. It is littered with notorious migrating sandbanks and shoals and the charted hazards to navigation increase. The Dover Strait is continuously monitored by UK and French agencies. The Channel Navigation Information Service (CNIS) provides a 24-hour radio and radar safety service for all shipping in the Dover Strait. As a mandatory reporting area, vessels over 300 gross tonnes have to report to either the British or French authorities before proceeding through the Strait.
>
> A system of traffic separation schemes was devised for heavy traffic areas and choke points worldwide. Shipping traffic 'drives' on the right-hand side of the 'road'. Rule 10 of the International Regulations Preventing Collisions at Sea (1972) explains who can and cannot use such a scheme, as well as the relative responsibilities of different types of vessel. I was pretty au fait with Rule 10 as I'd had it signed off in my Task Book. No excuses, then!
>
> Obtusely, as the width of the English Channel narrows to its minimum, traffic management becomes easier. Merchant ships remain in the correct lane for their direction of travel, while ferries cross perpendicularly to the separation scheme, as required by Rule 10. Safe passage relies upon all ships complying with Rule 10 and life becomes easy. But you must remain focused and keep a good lookout in case another ship fails to adhere to the Rules. The English Channel widens after Dungeness and Cap Gris-Nez and vessel traffic density decreases. The western end of the traffic separation scheme is marked by the Greenwich Light Vessel, south of West Beach, Brighton.

When *California Star* was free of the constraints of the scheme she altered course to port, to head directly for Le Havre, where we berthed on 6 August. Another quick turnaround and we steamed away from Le Havre, headed north-east in the other lane of the Dover Strait traffic separation scheme, and into the Thames estuary.

California Star berthed on 8 August at Tilbury. As promised, three cadets signed on, deck cadet Richard Chivers and two engineer cadets. Richard was a tall, slender bloke, dark-haired with a matching moustache. I gave him the ship's tour and we hit it off immediately. He was a little senior to me in his cadetship but we worked well on deck throughout the trip. We even managed to get up the road together during a couple of port visits, notably Disneyland in Los Angeles. The engineer cadets disappeared down below. We four day-working cadets usually enjoyed morning and afternoon smoko together, shared a table for meals and a couple of sherbets in the bar in the evenings. It was a pleasant change to have something of a social life on board after my trip on *Benedict*.

Spike Milligan also paid off and his replacement as Chief Mate was Ken Pyket. I enjoyed working for both of them but had more time with Ken, who was an excellent senior Mate, very thorough, decisive, and professional. Captain Daniel took over from Captain Newlin.

The new Lecky was George Smart. A bluff, Scot with a moustache and an unruly mop of curly dark hair. A great dry sense of humour lurked within his broad Scot's accent. I always remember his intense irritation when you wanted to change a light bulb. He vociferously exclaimed: 'LAMPS, LAMPS! They're called LAMPS! Yee poot bulbs in the groond! LAMPS go in light fittings!' Of course, when we realised his sensitivity on this subject, we inevitably talked of bulbs. He was too easy to wind up, as he just couldn't help himself and occasionally reached a fever pitch of outrage at our deliberate 'ignorance'. Despite it all, George was a jolly good bloke and took our ribbing in good heart. It was part of life at sea to do a bit of goading.

We left Tilbury, retraced our track to rejoin the south-westerly traffic separation scheme and on through the Dover Strait. After passing the Greenwich Light Vessel, *California Star* maintained her west-south-west course, skipped through the short traffic separation scheme off the Channel Islands and the Channel Light Vessel fell away astern. The English Channel opened up wide so it wasn't long until the French and English coastlines were over the horizon as we headed south-west into the Atlantic.

Another transatlantic crossing – crikey, how blasé was I getting having been at sea for only a handful of months? Mind you, it was my fourth, and then my fifth on the return trip. It was two weeks to Panama and we cadets settled into a decent daily routine. Richard and I worked on deck, either with the Bosun and his deck crowd, or Ken Pyket gave us specific tasks in the morning. The brace of engineer cadets spent all their time down below in the mechanical garden (engine room), getting grubby, oily, and smelly. Our quartet met for morning and afternoon smokos and a sundowner or two on the boat deck before shower and dinner. We always kept a keen eye out for the brief but legendary 'green flash', an optical phenomenon observed shortly after sunset.

> The green flash occurs when the sun is almost entirely below the horizon, with the barest upper edge still visible, which for a second or two sometimes appears green. Two criteria are necessary: no haze or cloud on the horizon; and a distinct edge to the distant horizon, best found at sea. Once I learnt of the green flash, I always hoped to see it whenever I was at sea and on deck or the bridge around sunset. One of those fascinating natural phenomena observed infrequently and, uniquely, only at sea. I was fortunate to witness it many times in my seafaring career.

Occasionally, someone would set up the Bell & Howell projector that all our ships had, and we enjoyed a film night in the Mess. Walport supplied films to British merchant ships for many years. Usually, the Radio Officer arranged an order from Walport for delivery at a particular port, where the old films were exchanged for the replacements. Each feature film was in a square galvanised metal canister, within which each reel was in its own circular canister – usually three reels per movie. I think there was a limit per delivery and an annual allowance per ship. On *California Star*, we watched films in the Mess. On general and refrigerated cargo ships in good weather (warm, balmy nights in the tropics), a white canvas or a huge linen tablecloth was stretched between the samson posts of a derrick for outdoor viewings. Ah, the good old days. No mail, no email, no internet, no DVDs, and, at home, videos just becoming affordable and readily available. An entirely different, simpler, and happier world compared to today!

On transoceanic voyages, I spent time during lunchtime and after work up on the fo'c'sle in the sunshine where silence reigned. I was alone and in peace, except for the distant throb from the engine room. I relaxed against the bulwark or I knelt and looked through the centre line fairlead, through which the head-ropes passed to secure the ship to the wharf in port. Many feet below, I watched the bow cleave through the sea to create the wake.

The sea spilled over the bulbous bow, a thin transparent sheen of water. Occasionally, flying fish shot out of the sea, flew for a few feet, then they dived back into the sea. This view fascinated me. I was almost drawn or hypnotised into the lure of falling in – quite compulsive.

During my time in BSSM, the split between container ships and general and/or refrigerated cargo ships was about a third to two thirds. But containerisation was continually increasing globally.

> The first standard shipping container was invented and patented by Malcolm McLean in 1956. Although he wasn't involved in merchant shipping, he owned the largest trucking company in the US. He developed an idea to make intermodal transportation seamless and efficient. Historically, cargo was loaded and unloaded in odd-sized wooden cases. McLean observed stevedores unload freight from trucks and transfer it to ships, noted the inefficiency of the method, and concluded that trucking and shipping companies would benefit from a standardised process of cargo transfer. So, he purchased the Pan Atlantic Tanker Company with all its shipping assets and experimented with better ways of loading and unloading trucks. Ultimately, he designed what became a shipping container – strong, theft resistant, reliable and easy to transfer.
>
> In April 1956, the first container to be shipped departed from Port Newark and arrived in Houston. Standard containers revolutionised freight transportation and significantly changed international trade. Cargo was sealed and safe, reducing pilfering and damage throughout its journey. The labour required to load and unload containers was reduced and dramatically changed the character of ports worldwide. Increased efficiency in cargo operations reduced the time a ship stayed in port, so shipping companies saved money and were happy.
>
> Ports adapted to accommodate containerisation: portainer cranes and straddle carriers replaced manpower. Sometimes, completely new ports were built specifically to handle containers, such as Royal Seaforth Dock in Liverpool. This inevitably meant that we poor merchant seamen found ourselves miles away from the throbbing action, just outside the dock gates in traditional ports.
>
> Overall, containerisation reduced the expense of international trade and increased its speed by greatly shortening shipping time. Today, container shipping transports about 90% of the world's cargo.

A standard container (TEU or 20-foot equivalent unit) is 20 feet (6.1 m) long, 8 feet (2.4 m) wide and 8 feet 6 inches (2.6 m) high. There are a variety of adaptations to the basic 'general purpose' TEU to accommodate different cargoes: flat-racks, tanks, refrigerated, open top (for goods too tall for a standard container). A longer 40-foot (12.2 m) version is also in common use.

Containers carried on deck must be secured to prevent their falling into one another or overboard when ships pitch and roll in heavy weather. In HMS *Fox* in 1987 and 1988, we surveyed the Celtic Deep and South West Approaches. Our sidescan sonar detected about twenty containers on a patch of flat sandy seabed. During storms, containers can get washed overboard and sink. Sometimes their buoyancy keeps them afloat and they drift on to beaches where locals 'investigate' their contents, similar to Compton Mackenzie's *Whisky Galore*.

In January 2007, a real-life *Whisky Galore* occurred when *MSC Napoli's* hull was breached during a storm some 50 miles (80 km) off The Lizard in Cornwall. The Master sent an SOS, the crew abandoned ship in lifeboats and were rescued by search and rescue helicopters. The salvors decided she was to be towed to Portland Harbour. After much discussion with authorities, *MSC Napoli* was beached at Branscombe Bay in East Devon. About 100 containers were washed ashore along with sundry loose items of cargo. The locals had a field day; BMW motorbikes were among the most prized 'goodies' lifted by people variously described as scavengers, looters, or beachcombers. The scene was a cross between a bomb site, a car boot sale and an Aladdin's cave. *MSC Napoli* (53,409 gross tons, 904 feet (275.66 m) long and 4,734 container capacity), was eventually broken up and removed from Branscombe Bay by July 2009.

The container lashing system comprised stacking cones, twist locks, lashing rods, and turnbuckles (or bottlescrews), effective in lashing containers on deck to the third tier, above which only twist locks were fitted. A twist lock is a special double pin to secure stacked containers. The pins are conic in shape and snugly fitted the oval openings in the corner posts of a container. By turning the pin 90°, it is secured. By securing the two pins in two containers stacked alongside or on top of each other, the containers are connected.

Ken tasked Richard and me to check, and tighten if necessary, the lashings every other day during the Atlantic crossing. We also greased the turnbuckles in situ, as well as the unused, spare turnbuckles and twist locks in their storage bins on deck. A good couple of day's methodical and worthwhile work.

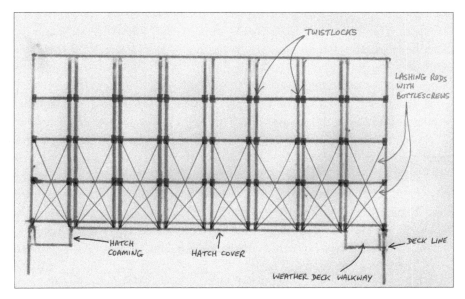

Fig 6.8 Securing containers on deck: turnbuckles with short lashing rods for first tier, turnbuckles with long lashing rods for second tier, twistlocks for all containers athwartships and in the stack

We briefly made our first landfall since the English Channel as we steamed through the Mona Passage between Hispaniola and Puerto Rico. On 21 August, we anchored off Colon overnight before transiting the Panama Canal. As there were two of us deck cadets, Richard and I could alternate between bridge and fo'c'sle for stand-by at each port. I was lucky enough to join Ken the Mate on the fo'c'sle for anchoring.

There's a set procedure for anchoring, practised throughout most of the merchant navy. Manpower on the fo'c'sle was the Mate, Bosun, a couple of ABs, and, if dispatched forward to learn, a deck cadet. At sea, no power was required up for'ard so it was essential the engineers provided 'power on deck' for the windlass using the necessary tools : spike, hammer, crowbar, oil can, goggles, and torch for night-time anchoring.

The process of 'clearing anchors' began. First, the hawse pipe covers were removed (hawse pipes are the conduits through which the cable passes outboard in the flare of the bow), then lashings in the chain locker were released.

The Bosun ensured the windlass was out of gear and its brakes were on. The primary use of the windlass is to heave the anchor from the seabed when weighing anchor. Still out of gear, the Bosun slowly 'turned over' the windlass to oil its moving parts. He checked that the gears were disengaged before putting an anchor into gear. An AB cleared the devil's claw (a two-pronged hook used for securing the anchor cable while at sea), other lashings, and the compressor bar (a mechanical device to hold the cable) from the spurling pipe (the conduit through which the anchor cable passed from cable locker to deck).

The Bosun checked that the anchor's weight was held by the windlass brake and the gear disengaged. In case the primary anchor failed to work for some reason, the second anchor was similarly prepared. The Bosun told Ken that both anchors were ready to veer (lower) clear of the hawse pipe. The prime anchor's gear was engaged and, on Ken's command, it was veered slowly under power until the anchor was 'a'cockbill' (clear of the hawse pipe) and 'dangled' vertically at the end of the anchor cable. The windlass brake was applied and the gear disengaged. Ken reported the anchor 'ready for letting go' to Captain Newlin via the walkie-talkie.

There usually followed a lengthy pause until the ship approached her anchoring position, as directed by the port authority controlling the anchorage or roads. This was an opportunity to gaze at the view of the port, city, shore, and other vessels in the anchorage. This leisurely 'waiting game' was quite a contrast from the constant activity on the bridge that I was used to from my first two trips to sea.

The Master told Ken to get ready. Bosun slipped on his goggles and, when ordered by the Old Man via Ken's walkie-talkie, let go the brake. There was an extraordinarily loud clanking of forged steel cable against ship's steel as the weight of anchor and cable, combined with gravity, caused the cable to race from the cable locker a couple of decks below, up the spurling pipe, over the windlass 'cogs', along a short stretch of deck, and down the hawse pipe. This racket was accompanied by clouds of dust and small lumps of dried mud thrown from the cable on its exit from the cable locker and spewed into the air.

As the cable raced away, it was important to note how much had gone. Anchor cables were divided into shackles, each of 15 fathoms (90 feet or 27.5 m). A lugless joining shackle joined the shackles together. They were quite distinct and easy to spot, despite the speed at which the anchor cable exited its locker and disappeared down the hawse pipe. As each shackle appeared 'on deck', an AB struck the ship's bell: one shackle, one bell; two shackles, two bells, and so on, in addition to Ken notifying the Master by walkie-talkie. I'd heard the bell-ringing quite clearly when anchoring on

ACT 5, despite the great distance between fo'c'sle and bridge and visibility restricted by on-deck containers.

When the correct number of shackles to be veered were 'on deck' or 'at the waterline', the compressor bar was put on, the brake tightened, and I hoisted the wicker anchor ball. Rule 30 of the International Regulations for Preventing Collisions at Sea stated our obligation to 'exhibit where it can best be seen in the fore part, an all-round white light or one black ball and, at or near the stern and at a lower level than the forward light, an all-round white light'.

There was a bit more to anchoring. Ken stood on the built-in step on the fo'c'sle bulwark to get a clear view of how the cable was 'growing', the way it was leading from the hawse pipe. Ken reported whether the cable was at 'short', 'medium' or 'long stay'. At 'short stay', the cable was taut and close to vertical, while 'long stay' meant the cable was still taut but nearly horizontal. 'Medium stay' was between these two extremes. Eventually, you could tell that *California Star* had settled as the cable slackened and Ken reported she 'had her cable'.

It was very interesting to observe up-close the mechanics of anchoring a merchantman. Each day, I was learning more and more about seamanship and navigation, and a myriad other stuff that was unknowingly captured and stored away in my memory. Every aspect of my working life was fantastic training and experience.

Richard was up forward for weighing anchor when *California Star* transited the Panama Canal the next day. Leaving Panama City astern, the ship navigated along the Central American coast. The coast curved away to starboard to become the Isthmus of Tehuantepec, the shortest distance between the Gulf of Mexico and the Pacific Ocean, before we made our Mexican landfall. With the Mexican coast to starboard, *California Star* passed Acapulco before she entered the port of Lazaro Cardenas, accessed between two short narrow breakwaters. It seemed a relatively petite port as, after about 550 yards (500 m), we turned tightly to port and berthed at the container wharf on 26 August. It was a short visit, so neither Richard nor I got up the road. We sailed later that evening.

The passage to Los Angeles was unremarkable. There was nothing noteworthy to be observed towards the coast, which curved away from us and disappeared over the horizon. Landfall was regained as Cabo San Lucas hove into view after being detected by our radar. This was the southernmost point of the Baja California peninsula, which separates the Pacific Ocean from the Gulf of California. The ship continued to hug the coast, about ten miles (16 km) off. The border between Mexico and the USA was apparent as, after Tijuana and San Diego, the coast was perpetually filled with light pollution, in contrast to the somewhat barren Mexican coast.

Because I'd been an Apollo space buff as a boy, I'd noticed on the chart a set of artificial islands in San Pedro Bay known as the Astronaut Islands, named after Freeman (the first NASA astronaut to die on active duty when his T-38 training jet crashed), Grissom, White, and Chaffee (the three astronauts who perished in the Apollo 1 launch pad fire in 1967).

On 31 August, *California Star* entered the breakwater and followed the channel to Terminal Island. I was up forward with Ken the Mate again, this time for our berthing. Whether on the fo'c'sle or poop deck, the same kit was required: two heaving lines; ratguards; rope and chain stoppers; oil can or grease gun.

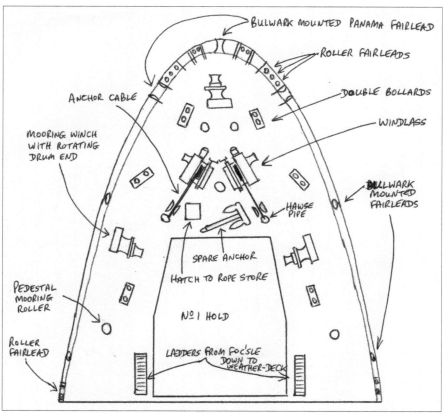

Fig 6.9 Fo'c'sle mooring arrangements

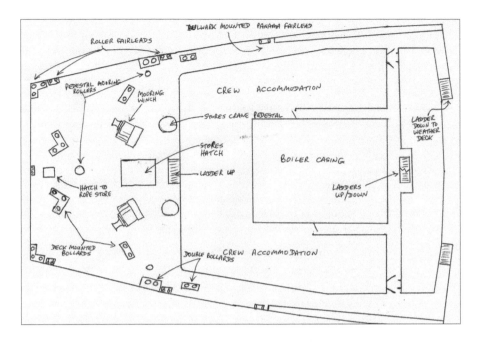

Fig 6.10 Poop deck mooring arrangements

On some ships, mooring lines remain on deck, secured on pallets (to prevent their erosion or damage) covered by tarpaulins as protection against weather. On some, they're stowed in a locker directly beneath the working deck, and on others they are permanently on mooring winches, with canvas covers to protect them. Regardless, mooring ropes and wires are brought on deck and flaked out to ensure ease of passing them outboard to the wharf. Their 'eyes' (the loop spliced at one end of a mooring rope or wire) are fed through the fairlead and hung back over the bulwark or guardrail, ready for use. On the fo'c'sle, an anchor is always prepared for 'letting go' in case of emergency.

Both fo'c'lse and poop were hives of activity. Except for the helmsman on the bridge, all ABs (about ten) were required for 'stations', evenly split between for'ard and aft.

The engineers provided 'power on deck'. Roller fairleads and the working parts of windlass, capstan and mooring winches were lubricated. It was vital to ensure the deck working space was free of debris and clutter. Importantly, walkie-talkie communications were tested between bridge, fo'c'sle, and poop deck.

It was usual to take a tug fore and aft. When directed, an AB threw a heaving line down to the tug. The tugboat crew secured their tow rope to the heaving line. The tow rope was hauled in board by hand and its eye dropped over a bollard on deck. *California Star* slowly approached the berth. As pilot, tugs, and Master manoeuvred her onto the berth, at a suitable range, a couple of ABs launched their heaving lines towards the shoreside line handlers. Pride was at stake when throwing a heaving line. If it fell short of the wharf, the AB was the butt of ribald humour as he recovered the heaving line and tried again. When caught ashore, the shore-siders heaved it in until the mooring line's eye was in their hands. They looped it over a bollard and we tightened the line on board using the drum-end of a mooring winch.

> A heaving line is a length of rope, usually ¼" (0.625 cm) diameter, with a monkey's fist at one end. This knot is formed over a core to increase its mass, diameter and aerodynamic properties (roundness). In the old days, the core material might have included lead shot, ball bearings, bolts, glass marbles, and the like. These were made illegal under maritime law, because of serious injuries and substantial property damage caused by a 'loaded' heaving line. A heaving line can be thrown long distances across the water attached to, and used for sending, a much heavier mooring line from a vessel to a wharf, or sometimes between two vessels.

This process was repeated for each of our lines, fore and aft, and reported to the bridge. Using the mooring winches, their drum ends and, down aft, the capstan, *California Star* edged ever closer until she nestled alongside the wharf. When she was judged to be in position, the bridge told Ken up for'ard and the Third Mate on the poop deck.

When a mooring rope was heaved taut on the drum end of a winch, it was bad practice to secure it there for the duration of the ship's berth. It was considered unsafe, even dangerous. Mooring lines were heaved in and 'stoppers' were used to maintain their tension until they were 'figure-of-eighted' around the deck bollards.

> A stopper maintains the accrued tension in the mooring rope to allow an AB to transfer the mooring rope from the drum end to 'figure-of-eight' it around adjacent deck bollards. Stoppers are tails of rope or chain with an eye at one end to which a shackle is attached. The shackled end is then secured to an eye bolt on the deck base of the bollards.
>
> There are three types of stopper:

1) a rope stopper of manila or sisal rope to be used on natural fibre ropes, never on synthetic fibre ropes; an initial half-hitch is made, then the remainder of the stopper's tail is wrapped over and under along the mooring rope;

2) the Chinese or West Country stopper is made of synthetic fibre rope and is always used on synthetic fibre ropes, like polyamide; it has two tails which are half-hitched before each tail is wrapped over and under the mooring rope;

3) for mooring wires, usually of flexible steel wire rope, a chain stopper is used with a cow hitch near the eye bolt, followed by the chain tail against the lay of the wire; this prevents the chain from jamming or opening up the lay of the wire.

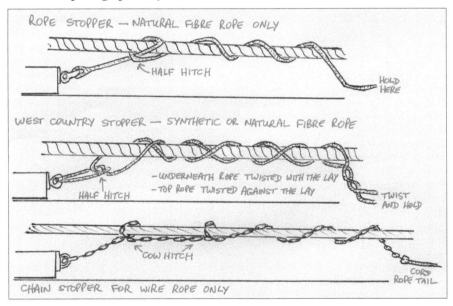

Fig 6.11 Types of stoppers

After application, an AB simply holds fast the tail of the stopper while the mooring rope or wire is moved onto the deck bollards and turned up. Amazingly, the mooring rope's (or wire's) tension iisn't lost. The stopper and AB are sufficient.

I was slowly learning that much seamanship was achieved via the application
of simple but very effective and ingenious solutions that evolved over
centuries of seafaring experience and seamanship expertise.

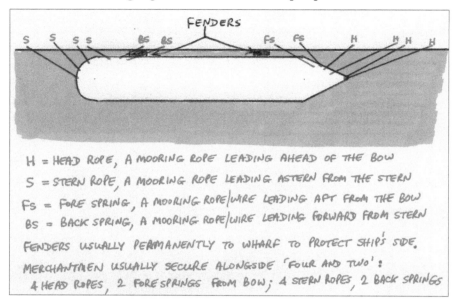

FENDERS

S   S   S S   BS BS   Fs   Fs   H   H H   H

H = HEAD ROPE, A MOORING ROPE LEADING AHEAD OF THE BOW

S = STERN ROPE, A MOORING ROPE LEADING ASTERN FROM THE STERN

Fs = FORE SPRING, A MOORING ROPE/WIRE LEADING AFT FROM THE BOW

BS = BACK SPRING, A MOORING ROPE/WIRE LEADING FORWARD FROM STERN

FENDERS USUALLY PERMANENTLY TO WHARF TO PROTECT SHIP'S SIDE.

MERCHANTMEN USUALLY SECURE ALONGSIDE 'FOUR AND TWO':
4 HEAD ROPES, 2 FORE SPRINGS FROM BOW; 4 STERN ROPES, 2 BACK SPRINGS

Fig 6.12 Berthing scheme: 'four-and-two' at bow and stern

When the bridge informed the fo'c'sle and poop deck that *California
Star* was in position on the wharf, the ship was secured and the tugs were
let go. A ship never sat directly against the wharf as her sides would get
scraped to bits, or even holed by the constant surge and movement against
the wharf as the tide ebbed and flooded, as well as by the wash and wake of
passing ships. Therefore, it was usual to see large fenders permanently fixed
to the wharf to prevent any damage. These cylindrical, pneumatic, rubber
'Yokohama' fenders, invented after World War II, were typically ten feet
(3.3m) diameter and 21 feet (6.5m) long.

Securing *California Star* took a few minutes using the limited manpower
at each end of the ship. The normal berthing scheme was 'four-and-two'.
This meant four head ropes and two springs from the bow, and four stern
ropes and two springs from the stern. This combination of mooring lines
prevented ship's moving in fore and aft directions, along the wharf. Breast
ropes could be used to prevent athwartships movement. A vessel bouncing
against the wharf could cause damage, despite the cushioning effect of
Yokohama fenders. I don't recall we ever used breast ropes.

Seamen take great pride in keeping work areas clean, clear, and tidy, especially as it helps prevent accidental injuries, so all unused kit (heaving lines, stoppers, oil-can, etc) was stowed away. The final action was to fit ratguards on every line. These circular metal cones prevented rats boarding the ship. Ports were notorious for being rat infested.

The entire process was fraught with danger as a rope or wire could part if too much tension was applied. I constantly recalled Captain Moore's parting advice at the end of our induction at Liverpool Polytechnic: never stand in the line of recoil of a mooring rope or wire under tension, if it parts the whiplash could easily kill or maim you if you are in the line of fire; never stand in the bight of a rope, if it is suddenly hove taut, your foot/ankle could get caught and squeezed as if by a boa constrictor; if you are struck by a heaving line being thrown back on board, you'll get a nasty shock, bruise, or bump from the monkey's fist. I strictly adhered to Captain Moore's advice throughout my seafaring career. I never witnessed any such accidents, thank goodness!

Although it was labelled Los Angeles in our itinerary, we were miles from the famous tourist spots of LA, in a vast industrial area split between the ports of Los Angeles and Long Beach. Ken Pyket released Richard and me from cargo watch duties so we set off to Disneyland. I don't recall how we got there – probably by taxi as a map showed it was some 15–20 miles (24–32 km) from the port as the crow flies. We had a great day out and enjoyed the various rides, although I avoided all the really scary, fast, whizzy ones. The queues for rides weren't too long and nor were those for fast food outlets. I'm not one for theme parks, but it was exciting to have actually visited the original Disneyland – something that was probably prohibitively expensive and beyond reach for UK families in the early 1980s.

It was 470 miles (757 km) and a day's steaming to San Francisco. I spotted the city on our starboard side, its densely populated hills rising up from the coast and then over the crest to the hidden slope down to San Francisco Bay. *California Star* rounded Lands End Lookout, with Point Bonita Lighthouse on the port bow, and the magnificent Golden Gate Bridge appeared, unmistakable in its rust-red colour. I'd heard about the foggy conditions typical of this bay area and, sure enough, the tops of the pylons supporting this famous suspension bridge were shrouded in mist. Air temperature had noticeably decreased so it was now quite chilly. Gradually, with the pilot's guidance, *California Star* made her way ever closer to the bridge. Soon it towered over us as we steamed under its vast span and emerged into San Francisco Bay itself.

Fig 6.13 Approaching Golden Gate Bridge

Following the channel, I was awestruck as we passed Alcatraz a few hundred yards down our port side. On the opposite side, Fisherman's Wharf was a similar distance off. Turning to starboard, the ship approached the Oakland Bridge which connected Oakland to San Francisco. As was now typical of my box boat experience, we berthed at Oakland Container Port, across the bay from the delights and sights of San Francisco. Again, our short turnaround time ensured that I didn't get up the road here either. Still, what was there to complain about? I had a great job that paid me to go to such famous places. People dream about going to San Francisco and seeing the Golden Gate Bridge. Never mind that, I'd steamed beneath it on my large ship. I considered myself extraordinarily fortunate.

No, I wasn't slightly blasé when we departed Oakland and steamed past Alcatraz and under the Golden Gate Bridge again! I remained tremendously thrilled, at my station on the bridge and looking directly above me at this enormous structure. We headed further north to Seattle, nearly 1,000 miles (1,610 km) away. The coastline was unremarkable, viewed from a range of some ten miles (16 km).

On 4 September, *California Star* edged to starboard around Cape Flattery and entered Salish Sea, divided down its centre by the US-Canadian border. Vancouver Island was to port, the Olympic National Park to starboard, and the snow-capped Rockies rose up ahead. The channel narrowed as we turned to starboard and Victoria, the city on the south-east tip of Vancouver Island, receded astern. The seaway between the islands of Puget Sound, the third-largest estuary in the United States, slimmed to about two and a half miles (4 km) wide. On the coast were large, expensive homes and small settlements, interspersed with forest right down to the shore as Seattle's skyline pierced the blue sky. The waterfront grew closer when we entered Elliot Bay and steered south-east to the container berths at Harbor Island, barely a mile (1.6 km) or so from the city centre.

This time, I managed to get ashore and strolled into the city, built on a solid chronological history of timber, gold rush, and the Boeing factory. A typical modern city with high-rise office and apartment blocks and wide streets – nothing much noteworthy as far as I could tell. I found my way to the Space Needle (built in the Seattle Center for the 1962 World's Fair) and took the lift to the observation deck, 525 feet (160 m) above street level. I enjoyed a panoramic view of downtown Seattle, the Olympic and Cascade Mountains, Mount Rainier, Mount Baker, Elliott Bay, and the islands in Puget Sound. Magnificent!

I was back on board for dinner and *California Star* sailed in the early hours. She retraced her track out of Puget Sound and continued north, passing Victoria to port. The channel to Vancouver wound between the San Juan Islands, criss-crossing the US-Canada border en route, and emerged in the Strait of Georgia. The seaway became considerably wider and, after passing Point Roberts to the east, we were in Canadian waters. As had become normal, *California Star* turned to starboard, rounded Stanley Park and passed beneath Lions Gate Bridge, the entrance to Vancouver Harbour. Fortunately, the container terminal was only a short distance from the city centre.

Amazingly, I wasn't required for cargo watch so, after a relatively short walk up the road, I was in Downtown and, a little further, Gastown – Vancouver's original name and from where it developed and expanded into today's large thriving city.

> Gastown is touted as an historic area for tourists with a notable feature: a steam clock. It was built in 1977, in 19th century style, to cover a steam grate (part of Vancouver's distributed steam heating system), to harness the steam and to prevent people from sleeping on the spot in cold weather. It is powered by a steam engine and electric motors, and displays the time on four faces. The quarter hours are marked by a whistle chime playing the Westminster Quarters, a melody heard in the Palace of Westminster. The clock also emits a puff of steam from its top on the hour. An unusual feature, but a misleading con rather than an icon, methinks.

Onwards I strode until I passed through the entrance gates of Stanley Park, a beautiful public urban park atop a promontory overlooking Vancouver

Bay, Burrard Inlet to seaward, and the Rockies across Lions Gate Bridge. It is densely forested, with firs, spruce and cedars, among which were many trails and grassy picnic zones. To cap it all, a seawall promenade went around its perimeter. An absolute delight to spend a couple of hours just wandering around. The highway threaded through Stanley Park and, between a pair of cast concrete lions, onto Lions Gate Bridge (opened in 1938). Time pressure forced me to retreat to the ship as we were sailing that evening.

California Star reversed her route, southbound back to Seattle, San Francisco and LA (on 6, 8 and 10 September respectively). I went up the road briefly in LA to visit the old *Queen Mary*, berthed at Long Beach since 1967. Her sailing days were long gone but her life had been refreshed and extended in a new career as a museum and hotel with restaurants. She was a magnificent ship in her distinctive Cunard livery. Nearby I saw Howard Hughes' Spruce Goose, his giant sea-plane had been designed for transatlantic flight but never managed it. Alas, no time to visit her as were sailing that evening, 10 September.

During our trip along the west coast of North America, I observed that port buoyage was opposite to that elsewhere. On entry, channel buoys showed green to port and red to starboard, whereas in Europe and Australia, red buoys were to port and green to starboard.

Historically, although many maritime nations used buoys to mark channels and dangers, their schemes differed. The International Association of Marine Aids to Navigation and Lighthouse Authorities (IALA), sought to establish a standardised buoyage system for adoption worldwide. By 1980, IALA's system was recognised by signatory maritime nations. A seafarer now had to learn or recognise only one set of buoyage, regardless of location.

There are several types of buoy:
- Lateral marks in red or green to denote each side of a channel;
- Cardinal marks to indicate the direction of safety as a cardinal compass direction (north, east, south, or west) relative to the buoy; each cardinal buoy has a distinctive orientation of two black, conical, top-marks. Both cones pointing up is north; the opposite for south; cone bases together is east, points together means west, which is easy to remember the apexes together forms a wine-glass shape and 'W' is for wine and west. The top-mark design is reflected in the yellow and black horizontal banding of the buoys, with black symbolising the cone's apex, and yellow representing the base;

- Isolated danger marks are black buoys with a red horizontal band and a top-mark of two black balls in a vertical line; they indicate the position of a single point hazard (such as a partially submerged rock) surrounded by navigable water;
- Safe water marks are painted in red and white stripes and indicate navigable water; they are used as fairway, mid-channel or landfall marks, such as Liverpool's Bar Light;
- Yellow special marks indicate other areas of particular usage (such as recreation areas) as marked on nautical charts.

Buoys come in a variety of shapes: can, pillar, spar, or cone. At night, depending on the category, a buoy displays a specified coloured light (white, red, green, yellow); to avoid confusion, a light's rhythm is designed to distinguish it from those with a similar purpose in the vicinity, such as a series forming a buoyed channel. Each buoy's characteristics are shown on the chart and provided you marry up the features of the light you are passing, you know how far you are along a buoyed channel.

But beware! There are two regions in this neat worldwide system, A and B, whose only difference is the colour of the lateral marks. IALA A uses red for port and green to mark the starboard side of the channel when entering a port – in force in Africa, most of Asia, Australia, Europe, and India. Conversely, IALA B uses green to mark the port and and red the starboard sides of the channel when entering port – as in North, Central and South America, Japan, Korea, and the Philippines.

Another custom at sea I'd picked up was 'dipping the ensign', a mark of courtesy or respect when a merchantman was in close proximity to a warship. Along the Californian coast the US Navy had large naval ports and, with such a huge fleet, it was inevitable that we'd come across one or two. When we did, we lowered our Red Ensign to about half-mast. In return, the warship lowered her ensign and then re-hoisted it. We then returned our 'red duster' to its close-up position. On such occasions, there was often a quick call to either Richard or me to race down to the poop deck to conduct this courtesy. Just another little job for a deck cadet.

I had now experienced a typical container ship trade route: seven ports in eleven days on the North American coast. I'd been determined to go up the road whenever possible and was pleased with my shoreside meanderings.

It was almost a pleasant relief to have a week at sea, steaming at 21½ knots, to arrive at the Panama Canal on 18 September.

I was on the fo'c'sle for weighing anchor before our transit. Similar tools were required as for anchoring, although a hammer or crowbar, plus a hose, were added. The engineers provided power and water on deck. The hose was connected and laid to the hawse pipe. The Bosun checked the windlass wasn't in gear and the brake was on. He slowly turned the windlass over and oiled its moving parts then put it into gear. An AB removed the compressor bar. Over the walkie-talkie, I heard the bridge tell Ken to start heaving in the anchor, which the Bosun did after he'd taken off the windlass brake. The AB turned on the hose and played it down the hawse pipe to wash off any mud and detritus on the cable. As each shackle appeared on deck, another AB rang the ship's bell.

Ken the Mate perched on the step and looked over the bulwark. He reported how the cable was 'growing'. All was well, as it led ahead rather than around the bow or astern. The cable grew at long stay initially but as more of it was heaved on board, that changed to short stay. Eventually, the cable was 'up and down' and we saw a 'clear anchor' when it emerged from the water. The Bosun continued to slowly heave in until the anchor was 'home'. He then applied the brake, threw the compressor bar across the cable, and disengaged the windlass gear.

Ken told me to lower the black anchor ball. After which, I unclipped it from its halyard and stowed it in the fo'c'sle locker. Meanwhile, the Bosun and ABs secured the fo'c'sle: devil's claws on the cables; bottle screws tightened up on both anchor cables; covers snugly fitted over the hawse pipes and spurling pipes; and the hose drained of water, rolled up neatly and stowed in its basket.

California Star joined the northbound convoy. At the other end of the Canal, she headed off on the 4,540 nautical mile (8,410 km) voyage across the Atlantic to Liverpool.

It was always 'Channel night' the evening before arrival at a UK port. Richard and I, with the engineer cadets and a couple of the day-work Engineer Officers (Stephen Moore and Howard Stringer), enjoyed a few sherbets. We embarked the pilot on 29 September, sailed past the Bar Light, Liverpool's familiar skyline dead ahead, entered the Mersey and manoeuvred into Gladstone Lock. With the assistance of a couple of tugs, *California Star* berthed at Royal Seaforth Container Terminal. I was definitely something of a Liverpudlian seaman, having signed on or paid off here for my three trips!

I reported to Captain Daniel. He signed me off Ship's Articles, signed and date-stamped my Discharge Book, and gave me a good debrief of my progress during this trip. We shook hands and said cheerio. He was a good Old Man and I wondered whether I would sail with him again. I bid farewell to Ken Pyket, an excellent Mate. I found Richard and the engineer cadets with whom I'd enjoyed so many laughs and good times throughout the voyage. We bade farewell with hopes of sailing together again on a future trip.

I toddled down the gangway, dumped my kit in the boot of the waiting taxi, climbed in, and headed for Liverpool Lime Street station, where I caught the train to Euston. I crossed to Waterloo via the underground, took the Pompey train and my folks picked me up from the Gosport ferry. Home again for a spot of leave after a great trip. I kept pinching myself in disbelief that I had such a great job.

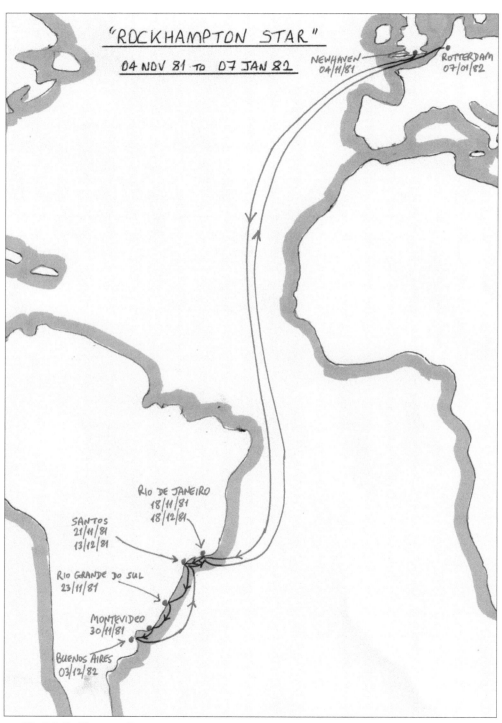

Fig 7.1 *Rockhampton Star* voyage

7 To Rio with *Rocky*!

Fig 7.2 *Rockhampton Star* (aka *Rocky*) (Fotoflite)

I travelled on the train from Pompey Harbour to join *Rockhampton Star* in Newhaven, East Sussex, on 4 November 1981. It made a change from flogging all the way to Liverpool by rail.

At last, I was on board a 'proper' Blue Star ship. *Rockhampton Star* (affectionately nicknamed *Rocky*) was a refrigerated cargo ship, or reefer, designed to transport perishable commodities (fruit, meat, fish, vegetables, dairy) that required temperature-controlled environments. Built by Cammell Laird, Birkenhead, in 1957, *Rocky* entered service in early 1958. We had a link as I was born in that year. Of 10,619 gross tons and 6,407 net tons, she measured 507 feet (154 m) in length, 68 feet (21 m) in the beam, and a draught of 30 feet (9 m). *Rocky* was powered through the sea at 17½ knots by a 13,300 bhp, 8-cylinder engine driving a single screw.

She was from an older era of ship design and the superstructure and engine room were amidships, which divided the five refrigerated holds into three forward and two aft. Lifting gear comprised a mast and a pair of derrick booms per hold. This enabled cargo operations in either single derrick or union purchase mode. Similarly, rather than the transom (flattened, vertical) sterns of my previous, modern ships, *Rockhampton Star* had an old-fashioned cruiser (rounded) stern.

Rocky's white superstructure was atop the engine room. Crew accommodation, mess and galleys were on the main deck, above which were the officers' cabins on port and starboard sides with the officers' mess and bar across the for'ard end. The boat deck was the spacious accommodation for the Master and Chief Engineer, abaft of which were two lifeboats on each side, instead of the usual two in total.

Surmounting the boat deck was the bridge. It was small and cluttered with rather ancient-looking equipment, including the helm and the engine telegraph. The chart table, with its wide, deep drawers in which the folios of navigation charts were stowed, was a solid, varnished, dark mahogany. *Rocky's* charts were divided into folios that covered a particular region or coast, such as Europe or the east coast of South America. Each folio was kept in a canvas cover. Very neat and certainly eased the search for charts.

Similar cabinetry housed the ship's two chronometers, each of which was wound a prescribed number of turns daily, their error recorded by checking against the Greenwich time signal. The chronometers were the time reference when using a sextant to observe the sun and stars to calculate a ship's astronomical position.

A couple of long mahogany bookshelves were fixed to the aft bulkhead, behind the chart table. They held the numerous essential UK Hydrographic Office's Admiralty publications (tide tables, the current annual *Nautical Almanac*, *List of Lights*, *List of Radio Signals*, *Sailing Directions*, *Annual Summary of Notices to Mariners*, *Chart Symbols and Abbreviations*, three volumes of *Distance Tables*, three volumes of *Ocean Passages of the World*, and, my personal favourite, *The Mariner's Handbook*), *Norie's Tables*, *Marine Observer's Handbook* (for meteorological guidance), and operator manuals for bridge equipment and systems.

> *Admiralty Sailing Directions*, **also known as** *Pilots*, **are a great source of information to support port entry and coastal navigation for all mariners. They're split across 75 volumes and cover the world's main commercial shipping routes and ports. Each volume includes information on navigational hazards, buoyage, pilotage, regulations, general notes on countries, port facilities, seasonal currents, ice and climatic conditions.**

Tucked behind the bridge was the radio shack where the Radio Officer (Sparks) monitored prescribed frequencies and radio traffic. Ocean-going ships were required by maritime law to carry at least one fully qualified Radio Officer. He was usually an employee of one of the major marine radio companies (such as Marconi Marine, Redifon, IMR, Kelvin Hughes) although some were employed directly by the shipping company.

When at sea, Sparks went on watch in his shack. He monitored the international distress frequency (500 kHz) for any distress or urgency signals and conducted his standard duties: sent traffic reports to local coast radio stations; listened to 'traffic lists' for messages specifically for his own ship; and passed on weather reports, navigational warnings, urgency signals, and distress messages to the Master and the Mate on watch. However, during 15–18 minutes and 45–48 minutes past each hour (the silence periods), his focus was entirely on listening to 500 kHz. All ships and coast radio stations were legally obliged to listen on this frequency in case any vessel transmitted a distress message.

Sparks were a strange breed, cocooned alone, head clamped by headphones, in a cramped office, bulkheads filled with metal panels of dials and switches, a table for the teletext and fax machines, other miscellaneous bizarre machinery and equipment, plus enough space for his desk and chair.

Advances in technology and the associated simplification meant 'old-fashioned', often temperamental and mysterious, equipment was gradually phased out. New rules and regulations came into force after I left Blue Star. The advent of satellite communications, plus the evolution of the Global Maritime Distress and Safety System (GMDSS) combined to make Sparks' job redundant. New systems were installed on bridges and all deck officers were trained to use them. Therefore, after a little less than a century, the Radio Officer was consigned to seafaring and maritime history. Sad, but that's man's progress into the digital age.

From the bridge wings, the view for'ard was only partially obstructed by the masts and rigging for the derricks. Abaft the bridge was dominated by the distinctive outsize funnel displaying the Blue Star logo – it was great to finally embark on a traditional Blue Star reefer. On the monkey island, a protective waist-high wooden wall enclosed the old-fashioned magnetic compass binnacle.

A significant difference from my previous ships was the lack of air conditioning in the accommodation. This made life a little uncomfortable in tropical latitudes, but at least our cabins had a decent sized port (window) for ventilation, fitted with wooden shutters. The crew's cabins were on the weather deck, while the officers occupied the deck above, with a narrow teak promenade deck from forward to aft on port and starboard sides and then around the aft end. Our cabins were only fitted with a washbasin, as heads (toilets) and showers were on the internal side of the alleyway. Wardrobe, chest of drawers, bunk and other furniture were of varnished mahogany and showed their age.

Rocky was manned by British officers and Chinese crew. – invariably escapees from Mao's China who had settled in Singapore with their families. They were all late middle-aged, some comfortably in their fifties or older. At dinner on my first evening on board, it was obvious the Pantry Boy – short, skinny, and wizened – was at least 60. To a man, they served in the same ship for several years at a time and sent their pay home. Despite being on board British ships for so long, their command of the English language remained basic. Bang, one of the stewards, barely spoke a word of English. If you ordered scrambled eggs at breakfast, he arrived at the table, slammed the plate down in front of you, and exclaimed 'SKAMBO!' Nevertheless, they were collectively friendly, courteous, invariably polite, and hard-working in a plodding methodical way.

Nicky Barr was Chief Mate. He was one of Blue Star's senior Mates and was a well-spoken, personable bloke. We had a chat about my experience to date and what he expected of me this trip. Another O/T was already on board and, at last, I was senior to a fellow cadet, as 'Doddy' Tapper had joined BSSM a year after my intake. I don't clearly recall, but he may already have had a brief trip on another ship. Regardless, I was in charge. Crikey, such responsibility!

I popped up to see the Old Man and was pleased to meet Captain Daniel again. He must have had an equally short period of leave as mine after *California Star*. It was great to sail with a previous shipmate again. We enjoyed a short chat about our last trip and looked forward to this trip on *Rockhampton Star* to South America. I'd got as far as Belém on *Benedict*, but *Rocky* was bound for ports further down the coast.

The Second Mate was Mark Daniels, one of the first intakes of officer trainees. A neat, smart, conscientious officer from Brighton. In the Deck Department was Mike Gaudion, Third Mate and a Guernseyman. A stocky young bloke with a shock of unruly blond hair. On the South American coast, Mike and I teamed up for one cargo watch, while Mark and Doddy formed the opposite watch.

I don't recall much about either the Chief or Second Engineers, but I enjoyed much interaction with the junior engineers. Dick Hills was

Third Engineer, a Falkland Islander settled in Southampton, where many Falklanders apparently lived if they moved to the UK. His native islands were, at that time, insignificant. Little did any of us realise that our visit to Buenos Aires wasn't too long before tension between the UK and Argentina increased and led to the Argentinian invasion of, and subsequent war in, the Falklands. Pete Glossart (Scotsman), Ian Robertson, and Steve Lloyd (northerners) were the Fourth, Fifth, and Junior Engineers respectively. Nick McKinnon was the sole engineer cadet and he possessed a strong West Country accent. With this gang of reprobates, I enjoyed quite a social life at sea and, particularly, alongside.

Chief Refrigeration Engineer (Fridgie) was 'Willy Wombat' McDonald, an older, bespectacled Scotsman with a soft accent who permanently wore a navy-blue bobble hat on board. Greg Sadler was his wingman as 2nd Refrigeration Engineer.

The Purser was responsible for catering and ship's victualling. He was an ancient bloke, tubby, with thinning white hair, and an obnoxious personality. I avoided him if at all possible as I'm afraid I just didn't like him at all. Such is life!

Adrian was the Radio Officer, an Irishman who was entirely competent as Sparks but seemed to inhabit a different world to the rest of us. He enjoyed a jolly good soaking of booze in port. When tasked with the 'All on Board' book, it was always interesting to check Adrian. Knocking on his cabin door, I faked an Irish accent, 'Are you on board, Adrian?' 'Yes, to be sure, I'm all there', he always replied in a thicker Irish accent than usual. Present in body but not necessarily in mind, methinks.

So, overall, a good ship, with a crew to match and an exciting trip: coasting in South America!

In those days, Newhaven was a quiet little town on the Sussex coast, astride the River Ouse, midway between Brighton and Eastbourne. It was a small commercial port but with a long history of cross-Channel ferry traffic to Dieppe. The only interesting thing to me was the realisation that, as the tide ebbed, *Rocky* settled on the river's mud banks until the tide flooded and she refloated herself. The slight list to port was a little unnerving and, inconveniently, meant the washbasin, showers and heads didn't drain properly until the ship attained an even keel again as the tide rose.

Rockhampton Star sailed on 5 November and, after dropping the pilot, set a south-westerly course down the English Channel. The ship was lightly loaded with powdered milk, whisky, and glass products for this transatlantic voyage, although it wasn't uncommon for a westbound voyage to be 'in ballast' (no cargo). Occasionally in the old days, pedigree cattle were penned in on deck, for delivery to Buenos Aires. I sympathised with the poor devil nominated to ensure they were 'fed and watered' daily. No doubt a cadet's job, I reckoned. I could scarcely imagine the mess on deck after their off-loading!

Fig 7.3 *Rocky* at Newhaven

Doddy and I worked with the deck crowd most days. Nicky Barr also tasked us with stripping, cleaning, greasing, and reassembling hatch and watertight door 'dogs'. All weather deck openings obviously had to be watertight. Doors and hatches tightly fitted in their place with a rubber gasket in a groove around the rim, secured by four or six 'dogs' (handles). By pulling each dog in turn, the door or hatch was clamped increasingly firmly to make the opening watertight. With time and usage, the dogs naturally loosened and their lubrication dried and dirtied. Hence, periodic maintenance was essential.

It took Doddy and me a few days, as we discovered 'dogs' were everywhere! Not just the obvious places, like doorways into the accommodation and around hatches, but on the mast house between each hatch, cargo winches on mast house roofs, windlasses on the fo'c'sle, capstan on the poop deck, miscellaneous lockers in the fo'c'sle head, like the paint shop. It was never-ending! Doddy and I were methodical and painstaking. With engineers' rags and a wire brush, we ensured the dogs were pristine and then freshly greased before we refitted them, watertight once again.

Rockhampton Star steamed south-west across the jaws of the Bay of Biscay. Sea and weather were kind to me again. *Rocky* then altered to a more southerly course and slipped between the Azores on one side and the Canaries on the other. Both archipelagos were unseen, far over the horizon. Onwards we sailed until landfall was made off Farol da São Thomé. We followed the Brazilian coast to starboard and rounded Arraial do Cabo, and finally saw Rio de Janeiro's skyline in the distance on 18 November.

Doddy and I met the pilot and escorted him to the bridge. *Rockhampton Star* continued into Guanabara Bay, on the west side of which sat Rio de Janeiro. From the chart, I knew we'd seen Ipanema Beach ahead before turning to starboard. On the port side, we passed Copacabana Beach. High above the city, the statue of Christ the Redeemer perched on Corcovado surveyed the throbbing metropolis below. Proceeding further into the bay, I spied Pão de Açucar (Sugarloaf Mountain). I couldn't believe my immense good fortune in coming to Rio, and getting paid for it!

We were there for three days, loading coffee and fruit. The former in large bags secured to pallets and stowed in the lower holds; the latter boxed and loaded into the smaller tween deck refrigerated compartments. Mark and Doddy, Mike and I split into our two shifts and settled into the routine. Fortunately, the port didn't work 24 hours per day, so we split our shifts evenly from 0700 to about 1900 daily. Stevedores (wharfies) clambered aboard – a motley collection of blokes, dressed in everyday shirts and jeans, some in safety boots, most in flip-flops.

The Chinese ABs opened the MacGregor hatches by attaching a wire rope to the securing point on the hatch and used a derrick winch to pull the hatch covers along the hatch coaming rails to their vertical stowage position at one end of the hatch. *Rockhampton Star's* hatch openings were smaller than *Benedict's*, typical of a refrigerated ship compared to a general cargo vessel. This design limited the loss of cold air from the chilled hold and reduced ingress of warmer and more humid ambient air during cargo operations.

Ships' cargo holds extended from the weather deck to the tank top, oddly this described the 'deck' of the lower hold, which was therefore also the 'top' of the double-bottom tanks. On reefers and general cargo ships, an extra deck or two, tween decks, were fitted with hatches between the tank top and weather deck. Each of *Rocky's* holds comprised an upper and lower tween deck and lower hold, the latter a large space for a large volume, single 'fridge' cargo or for a variety of break bulk general cargoes. The tween decks had a lower headroom to create small refrigerated compartments in the wings of each deck of the hold. This enabled a variety of 'fridge' cargoes to be carried, which needed to be at a specific temperature.

As the hatch square was also a refrigerated cargo space, its deck similarly required insulation. In *Rockhampton Star*, the hatch covers for the tween decks were of an old-fashioned 'beam and plug' design. Several wooden beams sheathed in protective galvanised steel slotted into short grooves along the longitudinal edges of the hatch square. The plugs were small thick squares of cork insulation, bevelled and edged with galvanised steel, which were then snugly placed between the bevelled sides of the beams. They fitted together like a jigsaw puzzle to seal the hatch square. Each plug was numbered to ensure they were returned to the correct hole. Beams and plugs were heavy, so the ship's derricks were used for removal and refitting.

Deck officers had to monitor the refitting as the wharfies could be slapdash. When loading was completed, all they wanted to do was plop the beams and plugs in as quickly as possible so they could get home. Due to *Rocky*'s age, the plugs were no longer in mint condition, which made the task awkward at times. We had to be on our toes at all times so these essential items were fitted correctly and the refrigerated compartments were sealed as tight as practicable.

With the hatches open, we rigged stanchions and looped safety ropes through their tops to make the edge of the exposed hatch square as safe as practicable to prevent wharfies falling to the bottom of the vast lower hold. The stanchions and ropes were stowed in lockers on the weather deck so we manhandled everything down the hatch ladders and then erected them as safety barriers.

There were no fitted lights in the holds so, during twilight and night watches, we rigged portable lights (clusters) around the hatch coaming, secured so their light shone down into the darkness of the tween decks and lower hold. Each cluster had a short sisal rope spliced onto it to fix it to a suitable bit of hatch coaming. In the tween decks, clusters were attached to the stanchions to shine light more directly into the lower hold. Inevitably, a lamp in a cluster 'popped' and needed replacing.

It was time-consuming and tiring to rig all this stuff in tropical heat and humidity, day or night, and to remain abreast of everything. During a cargo watch, we had periods of intense, high-speed activity interspersed with a more relaxed pace. Cargo watch passed quickly.

On our second afternoon, Mike and I took a taxi to Sugarloaf Mountain. The cable car carried us to the summit, almost 1,300 feet (400 m) above the city. There wasn't much to do at the peak, except enjoy panoramic views of the city, the bay, and its eastern side beyond.

On our last afternoon, we were irresistibly drawn to Copacabana Beach – who wouldn't be? The taxi wound its way through the heart of downtown Rio and along the bay's edge. Like any 'world' city, high-rise office blocks and trendy and expensive malls and shops were evident. We also saw poorer suburbs with litter-strewn pavements, shabby unkempt people, tatty shops and bars. We got out of the taxi at the north-east end of Copacabana, at the Hilton. The golden arc of this famous beach stretched away to the south, filled with glistening tanned Brazilians. A sprinkling of beach volleyball games were in progress, folks in the sea, and others loafing on the beach. Sandals in hand, we strolled slowly along the beach, our feet warmed by the sand. There were plenty of young women in the tiniest of bikinis, 'flossing' – certainly not a sight I was used to at Hayling Island or on the Isle of Wight! We scuppered a cool Antarctica beer (a Pilsner brewed in Brazil) in a bar at the south end of Copacabana and then continued round the headland to visit Ipanema too, before returning to *Rocky*.

Night-time proved a typical example of traditional merchant navy social life. With Pete, Ian, Steve, and Nick, we went up the road by taxi. VW Beetles were ubiquitous throughout Brazil, still being built under licence many years after production ceased in Europe. This was many years before the reincarnation of the Beetle in the mid-1990s.

We arrived at the 'skids', merchant navy parlance for the dodgy, down-at-heel areas full of bars and 'knocking shops' (brothels) that attracted visiting seamen and local whores alike. The bars did a permanent roaring trade, with long daily opening hours, to fulfil a seaman's requirement for booze, fun, laughter, cabaret, and girls.

We spent the evening in the Scandinavia Bar (shortened to Scandi Bar) and the Florida Bar. We scuppered large bottles of Antarctica beer, a rather nice Brazilian-brewed beer. The alternative Brazilian beer was Brahma Chopp, which I didn't find quite so palatable. Those more alcoholically adventurous than me enjoyed Cuba libre, a highball cocktail of Coca-Cola, Bacardi, and lime juice on ice. It was waitress service and they reappeared frequently at every table to replace empty glasses with filled ones. Cash changed hands.

The cabarets were usually strippers rotating through their limited repertoire. Many punters were transfixed by the strippers' gradually exposed bodies. Others completely ignored them, and focused completely on the bottom of successive shot glasses or beer bottles. All the while, 'girls' roamed among the tables of increasingly inebriated seamen, doing their best to attract custom. Like all Brazilian girls I'd seen so far, they were lovely to look at: tanned, luscious, firm, young bodies with immaculate hair and make-up. Occasionally, a punter was drawn into their web of charm by unbridled, desperate lust and desire. A conversation would take place, limited by the mutual grasp of the English language. Eventually, a punter would weaken and accompany 'his girl' to the 'bag-off hotel' nearby.

Fig 7.4 Business card: Scandinavia Bar, Rio

In rare instances, booze caused an argument or even a fight to break out among some of the clientele. Nothing much would come of it, as it usually petered out or shipmates broke it up and everyone was friends again. It was all so innocent compared to the naked, drug-fuelled aggression and violence witnessed today in any town centre worldwide.

It was known that one or two of the Chinese crew saved some of their wages to spend the entire port visit in a 'bag-off hotel' with a girl. Understandable I suppose, as the Chinese crew signed on for at least twelve months, a long time away from wife and family.

The whores possessed a principle of loyalty to customers. This was expected to be reciprocated by the punter. But if he strayed to an alternative option, his girl became aggressive, even violent. I witnessed this a couple of times. The girl typically launched into a verbal assault. To be called a 'butterfly' by a Brazilian whore was just about the worst insult a seaman in the skids could suffer! A bit of slapping occurred as her fury and volume increased. Eventually, the scene subsided and she retreated, the poor chap was left embarrassed and almost untouchable to the other whores. An interesting code of honour.

Conversation at our table on these nights in the skids was always fruity, with many yarns spun, accompanied by much laughter. Names were mentioned in these tales of derring-do in the skids and on the coast worldwide. The Ozzie and Kiwi coasts were particularly noteworthy. In the old days, merchant ships were 'on the coast' of either or both countries for a couple of months or more. The working day (for Deck and Engine Departments) ended at 1600 or so, and left many empty evenings and nights to fill.

Blue Star Line ships, like other shipping lines, attracted a certain type of Antipodean 'party-girl' (moll). Almost nightly, molls were welcomed on board and a party started. It wasn't uncommon for 'romantic' pairings to develop. Often, the moll remained on board not just in her home port but for the duration that the ship was on the coast, secreted in his cabin by her paramour. The moll was then said to be 'ring-bolted'. One (in)famous Blue Star Engineer, nicknamed 'Billy Bag-Off' (I never knew his real name), was notorious for taking a smoko-poko during the morning and afternoon tea breaks in port and at sea! I realised that my seafaring career was at the crossroads between this traditional era and the new-fangled box boat epoch.

There were only so many (or more accurately, few) large Antarcticas that I could drink in an evening. I was incapable of drinking my own bodyweight nightly, unlike so many other blokes. The others remained in situ when I told them I was heading back to the ship. I disliked taxis so, on both nights in Rio, I walked back to *Rocky* alone – in hindsight, an incredibly foolish thing to do. In my defence, I wasn't drunk, fully retained my faculties, and felt confident I could outrun any threat en route. I never found out if this was true. I kept my eyes and ears wide open during the steady trudge through the dark, poorly lit, cobbled, pot-holed streets, past a series of silent warehouses. Relieved at sighting the dock gates, I passed through security and got back on board.

We sailed from Rio in the early morning light of 21 November for the half-day steam to Santos. There wasn't much to see during this short passage. The land swept away some 17 miles (30 km) from us until landfall was made at Ilhabela, an island beyond which was Santos, famous as Pele's hometown football club and the port for São Paulo. Stand-by was quite short as the port was only about 1½ miles (2.5 km) up the River Santos estuary, on our port side.

Fig 7.5 Departing Rio

Unlike on container ships, cargo operations didn't start immediately. There was always a lag after berthing at the wharf because the Deck Department had to complete preparations for cargo work. Depending on the weather and sea state, the crew might have opened the hatches before stand-by and got the derricks up and running. Otherwise, this was done when berthed.

Mark and Doddy chose the day shift. Mike and I were on nights, which he preferred, particularly as sometimes loading of frozen or chilled cargoes halted at odd times during our shift until deliveries from source resumed in the morning. The stevedores' night shift usually took a break of a half to a full hour. We enjoyed a relaxed mug of tea during the slack periods and had a modicum of success raiding the galley or pantry for tasty bits and pieces.

During cargo operations we were constantly busy. We flitted from one hatch coaming to another, peering over to observe the wharfies at work. We scampered down and up ladders in the holds to fix any stanchions and safety ropes that had come adrift. At night, the clusters were critical and required frequent re-siting as loading developed to illuminate the dark recesses that were being filled with cargo. Lamps exploded or extinguished if they were struck by cargo pallets and had to be immediately replaced. Frequent descents into the holds to inspect the loading and securing in refrigerated compartments meant that our bodies were continually adjusting to the chill down below and the humid tropical heat on deck. Sweat constantly poured off us and dried in our boiler suits. It was quite a relief when our shift ended and Mark and Doddy took over.

Fig 7.6 View for'ard from port bridge wing: masts, derricks, standing rigging

Mike and I enjoyed a swift breakfast and slept until lunchtime. In the afternoons, we went up the road. It was a short walk to the cross-river ferry terminal. On the opposite side of the river, we got a taxi to the coastal town of Guarujá, possessed of several fabulous long sandy beaches. We based ourselves at a bar overlooking Praia das Pitangueiras and, beyond, the vast empty expanse of the Atlantic Ocean. Life was good: Antarctica beer, steak and chips, golden sandy beach, lots of lovely, deeply tanned, bikini-clad Brazilian girls to observe. What more could a chap want?

Sadly, each afternoon evaporated. Inevitably, we returned to *Rockhampton Star* for our night shift. However, we always succumbed to an Antarctica beer in The Love Story, a popular seamen's bar on our way back to the ship. We loaded oranges, sugar, and coffee. It was a day-and-a-half's steam down the coast to our next port.

Rockhampton Star passed between mile-long (1.5 km) breakwaters and berthed at a wharf about six miles (10 km) up the Rio Grande on the western side. The town of Rio Grande, small and full of industrial estates, didn't have much to recommend it and we didn't bother to go up the road.

Beyond the town, the narrow waterway opened up and became Lagoa dos Patos, an estuarine lagoon some 93 miles (150 km) long and varying in width from six to twelve miles (10 to 20 km). At the northern end was Porto Alegre, the state capital and prime port of Brazil's southernmost state, Rio Grande do Sul, which borders Uruguay to the south and Argentina to the west and is dominated by farming and cattle. For about five days, we loaded frozen concentrated orange juice manufactured by Cutrale, a world leader in the industry, and leather products.

Fig 7.7 View aft: outsize Blue Star funnel, port lifeboats, more masts, derricks, standing rigging

Concentrated orange juice, perhaps surprisingly, was a very valuable cargo. It was shipped in 40-gallon drums, hoisted aboard on pallets, and lowered to the bottom of *Rocky*'s huge lower holds. There were Blue Star tales about a drum being dropped during loading and splitting open on deck. The content was so concentrated and potent that it stripped the paint off the steel deck. On another occasion, wharfies 'sampled' the orange juice and ended up in hospital and, reportedly, one died. Dangerous stuff, orange juice – stick to wine and beer is my advice, although Cutrale as a well-diluted mixer in a half-pint pot of vodka does quench your thirst!

The leather products were a miscellany of footwear, bags, and coats. In another Blue Star yarn, the load included shoes, so the entire crew wore brown leather loafers for the voyage home.

The port of Rio Grande had no dockside cranes, so we used our own derricks rigged in union purchase.

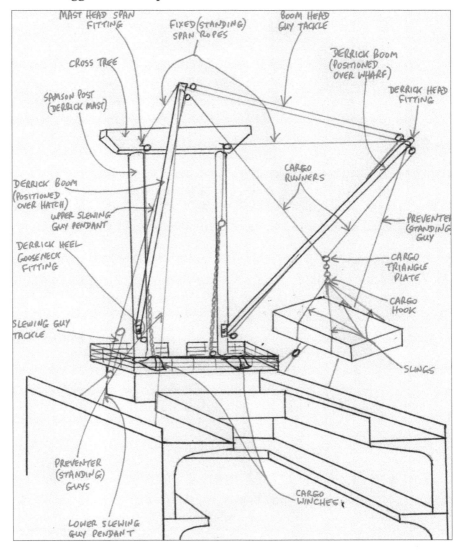

Fig 7.8 Union purchase rig

In union purchase, each pair of derricks is joined such that the inshore derrick plumbs over the wharf and the outboard derrick is positioned over the hatch square. The derrick booms are fixed in these positions using preventers or guy wires to keep them static. The derricks' cargo runners are coupled so the load can be swung from a position vertically under one derrick boom to a position vertically under the second. The winchmen operate in synchronicity to raise the cargo from the wharf, clear the ship's side, move it across the deck, and lower it into the hatch square where the wharfies unhook and stow the cargo.

Union purchase demands specific operating criteria and safety precautions. The operating angle of the derrick is not to be less than 30° to the horizontal. The maximum angle between the cargo wires should not exceed 120°, which minimises the forces within the rig. The cargo slings should not be unduly long. The winchmen are not to lift loads above a minimum required for safety but sufficient to clear guardrails and hatch coamings. Cargo runner wires mustn't chafe against the hatch coaming or guardrails. Winchmen have to be experienced and coordinate closely. Failure to adhere to these rules could cause an incident and possible injury to wharfies or crew. This highlights the hazards in working cargo on a merchantman.

It was another half-day's steam to the mouth of the River Plate. On 30 November, *Rocky* was alongside at Montevideo, where the port was conveniently located almost adjacent to the hub of Uruguay's capital city.

In December 1939, the German cruiser *Graf Spee* sought refuge from the Royal Navy in this neutral port. After a few days the Captain decided to scuttle the ship rather than face defeat and heavy loss of life to his crew if he tried to sail away from Montevideo.

I went up the road one day and strolled around the city centre. The streets and squares were lined with trees and provided welcome shade. By chance, I reached Plaza Constitución, a lovely green, peaceful space in the city centre. Eastwards, a tree-lined boulevard led me to Plaza Independencia, a vast square around which were government ministry buildings and the President's residence. There were many statues in this square, but the centre was dominated by the most important and venerated memorial: the mausoleum of José Artigas, national hero of Uruguay's independence movement.

I strolled south, past the Teatro Solis and reached the corniche and a refreshing sea breeze. I was now at the pleasant park of Plaza Republica Argentina. It was time to return to the ship, a good walk along the corniche, along the Rambla Gran Bretaña which morphed into Rambla Francia. I was soon at the dock gates and back on board. Montevideo was a pleasant, old-fashioned sort of place. I was struck by the prevalence of old cars on the streets – all about 20-odd years behind models in Europe and the UK.

Naturally, beef products made up the cargo we loaded during our three days in port, including Fray Bentos corned beef, which originated from the port of the same name up the River Uruguay. Boxed frozen beef for the UK and chilled horse on the bone for the Continent were also loaded. On one occasion we loaded a consignment of vintage cars (including Ford Model Ts) for delivery to the UK.

I saw *Bronte* arrive on our last afternoon. She was one of four L&H general cargo ships on the South America route. Her sisters (*Browning, Belloc* and *Boswell*) were all built by Austin Pickersgill, Sunderland, in 1979 to their Standard Ship Design 14 (or SD 14). With five holds, they were 472 feet (144 m) long, a beam of 65 feet (20 m), 29 feet (8.8 m) draught, and weighed in at 9,324 gross and 6,151 net tons. We didn't meet up or visit her as we sailed a couple of hours later. Still, it was nice to see another BSSM ship in a foreign port.

It took barely half a day to steam across the Plate estuary to Buenos Aires (BA), where *Rockhampton Star* slipped behind the protective breakwater and berthed on 3 December. We loaded tinned processed meat products, frozen beef carcasses, boxed frozen beef, and chilled horse meat. We were on deck for most of the time.

The spaces had to be thoroughly cleaned prior to loading. In particular, those for chilled beef were fumigated with formaldehyde 'bombs' to kill traces of fungus lurking in the woodwork. Dunnage was then carefully laid to ensure correct air flow throughout the locker or hold. Chilled beef was carried as fore and aft hindquarters hung on sterilised hooks at -1.6°C, with a tolerance of less than ±½°C. Frozen meat required carriage at -9.5°C. Freezing meat caused tiny blood vessels to burst, which then bled when thawed, which made chilled beef, untainted by this phenomenon, a more valuable commodity than frozen beef.

As loading of each tween-deck and locker was completed, it was important to fit our beams and plugs quickly and snugly. This helped 'Willie Wombat' and Greg to get on with reducing each compartment's temperature to the correct level.

Equally important, the quality of the loaded meat was monitored by 'Willie Wombat' and Greg, on the quay in spotless white boilersuits. They speared carcasses with a spiked thermometer as they came off the trucks and used a hand drill to get the thermometer into the bone to ensure that the meat was thoroughly frozen. If a ship accepted a cargo as being in good condition, but then unloaded it in a worse condition, the deterioration must therefore be the ship's fault. An insulated truck may have been delayed under harsh sunshine en route to the ship. If meat is loaded into the ship 'soft' it soon refreezes and becomes misshapen and it is unhygienic to refreeze thawed meat.

Occasionally in the old days, polo ponies were loaded in BA. Temporary stables were erected on the poop deck. Apparently, the ponies were very aggressive and bit you as you walked by. I understand that gauchos, some of whom had met or were acquainted with the then Prince Charles, embarked to tend them during the voyage to the UK. On occasion, the gauchos invited the crew to a polo match barbecue before sailing, where these cowboys showed off their equestrian skills. During unloading in Newhaven, animal rights activists were on the wharf to watch for any cruelty meted out to the ponies. The gauchos gave the polo ponies an injection, which pepped them up and made them a bit frisky after being cooped up during the transatlantic voyage in their temporary stables.

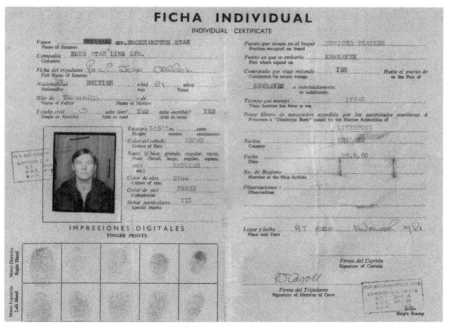

Fig 7.9 *Ficha Individual*

Fortunately, the port was only a short stroll from the city centre. Armed with my *Ficha Individual,* the identity document the authorities required in order to go ashore, I walked around the streets as usual. BA seemed a less shabby and wealthier city than Montevideo, on the opposite side of the River Plate. The main boulevards were much wider and the architecture more impressive and substantial.

Fig 7.10 Alongside in BA

I found myself in Plaza de Mayo, the city's main square, a large oval over 110 yards (100 m) long by about 55 yards (50 m) wide. Anchoring the eastern end was Casa Rosada, the President's Residence, an impressive building. Armed sentries patrolled its frontage. I knew that Argentina, like many other nations, took a sensitive, wary approach to photography of public buildings. At this time, tension was mounting between Argentina and the UK about the Falklands. The newly installed Junta was huffing and puffing and I didn't risk a photograph, in case I got arrested (or worse) for suspected spying.

One day, the ship's agent organised a crew trip to a ranch out in the country. Most of the off-watch officers jumped into the minibus and we enjoyed a lovely day away from the ship, the docks and the big city. My only clear memory was the late lunch provided at the ranch. Bife de lomo (tenderloin or filet mignon) was one of Argentina's most popular lean cuts of meat, with a milder beefy flavour compared to other cuts of steak. It was huge, succulent, extremely tender, juicy, and delicious, complemented by patatas fritas (chips), salad, and beer.

Rockhampton Star departed Buenos Aires on 10 December and set course for the coastal passage northbound to revisit Santos. It was an unremarkable two and a half day trip, with a slight sea, low swell, cloudy, fine and clear. These phrases were common for the weather and sea conditions in the ship's Deck Log at the end of each watch, often abbreviated to 'SS, LS, CFC'. As I had done since Rio, I doubled up with Mike for bridge watchkeeping, Doddy likewise with Mark.

The practical chartwork along the South American coast was great experience. I used 'fixes' that I'd taken of visual bearings of lighthouses and other charted features, plus radar ranges of prominent capes and headlands. I plotted these observations on the chart and was pleased that the position lines intersected at the same spot to yield our position. Occasionally, I got a 'cocked hat' – a rubbish fix because the position lines didn't intersect as hoped, but formed a blasted triangle. It was impossible for me to determine which of my bearings was wrong, so I had to quickly re-take the fix and plot it on the chart.

We loaded more of the same cargo in Santos and then Rio as on our southbound stops. Mike and I thoroughly enjoyed our afternoon excursions to the beaches at Guaraja. It made for long days and little sleep, but who cared? I didn't know when I might visit Brazil again. In fact, it was 1989 in HMS *Hecla*, on an eight-month geophysical survey deployment.

The correct temperature had to be maintained in the refrigerated compartments and holds to prevent our delicate cargo from 'going off' en route. Broadly, it cost more than twice to build a refrigerated ship than a dry cargo vessel. The extra cost came from fitting the required insulation and the ship's refrigeration plant. The insulation of hull, deckheads, and undersides of hatch covers mitigated the effects of higher external air and sea temperatures, especially in the tropics. Internally, the holds were compartmentalised and lockers were insulated from one another.

Rockhampton Star's indirect, brine cooling system comprised three separate but interconnected systems: a refrigeration plant (compressors, evaporators, expansion valves, condensers, control systems); a brine system; and an air circulation system. The refrigeration plant worked on the same principal as a domestic freezer, with the temperature adjusted by thermostat. On board, 'warm' brine (saltwater) circulated through the evaporator (equivalent to a domestic freezer) and exited at a predetermined lower temperature. The immaculately clean 'fridge flat' housed the refrigeration compressors. The 'brine room' was adjacent and contained evaporators, brine pumps, and associated pipework and valves. It was well insulated and maintained at near-zero temperature, ideal for storing drinking water to keep the engineers hydrated during their hot, steamy watches in the engine room. It also doubled as the Officers' beer store – bottles of Grolsch were the traditional beer of choice on *Rocky*.

Brine froze (or stayed liquid) at a lower temperature than freshwater. By increasing the salt content, brine's freezing point was lowered. The brine had to remain pumpable, so it couldn't be allowed to freeze. The cold brine egressed from the fridge plant and was circulated by brine pumps through cooling banks (or nests of tubes) in the holds. Circulating fans blew air through the cooling banks containing the cold brine and cooled the air. The cargo remained cooled or frozen by this constantly circulating air.

Certain cargoes, such as fruit, were 'alive' when exported and gave off carbon dioxide. This caused 'brown heart', seen when an apple is cut in half and the area around the pips is brown. Carbon dioxide levels were constantly monitored and, if too high, warmer outside air was introduced, which increased the hold's temperature. Rapid cooling, followed by decreasing the brine's temperature, reduced the hold temperature to the desired level.

Like a domestic freezer, the cooling banks were prone to icing up, indicated by a slight warming of the hold or compartment because the flow of cooled air through the bank was restricted. This was rectified by stopping the fans and circulating warm brine until the cooling bank defrosted. Monitoring and maintaining the system kept 'Willie Wombat' and Greg constantly engaged.

For quality control during loading, the on-watch Mate intermittently selected a case of fruit and inserted a thermometer with a long spike to check the cargo was being delivered at the right temperature. The same case was then opened and a couple of apples cut in half to ensure there was no 'brown heart'. Obviously, these opened cases couldn't be loaded as cargo as they were now 'spoilt'. There was always plenty of fresh fruit for the voyage home!

As *Rockhampton Star* departed the shores on 20 December 1981, I pondered my South American experience. It was a great place to live if you were rich but, having seen some of the favelas (slum areas), particularly in Brazil, it would be the complete opposite if you were poor – when a life of unadulterated misery, danger, poor sanitation, and ill-health awaited. I recalled our great nights up the road to the skids, with its bars and girls. Sadly, this traditional merchant navy way of life was disappearing as shipping focused increasingly on efficiency, economics, and the switch to containerisation. This resulted in shorter stays in new ports, often constructed miles from town and designed specifically to handle container ships.

It was some 6,500 nautical miles (12,040 km) to Rotterdam. This transatlantic voyage was busy for Doddy and me, but otherwise uneventful. Christmas Day passed by rather quietly, except for a few bottles of Grolsch with Pete, Ian, Steve, and Nick, our fellow day-working engineers. The crew organised a Chinese evening for the officers on New Year's Eve. They put on a terrific spread of traditional Chinese food from the crew galley, which was separate from the officers' galley. Despite the language barrier, we'd been together, particularly Doddy and me on deck, for a couple of months, so it was quite an uproarious evening with plenty of 'yam seng' (Cantonese for 'cheers' in traditional wedding ceremonies, but more specifically, 'drink to victory').

Nicky the Mate employed Doddy and me to holystone *Rocky*'s teak decks. This ancient practice was the scrubbing or scouring of a ship's wooden decks to whiten them. Holystone was a soft, brittle sandstone. In the old Royal Navy, sailors knelt in a line and, each armed with a brick of this stone, scrubbed the decks daily for hours. It was eventually banned as it was viewed only as a means to occupy sailors – and not very healthy either.

Doddy and I didn't have to kneel as our holystones were fitted into a metal framework on the end of a broom handle. We wetted the deck and used the broom-holystone contraption to systematically scour the decks around the accommodation and up to the boat and bridge decks. We may have managed the monkey island too, but I'm not sure. It was quite hard work, but at the end of each day we saw our progress as the teak deck certainly gleamed white. Character-building stuff!

We also helped Mike the Third Mate to check, muster, and scrub our lifeboats. It was Third Mate's perks to be responsible for ship-borne safety, the life-saving and firefighting equipment. *Rockhampton Star* had four lifeboats so, with Mike, Doddy and me on the job, it was a less onerous task. We emptied each in turn. They were sparkling clean after we'd scrubbed them.

We mustered and checked the expiry dates of the tins of condensed milk, barley sugar, and ship's biscuit. Boat lamps, compasses, torches, heliographs, balers, buckets, heaving lines, jack-knives, water dippers, drinking cups, whistles, plugs, and crutches were cleaned. Distress hand flares, smoke floats, and parachute flares were also checked for their validity. Finally, we changed the water in the lifeboats' tanks. In the tropics and mid-latitudes, it was a great job, like holystoning, to do in shorts and T-shirt in warm, bright sunshine. We certainly earned our sherbets at 1600!

Eventually, *Rocky* closed the English Channel and we enjoyed 'Channel Night'. The days were short, the nights long in the northern hemisphere winter. The weather a little less benign, but at least it pushed us from astern as it prevailed from the south-west, those familiar 'families of depressions' that transited the Atlantic Ocean in this season.

We berthed in Rotterdam, having negotiated heavy traffic and the traffic separation schemes in the Dover Strait and into the North Sea. Via a nautical traffic separation scheme 'roundabout' or two, *Rockhampton Star* entered the waterway at Hook of Holland and slipped into Calandkanaal, which led us to Europoort.

As soon as the ship had berthed, a diving team came on board to inspect the stern gland. A leak had slowly wept seawater through this collar of brass, designed to prevent the ingress of water where the propeller shaft exited the hull. The shaft tunnel, which protected the propeller shaft from Holds 4 and 5 above and around, had accumulated several inches of seawater during the Atlantic crossing. The ship's bilge pumps coped adequately so *Rocky* was never in danger of sinking.

During the couple of days before paying off, Doddy and I took the train to Amsterdam for a day trip. We strolled around a fair bit, took a canal-boat cruise, and enjoyed a pub lunch. In the evening, we played pool against a couple of locals and sunk a few sherbets. We caught a late train back to Rotterdam.

On 7 January 1982, I went up to the Captain's cabin. He debriefed me on my performance, and signed and date-stamped my Discharge Book. It had been a pleasure to sail with Captain Daniel again. I said my good-byes to the lads and to the Chinese ABs, clambered down *Rockhampton Star*'s gangway, and clattered into a taxi. I flew from Schiphol to Gatwick, caught the train to Portsmouth Harbour, and crossed to Gosport via the ferry. I rang my parents, who picked me up and brought me home.

Another great trip, on an old-fashioned British refrigerated cargo ship, with a Chinese crew, to a new part of the world, and I'd sampled something of the traditional coasting life of the merchant navy. I'd certainly gained excellent experience and invaluable sea-time across the spectrum of BSSM assets. My next trip wouldn't be until after completing our first college phase at Liverpool Polytechnic.

8 Back to the 'Bel' and College

In early February 1982, I drove up to New Brighton, Wallasey, for the first college phase at Liverpool Polytechnic. I hadn't seen any of my contemporaries since our induction nearly 18 months before. It was great to meet up again In the Belgravia Hotel bar, and share our global seafaring experiences across the BSSM fleet. We'd each completed several trips, varying from two to five months or so and accumulated roughly the same sea-time.

Mr Burke popped over that Sunday evening to welcome us back, briefed us about this phase, and gave us news about Blue Star and BSSM. A couple of older ships were to be sold, sadly this included *Rockhampton Star*, while a couple of newer ships were being acquired. With our limited knowledge of the company, BSSM seemed to be in a reasonably healthy state.

The following morning, we set off for 'school'. It was good to meet our lecturers again: Captain Moore, Captain Watson and, occasionally, Captain Holder. It didn't take long to get into the swing of things. It was a busy four months or so, with much to learn in the classroom, plus several practical courses elsewhere in Liverpool.

It was freezing in my room at the Bel. A harsh Scouse winter meant that occasionally ice formed on the inside of my window overnight. The Bel didn't have central heating. Each room had a meter which ate the 50 pence pieces that powered the little electric heater in the room. It was like revisiting my student days and the lodgings in Whitley Bay. My little quartz alarm clock froze and failed a few times. After thawing it under the bedclothes, it returned to functionality, seemingly none the worse.

Sue was at Liverpool University on the Postgraduate Certificate in Education course, a teacher training qualification. We were both busy in 'school' during the week, but spent most weekends together, usually in her hall of residence. Her accommodation was much more comfortable and warmer than the Bel. We had quality time together and Liverpool offered a pretty good social life, with plenty of pubs, cafes, restaurants, and discos. Yes, I think those night-time venues were still called discos! Sue occasionally stayed over with me in New Brighton, but it was, to be brutally honest, a rather sad, decrepit, depressed town. Its halcyon days long gone and, unfortunately, unlikely to be rekindled any time soon.

Our syllabus at Liverpool Polytechnic covered navigation, chartwork, meteorology, nautical applications of physics and mathematics, and the all-encompassing spectrum of general ship knowledge (GSK). In addition, we began to learn Morse code and endured daily ROR quizzes. There were also external courses to attend and to earn certifications as prerequisites for gaining our Second Mate's Ticket: lifeboat ticket, Efficient Deck Hand (EDH), radiotelephony, and firefighting.

The first such course to interrupt our classroom studies was four days on firefighting at Liverpool Speke Airport. The same Fire Service instructors gave us their usual comprehensive instruction and guidance through practical exercises. Their broad Scouse accents were laced with that renowned Liverpudlian sense of humour. We recapped much of the two-day course we'd done during our induction back in September 1980. The classroom instruction on firefighting equipment, techniques, and breathing apparatus, was followed by a series of practical exercises. The big steel fire box, with its compartments, ladders, hatches, and doorways was repeatedly 'attacked' and the fires extinguished. It was an enjoyable, if rather grubby, hot, sweaty, smoke-laden course. We were given our certificates on 11 March 1982. No time off on Friday, though! We returned to the classroom and got hammered by Captain Moore with ROR.

The following week was spent at the MNTB training facility in The Strand, diametrically opposite Albion House (BSSM headquarters), at the junction with James Street. During our sea-time, we'd experienced the weekly 'Board of Trade games', usually at 1500 on a Friday. Everyone secured at 1430. The ship's horn sounded the emergency signal (seven short blasts followed by one prolonged blast on the ship's horn). The crew mustered on the boat deck at either Lifeboat 1 (starboard side) or Lifeboat 2 (port side). One of the mates completed the muster, while the Bosun and an AB prepared one of the lifeboats for lowering. The lifeboats were used in alternate weeks. Slips released the lifeboat's securing ropes and the lifeboat was lowered by gravity, controlled by a handbrake. Ordinarily, it was only lowered to deck-edge level, where embarkation would occur. In my experience, the lifeboats were never launched, and the ship maintained her speed of 17 to 20 knots or so. At least this weekly exercise proved that the davits hadn't rusted in place, that the handbrake worked, and that the winch hauled the lifeboat back into its cradle, where it was re-secured with the ropes and slips. The crew were then dismissed for the day, the weekly Board of Trade legal requirement achieved.

Armed with our variety of experience of lifeboat drills acquired across the fleet, we had a decent grasp of lifeboats and life rafts. The syllabus was a blend of classroom instruction and practical work. CH Wright's *Survival at Sea* was the source reference book and contained everything we needed to know.

For lifeboat and life raft, we were required to identify permanent markings, including personnel capacity. We learnt the list of statutory equipment, its correct use, the location of instruction cards for important items (transmitter, first aid kit, pyrotechnics), and the minimum food and water allowances per person.

In the classroom, the launching and handling of the lifeboat was explained. Of equal importance were the procedures for preparing, swinging out, embarking, lowering, and launching a lifeboat, and the dangers involved. We were taught the method of clearing the ship when afloat, riding to the sea anchor, and the management of a lifeboat under sail. None of us had any expertise in sail as BSSM ships' lifeboats were fitted with engines.

Equivalent knowledge was required of life rafts, although their methods of launching and precautions to be taken before, during, and after launch were distinctly different from a lifeboat's. Our instructor (a hard-bitten, gnarled old Scouse ex-Bosun) demonstrated how to board a life raft from the ship and, more crucially and likely, from the water. Depending on sea state and wind strength, it was almost inevitable that it would capsize, therefore we learnt to right an inverted life raft.

The philosophy on survival procedure in lifeboats and life rafts included: rigging the covers on lifeboats to protect survivors from wind, spray, and sun; the comfort of passengers and crew; issuing food and water; and maintaining discipline.

For the practical element, we demonstrated to the instructor preparing and launching the training centre's lifeboat, hung on davits on an adjacent dockside. In March, the cold, wet, miserable weather hardly made it a pleasurable experience but realistically mirrored a real-life scenario. It was unlikely to be a beautiful day if your ship sank beneath you! We each successfully conducted the engine-starting procedure. Finally, we merrily rowed around the dock, steered the boat, and acted as coxswain until the instructor was satisfied.

He quizzed us on the orders commonly used during boat handling and we rigged and streamed the sea anchor. Fortunately, he didn't require us to set the sail. The importance of learning how to rig and sail a lifeboat struck me when I read Captain Taprell Dorling's *Blue Star Line at War 1939–1945*. After Blue Star ships were sunk, stirring tales of fortitude and feats of seamanship occurred as mates and masters sailed their lifeboats for weeks over hundreds of miles, heading to the nearest landfall. And mostly with success and many lives saved. Some of these skilled, gutsy officers were gazetted for honours (MBE, BEM, OBE). Courageous, brilliant sailors!

Thankfully, we all comfortably gained our lifeboat ticket on 19 March and resumed 'school' after the weekend. Another step closer to earning our Second Mate's certificate.

After a week in our classroom, we shifted to another room in the department for a week on very high frequency (VHF) communications and radio-telephony. It was dull but essential. The course covered the practical knowledge of adjusting the radiotelephone apparatus, its operation and procedure and of sending and receiving spoken messages correctly by telephone; and a general knowledge of the regulations pertinent to these communications, particularly relating to safety of life. We all passed – another important box ticked!

> Since the 1980s, the course content has morphed into a comprehensive syllabus under the title of Global Maritime Distress and Safety System (GMDSS). It incorporates the latest technology and associated gadgetry mandated in the Safety of Life at Sea (SOLAS) convention. A far cry from our 'noddy' course!

In April, the week-long EDH course was also held at the MNTB centre. The syllabus covered seamanship knowledge and practical work. It was intense and certainly not an 'attendance course' (turn up for a course, do nothing, and get a certificate at the end). We consolidated practical knowledge gained at sea with correct formal instruction from another old-and-bold seamanship instructor. He certainly didn't go easy on us and set a very high standard.

Nautical knowledge embraced: the meaning of common nautical terms; names and functions of parts of a ship; knowledge of the compass card; how to report the approximate bearing of an object in degrees or points on the bow; how to read, stream, and handle a patent log (which none of us had seen); markings on a hand lead line; how to take a cast of the hand lead and correctly report the sounding (depth) obtained; markings on the anchor cable; understanding helm orders; and the use of firefighting and lifesaving appliances.

The practical work was dominated by seamanship skills: knots, hitches and bends; whippings (binding the ends of a rope with marline twine to prevent fraying); seizings (binding two ropes, a rope to an object, or two parts of a rope together with marline twine); putting a stopper on a rope or wire hawser; splicing plaited and multistrand manila and synthetic fibre rope; putting an eye splice in a wire rope; slinging a stage; rigging a bosun's chair; rigging a pilot ladder.

In addition to demonstrating these skills, we were required to verbally explain: care in use and general maintenance of ropes, wires, blocks, and shackles; rigging a derrick; general precautions before and during winch operations when working cargo or warping the ship; using and operating a windlass in anchor work; safe handling of mooring ropes and wires, particularly synthetic fibre ropes and self-tensioning winches; precautions in stowage of anchor chain cable and securing the anchors for sea; knowledge of cargo gear and understanding its uses; and safe handling of hatch covers, battening down and securing hatches and tank lids.

The indispensable reference book was *The Efficient Deck Hand* by CH Wright, while *Ashley's Book of Knots* was also useful. Wright's book contained all you needed to know about such esoteric and extinct instruments as the patent log. We'd all participated in the majority of this syllabus at sea where, of course, short cuts in procedures inevitably occurred. The accuracy of the knowledge you gained depended on the Bosun or AB teaching you.

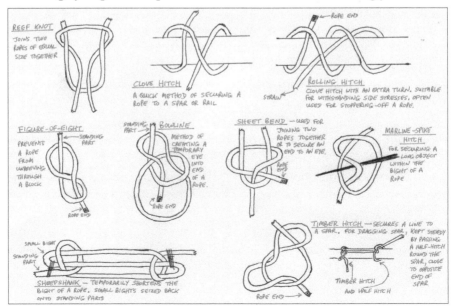

Fig 8.1 Knots and their uses

Most of us had used a rope and/or chain stopper in anger, but our instructor explained how to use them correctly. He demonstrated examinable knots, hitches, and bends. Luckily, we'd all used the majority of them. In my experience the clove hitch, bowline, and round-turn-and-two-half-hitches were the most used on board. Historically, all had a specific usage but, like most ancient skills, they were slowly falling out of use.

As the course progressed, it hammered home that the evolution of humdrum routines, about which you didn't really give much thought, were potentially dangerous, injurious, and even fatal. There were always horror stories of seamen being killed by cargo gear, opening and closing hatches, ropes parting, and heavy objects swinging about like wrecking balls.

Confined spaces were particularly hazardous. A compartment, tank, or cofferdam was a deathtrap if it was not adequately ventilated prior to entry. Noxious and toxic fumes accumulated and it took a specified period for a confined space to be safe for human ingress after opening. So many seamen had died as a result of not adhering to the rules. It was a crucial element in the 'Code of Safe Working Practice', of which we needed a sound working knowledge.

This intense and comprehensive week at 'school', plus self-study at the Bel, yielded passes for us all. Another prerequisite achieved. Much relief all round.

We learnt Morse code to attain the standard of 'reading Morse code from a flashing light at six words per minute'. I found it difficult. A few Morse signals were already familiar as they were used in single flag hoists in the International Code of Signals and in the ROR. The flag hoists themselves were relatively easy to learn, aided by the astute purchase of a pack of cards with the flags on one side and their meaning on the reverse. After shuffling them, it was a good test of memory to recognise not only the letter represented in the graphic but also its meaning.

I got the hang of Morse code by looking at patterns in the dots and dashes. Reading a flashing light at a speed of six words per minute didn't sound too fast, but our tuition started at a slower speed. We sat in our darkened classroom to observe and record the letters from a flashing light on the front wall above the whiteboard. Initially, it wasn't too bad, but as the speed and length of message gradually increased, it certainly became harder.

For me, the concentration required increased almost exponentially. As each message was tapped out, I found I fell almost into a trance, although I retained a good level of concentration, my eyes were transfixed on the flashing light without really 'reading' the dots and dashes. I learnt not to dwell on every letter if I was struggling, but to skip it and read the next one. At the end of the message, I hoped to have enough letters to interpret the blanks and derive the content of the message. It didn't always work. It was absolute torture and frustration. On exam day, I hoped to miraculously have a good stab and immense luck

Table 8.1 International Code of Signals: single flag meanings

Flag	Phonetic	Meaning	Morse
	A – Alfa	I have a diver down; keep well clear at slow speed	• —
	B – Bravo	I am taking in or discharging or carrying dangerous goods	— • • •
	C – Charlie	Affirmative	— • — •
	D – Delta	Keep clear of me; I am manoeuvring with difficulty	— • •
	E – Echo	I am altering my course to starboard	•
	F – Foxtrot	I am disabled; communicate with me	• • — •
	G – Golf	I require a pilot	— — •
	H – Hotel	I have a pilot on board	• • • •
	I – India	I am altering my course to port	• •
	J - Juliet	I am on fire and have dangerous cargo on board: keep well clear of me	• — — —
	K - Kilo	I wish to communicate with you	— • —
	L – Lima	You should stop your vessel instantly	• — • •

Flag	Letter	Meaning	Morse
	M – Mike	My vessel is stopped and making no way through the water	— —
	N – November	Negative	— •
	O – Oscar	Man overboard	— — —
	P – Papa	All persons should report on board as the vessel is about to proceed to sea	• — — •
	Q – Quebec	My vessel is 'healthy' and I request free pratique	— — • —
	R – Romeo	No meaning as a single flag hoist	• — •
	S – Sierra	I am operating astern propulsion	• • •
	T – Tango	Keep clear of me; I am engaged in pair trawling	—
	U – Uniform	You are standing into danger	• • —
	V – Victor	I require assistance	• • • —
	W – Whiskey	I require medical assistance	• — — •
	X – Xray	Stop carrying out your intentions and watch for my signals	— • • —
	Y – Yankee	I am dragging my anchor	— • — —
	Z – Zulu	I require a tug	— — • •

We studied the principles of the gyro compass, used to steer by hand and in autopilot. We took visual bearings for coastal navigation and of nearby ships to 'determine if risk of collision existed'. Sadly, I found it an almost incomprehensible topic. A gyro compass contains a gyroscope motor that registers the direction of true north along the surface of the earth, independent of the Earth's magnetic field. If you're desperate to learn more, use Google, as even now, four decades later, the principles remain utterly baffling to me.

Variation and deviation are two factors that directly affecting a ship's magnetic compass. Both had to be taken into account when setting a course, as mariners always steered a true course, not a compass course.

Variation is the angular difference between true north and magnetic north. This angle varies, depending on your position on the Earth's surface and on changes over time. The magnetic North Pole isn't located at the true North Pole, as 'polar wandering' has placed it in Hudson's Bay. The magnetic South Pole acts similarly near Antarctica. Academics have studied and mapped this phenomenon for centuries and the UK Hydrographic Office publishes annual variation charts.

DEVIATION CARD 1 NAVIGATION		
Magnetic Heading	Deviation	Compass Heading
353°	6°W	000°
014°	6°W	020°
035°	5°W	040°
056°	4°W	060°
078°	2°W	080°
099°	1°W	100°
120°	0°E	120°
142°	2°E	140°
164°	4°E	160°
186°	6°E	180°
208°	8°E	200°
230°	10°E	220°
247°	7°E	240°
266°	6°E	260°
283°	3°E	280°
301°	1°E	300°
317°	3°W	320°
336°	4°W	340°
355°	6°W	360°
This table should not to be used for navigation.		

Fig 8.2 Example of a deviation card

Deviation is the angular difference between magnetic north and the compass needle due to interference from the ship structure, particularly derricks and cranes. It can greatly affect the magnetic compass, but can be reduced by 'swinging the compass'. A ship is moored to a buoy and, under the direction of the 'Swinging Officer' (no sniggering, please), is manoeuvred and held steady by a tug. Adjusting magnets in the compass binnacle on the bridge roof to minimise the effect is a lengthy process. A deviation card tabulates the results. The SOLAS convention requires a biennial compass swing and adjustment and a new deviation card.

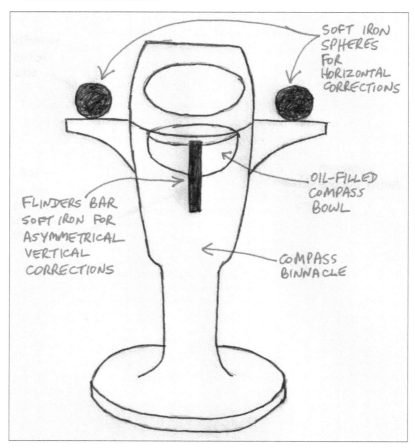

Fig 8.3 Magnetic compass binnacle

Variation and deviation are important for accurate observed bearings and courses steered. A simple phrase is used: Compass, add East to get True (or CAdET). To apply variation and deviation in the correct sequence, a memorable mnemonic is 'Timid Virgins Make Dull Companions'.

Timid	Virgins	Make	Dull	Companions
T	V	M	D	C
True	Variation	Magnetic	Deviation	Compass

Compass	Compass To True ⟶		True
C	A D	E	T
	Add	East	

For example, if the compass course is 080°, what is the true course to steer?

Compass = 080°

Deviation = -2°W (from the deviation card, above)

Magnetic = 078°

Variation = +6°E (from the compass rose on the chart, and applying the annual increment correctly)

True   = 084° is the true course to steer or set on autopilot

Combine both phrases and you can't go wrong!

The syllabuses for practical navigation and principles of navigation overlapped in places. Both involved relatively simple calculations using, for some topics, *Norie's Tables* and the *Admiralty Nautical Almanac*. Despite it being simple arithmetic, there was plenty of scope to misread a line in a table or inaccurately interpolate between several tabulated values. Considerable care was required but it was rewarded with easy gains in marks towards a pass. We used two great text books: *Munro's Navigation* by Captains Earl and Main; and *Practical Navigation for the Officer of the Watch* by Captain A Frost.

Captain Moore gave us practical problems on various types of 'sailing'. We used traverse tables (in *Norie's*) to obtain the ship's position at any time, given compass courses, variation, deviation and the run recorded by log.

Astronomical navigation included exercises to find latitude and then to derive a position line and a position through which it passes from an observation of the sun, moon, and any of the 57 stars listed in the *Admiralty Nautical Almanac*. For sextant observations of stars, position lines were obtained from at least four stars, and where these lines (hopefully) intersected when drawn on graph paper they indicated the ship's position.

We'd witnessed all this on many occasions at sea and, if lucky, had actually conducted them ourselves.

The principles of navigation concentrated further on the astronomical aspects of navigation: the shape of the Earth and the familiar lattice of poles, equator, meridians (or longitude) and parallels of latitude; an associated array of navigational terms and measurements, including direction, bearing, and distance. We used all these terms to calculate 'sailings' between two places on the planet.

For trans-ocean voyages, we learnt of great circles, great circle course and distance, small circles, rhumb lines, and composite great circles. We practised numerous examples in the classroom. Our knowledge expanded to the celestial sphere where, with Earth at its centre, terms like longitude and latitude were projected onto it and renamed hour angle and declination, plus many additional important terms.

There was something magical, mystical, almost romantic, about celestial and astronomical terms like equinox and solstice, right ascension, ecliptic and equinoctial, hour angle (local, Greenwich, sidereal), precession, inferior and superior planets, ascending and descending nodes, eclipses, occultations, constellations, Polaris (Pole Star), azimuth and zenith, rising, culmination, and setting of heavenly bodies. What about obliquity of the ecliptic? Or, the most peculiarly romantic, First Point of Aries? How could you not be intrigued? Their importance and usage in navigation were critical for a deck officer. And they were coupled with famous seafarers, navigators, and explorers – Magellan, Cook, Flinders, and Vasco da Gama for starters. Explanations of this intriguing terminology are found in any decent navigation text book.

Time is a crucial element in astronomical navigation so there was an emphasis on Greenwich, time zones, and the equation of time. This explained the importance of the ship's chronometer, its care, protection, and daily winding with a specific number of turns at the same time of day, and recording its error against the Greenwich time signal on the BBC World Service.

Captain Moore took us through the sextant, its construction, and how to use it correctly. Like any precise instrument, observations were affected by instrument errors and certain corrections were applied in the calculations.

Suffice to say, we covered much material, consolidated knowledge gleaned at sea, and learnt much. To me, it all made sense when Captain Moore explained it to us. It just required care, attention, and neat handwriting to avoid silly clerical errors in order to succeed at the two exams. As I possessed all those characteristics, I felt happy and confident.

Chartwork was closely allied to both navigation topics and it graphically consolidated all the elements and techniques of navigation when using worked examples on charts. I immensely enjoyed chartwork in the classroom and at sea. There was something innately rewarding in plotting data on the chart, drawing crisp lines, and annotating position fixes, courses, and speeds in a legible, clear hand, using the correct symbology.

We practised standard methods of fixing a ship's position by visual bearings, radar ranges, and a combination of both, and with positional information from electronic navigation systems. We'd all attempted these for real during our sea-time. Other, less frequently used techniques to ascertain position were explained.

We were introduced to complexities like the effect of current on speed, the allowance for leeway (the sideways drift of a ship to leeward of the desired course), and calculating the 'course to steer' by allowing for the current. The compass course, the ship's speed, and the current's rate and direction, determined the 'course made good' and were applied to the 'course to steer' to negate their effect. Given the course steered and the distance run, the set and rate of the current between two positions could be calculated, as could the current's effect on 'speed made good'.

It was essential to consolidate our on-board experience with classroom practice using *Admiralty Tide Tables* to find the time and height of high and low water at standard and secondary ports by tidal differences. We used tide tables and tide curves to find the time that the tide attained a specified height or the 'height of tide' at a given time.

We were expected to have a sound working knowledge of *Chart 5011*. This wasn't a traditional nautical chart, but an information booklet on nautical symbols, abbreviations, signs, and a key to all charted objects found on Admiralty charts.

We studied the contents and use of the *Admiralty List of Lights and Fog Signals* and *List of Radio Signals*. We delved into *Admiralty Sailing Directions* (*Pilots*). These 76 volumes embraced the world and contained a wealth of information on navigational hazards, buoyage, pilotage, regulations, general notes on countries, port facilities, seasonal currents, ice, and climatic conditions. They included high-quality diagrams and photographic views to help understand critical information during passage planning. Invaluable.

Admiralty *Notices to Mariners* were published weekly and included all the corrections, alterations, and amendments to update and maintain Admiralty charts and publications with the latest safety-critical information.

The *Annual Summary of Admiralty Notices to Mariners* was another important reference book. We knew of the former, but became au fait with both.

Throughout this first college phase, and the later one which culminated in examinations, the ROR was a constant presence. In the 1980s, the International Regulations for Preventing Collisions at Sea contained 38 rules in six sections, plus four annexes. We learnt the whole lot by heart during our cadetship. A rule was only signed off in your Task Book if the Mate or Master considered that, although you could spout it verbatim, you also understood its content and application. The 38 rules were divided between five parts.

Part A (Rules 1 to 3) were 'general' rules: where and to whom the rules applied; responsibility of the master, owner, and crew to comply with the rules; and a host of definitions, including types of vessel. Part B concerned 'steering and sailing', and Rules 4 to 10 applied in any condition of visibility. Crucially, Rule 5 (maintaining a proper lookout), Rule 6 (safe speed), Rule 7 (assessing risk of collision), and Rule 8 (action taken to avoid collision) were worked on ad nauseam in Captain Moore's ROR lessons. Rules 9 and 10 covered narrow channels and traffic separation schemes. Rules 11 to 18 explained actions to be taken by vessels in sight of one another, culminating in Rule 18's responsibilities between vessels and requirements for vessels which 'shall keep out of the way of others'. Rule 19 dealt exclusively with the 'conduct of vessels in restricted visibility', another rule that Captain Moore relentlessly hammered home.

Part C (Rules 20 to 31) described the 'lights and shapes' that vessels were required to display, their positioning on the vessel, and the arc and minimum range of visibility required for vessels of specific lengths.

Part D (Rules 32 to 37) explained the 'light and sound signals' applicable to vessels and specified the duration of a 'short blast' (one second) and a 'prolonged blast' (4 to 6 seconds).

Part E (Rule 38) covered 'exemptions' to the rules.

The four annexes were almost equally important as they explained the detail: 'Positioning and technical details of lights and shapes'; 'Additional signals for fishing vessels fishing in close proximity'; 'Technical details of sounds signal appliances'; and 'Distress signals' – also one of Captain Moore's pet subjects and he brooked no failures on this topic (we had to know all 15 listed).

There was plenty of scope for the principal examiner of masters and mates to catch you out during the oral examination. For instance, 'safe speed' (Rule 6) was long and convoluted with a multitude of elements, any one of which you could easily get wrong in the oral exam. It stated: 'Every vessel shall at all times proceed at a safe speed so that she can take proper and effective action to avoid collision and be stopped within a distance appropriate to the prevailing circumstances and conditions.' Not much there to get wrong, easy to learn. The pitfalls were in the sub-paragraphs.

> In determining safe speed the following factors shall be among those taken into account:
> (a) By all vessels:
>   (i) The state of **visibility** (V)
>   (ii) The **traffic density** including concentrations of fishing vessels or any other vessels (T)
>   (iii) The **manoeuvrability** of the vessel with special reference to stopping distance and turning ability in the prevailing conditions (M)
>   (iv) At night the presence of **background light** such as from shore lights or from back scatter from her own lights (B)
>   (v) The state of **wind,** sea and current, and the proximity of navigational hazards (W)
>   (vi) The **draught** in relation to the available depth of water (D)
>
> (b) Additionally, by vessels with operational radar:
>   (i) The characteristics, efficiency and **limitations** of the radar equipment (L)
>   (ii) Any constraints imposed by the **radar range scale** in use (R)
>   (iii) The effect on radar detection of the sea state, **weather** and other sources of interference (W)
>   (iv) The possibility that small vessels, ice and other floating **objects** may not be detected by radar at an adequate range (O)
>   (v) The number, location and **movement of vessels** detected by radar (M)
>   (vi) The more exact assessment of the **visibility** that may be possible when radar is used to determine the range of vessels or other objects in the vicinity (V).

My bracketed capital letters allied to the words in bold formed the absolutely invaluable mnemonics in learning Rule 6:

VTMBWD = Virgins Tickle Men's Balls With Delight;

LRWOMV = Large Robust Women Offer Men Virginity.

Each letter triggered the word in that sub-paragraph and the rest of the sentence spewed forth automatically. More than four decades later I can still recite Rule 6 in its entirety.

Learning and nightly revision of the rules became automatic. The more you read this thin booklet, the more you realised that the same words and phrases cropped up throughout. Once you used these little tricks, then memorising them magically became easier.

Daily, we had a ROR lesson with Captain Moore. If there were a few spare minutes before lunch or at the end of the day, he slipped in another few round-the-class ROR questions. He nominated the recipient of the question and there was no escape. We were expected to answer with a verbatim recitation of the rule or to apply a rule to his scenario.

We became confident of the seemingly unnecessary details in the annexes. We all thought it unlikely we would ever need to be quite so familiar with all this detail at sea. Rather, that it was meaty stuff the examiner could test us on. The pass mark for the ROR oral exam was 100%. No leeway for being lazy in learning every detail as your career and future depended on it.

With increased knowledge and application of the rules, I quite enjoyed Captain Moore's ROR lessons and his persistent quizzing. A few years later, I used his methods to instruct naval officers-under-training at Dartmouth, when I was a staff officer at Britannia Royal Naval College. Despite newfangled, computer-based training, I believed Captain Moore's traditional technique remained valid.

Overall, I enjoyed the first college phase. At the end of April, it was all over. We bomb-burst to home for some leave before our next trip to sea. Where was Mr Burke going to send me next, I wondered?

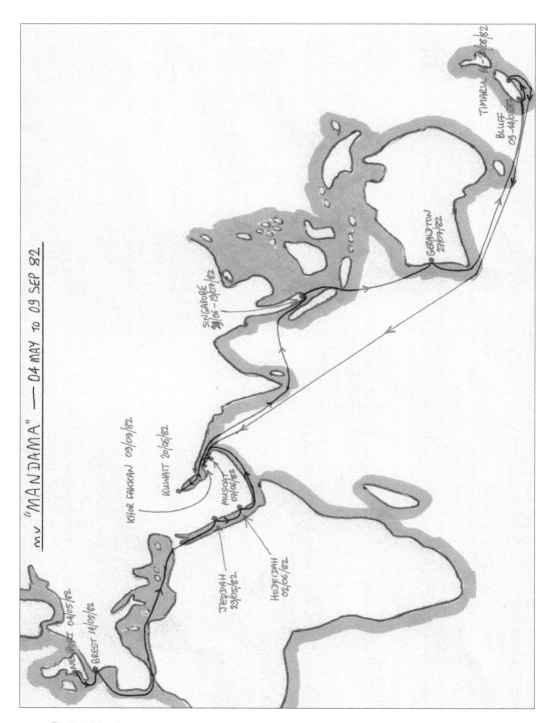

Fig 9.1 *Mandama* voyage

9 Frozen Chickens and Lamb to the Gulf

Fig 9.2 *Mandama*, bow view (Fotoflite)

Fresh from completing our first college phase, I joined *Mandama* in exotic Newport, South Wales, on 4 May 1982. She and her sister (*Mahsuri*) were BSSM's two Austasia Line reefers. It was love at first sight as she was the most beautiful ship I had ever seen. The clear, graceful line of her hull, cruiser stern, sharp bow, blue boot-topping at the waterline, grey hull, and then the pristine white mast-houses, derricks, and superstructure, topped off with a brilliant white funnel with a black 'A' enclosed by a black circle. The funnel was untarnished by exhaust soot, due to the protection afforded by the black ring around its top. Her weather deck was bright green. Sunderland-built in 1965 at Bartram & Sons, she was originally named *Taupo* for New Zealand Shipping Company and, via P&O and then Strick Line, renamed *Mandama* when bought by Austasia Line in 1980. At 528 feet (160.81 m) long, 71 feet (21.72 m) in the beam, and with a draught of 30 feet (9.05 m), *Mandama* weighed in at 8,219 gross tons and 4,474 net tons. She was powered by an eight-cylinder Sulzer engine, yielding a speed of 20 knots. The five refrigerated hatches were serviced by her seven distinctive Hallen derricks (one 30 ton, two 25 tons, four 10 tons SWL). She was the first British ship fitted with them.

Fig 9.3 *Mandama*, stern view (Fotoflite)

This was my fourth ship with a 'foreign' crew, this time they were Chinese. Blue Star and Booth Line had long histories of employing Chinese and Barbadian (Bajan) crews with British officers.

The Chinese were from Singapore and signed on for twelve months. The rationale was predominantly their cheaper wages, but this was counterbalanced by larger crews and huge amounts of overtime. The Chinese were a mixture of Singapore Chinese and Malay Chinese and were all in their fifties and even sixties. Generally, Singaporeans were in the engine room, Malays on deck, but I'm unsure of the cooks' and stewards' nationalities. Usually, our Chinese-crewed ships had two galleys (one for officers, one for crew), but some ships had a further separation with a galley for deck sailors and another for engine-room greasers, motormen, and donkeymen.

Many of the 'younger' Chinese spoke reasonable English, unlike their elders. Fortunately, all the ABs understood steering and helm orders. *Queensland Star* and *Rockhampton Star* initially carried chilled meat from Queensland to Europe via Suez and, because they passed Singapore, cheaper but larger Chinese crews were engaged. When Blue Star Line first started, eggs and pork were carried from China to South Africa and the UK and all these ships had Chinese ratings.

The Chinese sent most of their wages home. Those who were away for over a year, accumulated Singer sewing machines, which they carefully stowed in the poop, took ashore at crew changes, and sold off to tailors. They were great people to sail with, hard workers, and the Bosun was definitely the boss. The engine room was invariably spotless.

Fig 9.4. Typical Chinese AB

The Bajans crewed Blue Star's east coast of North America (ECNA) and Australia/New Zealand ships and Booth Line's Brazil/West Indies routes. They, too, signed year-long Articles and were mainly from Barbados, but there were occasionally other West Indians in the crew. I believe Bajan crews were signed on with the same conditions as British crews (wages, feeding rates, and even membership of the National Union of Seamen), therefore reduced running costs weren't a factor. Maybe it was the convenience of crew changes and historical inertia? The ECNA ships annually stopped in Barbados for a crew change, as Bridgetown wasn't a great detour on the passage between ECNA and the Panama Canal. Some Blue Star ships hardly ever returned to the UK. *Canterbury Star*, first of a class of five in 1960, traded between New Zealand and the West Indies, so it's possible that employing a West Indian crew was part of the deal which continued with later ECNA ships. Booth Line employed Brazilian crews in the mid-1960s, but switched to Bajans as they were cheaper. Bajan crews were great fun if a little unfocused. I enjoyed sailing with them as they were very gentle and relaxed, but they were good seamen.

A crew change in Bridgetown was an excellent opportunity to stock up on Mount Gay rum. During one crew change on *Canterbury Star*, all the officers were ashore, save for the Third Mate and the Fifth Engineer who were duty officers. They signed for a delivery of Mount Gay ordered by the Chief Steward, and there were two extra cases for 'whoever signed for it' – an unexpected bonus. There were tales of raucous all-hands barbeques and horse race nights on older ships like *Canterbury Star* and *Montreal Star*, four-hatch reefers of the 1960s and 1970s. When Barbados gained independence in 1966, a great party was held on board *New York Star* in mid-ocean. That must have been quite a night.

British crews were from all over the UK, with a majority from Merseyside and hefty minorities of Scots and Cockneys. They were also good for a laugh, worked hard on board, and partied equally hard ashore.

BSSM officers were predominantly British, but there was a large proportion of Ozzies and Kiwis, and occasionally other Commonwealth nationalities. The Antipodeans were invariably good fun, exactly as we Brits imagined them to be from television, cinema, newspapers, and magazines of the era.

For the duration of my time on *Mandama*, the Master was Captain John Igoe and the Second Mate was Keith Warmisham, an O/T from one of the first intakes. Fresh from my first college phase I was senior to my wing-man, Bill Mead, another O/T. All the other officers changed, mainly in Singapore, and later in Timaru. The Mate was Barry Truran, an absolute gentleman and a very senior Mate, while Third Mate Nick Hope-Inglis was a rather untidy chap, with an unruly mop of hair and a scruffy beard which belied his professional competence.

Mandama sailed from Newport, headed off down the Bristol Channel, nipped around Land's End, and crossed the English Channel to arrive in Brest on 14 May. The crew had prepared the holds after discharging the previous cargo (apples from Cape Town, I think) in Newport. *Mandama* was empty and ready to be fully loaded with nearly 4,500 tons of frozen Doux chickens.

Groupe Doux, established in 1955, ranked as one of the largest poultry producers in the world and was the first frozen and processed poultry exporter to Saudi Arabia, Qatar, and the United Arab Emirates. Hence our trip to the Gulf. Brest was an important commercial port situated in a sheltered bay in France's Finistère départément. It was home to the Académie de

Marine (Naval Academy) and to shipbuilding. I didn't see much of Brest as those frozen chickens were very swiftly loaded and filled our five holds.

Departing Brest, we trundled across a calm Bay of Biscay, down the west coast of Iberia, and entered the Mediterranean via the Strait of Gibraltar. A pleasant easterly passage culminated in anchoring off Port Said on 21 May to prepare for my second Suez Canal southbound transit.

Throughout this trip, Bill and I went to the bridge each morning at 0740 to get our jobs for the day from Barry the Mate. He was a keen listener to the BBC World Service and kept up to date with the news – even more so now that the Falklands War was in progress. It had begun during the last month at college and the day I joined *Mandama* was when HMS *Sheffield* was struck by an Argentinian Exocet missile. By now, the Task Force had been on station for a while and 21 May marked the initial landings at San Carlos Water and the loss of HMS *Ardent*.

Blue Star contributed to the war effort as *Avelona Star* and *Andalucia Star* (both reefers) and *Rangatira* (a troopship managed by Blue Star) were STUFT (Ships Taken Up From Trade), although I was unaware of this at the time. *Avelona Star* and *Andalucia Star* were modified by the Ministry of Defence with: a flight deck for helicopter operations added abaft the accommodation superstructure; a tannoy system fitted throughout the holds; military radio and encoding systems; plating over the swimming pool; and a fresh water-producing, reverse osmosis plant.

Barry gave us an update on the war each morning so we were reasonably well-informed of its progress. Bill and I had plenty of jobs to do on deck while enjoying the sunshine – chipping, painting, greasing, the usual deck cadets' tasks.

Mandama steamed through the Canal on 22 May, as 3 Commando Brigade completed its landing at San Carlos. Our southbound convoy anchored in the Great Bitter Lake to allow the northbound convoy to continue its passage uninterrupted.

> A few years later I read Captain Sandy Kinghorn's *Before the Box Boats*, his experience as Chief Mate on *Scottish Star* (a five-hatch, 10,000-ton reefer, built in 1950). She was one of the 14 ships in a northbound convoy that was trapped for several years in the Great Bitter Lake as a result of the Six Day War in 1967. Diplomacy failed to free them. As they were anchored closer to Egypt, their logistics and administration were controlled by the Egyptian authorities. Shore leave wasn't permitted but the crews could use ship's lifeboats within a 550-yard (500 m) radius of

the anchorage. Egypt allowed shipping companies to make crew reliefs. Financial reasons (double pay for some, or just simply to save money) led some men to remain for the duration. British crews got £2 per day each as hardship/danger money. Dysentery and sunburn were constant hazards.

The ships and their 220 men formed the Great Bitter Lake Association (GBLA). *Scottish Star*, like the others, maintained a daily routine to provide stability and purpose. The shipping companies allowed the crews to 'raid' their cargoes. On the first Sunday of the month, shopping lists were exchanged so Monday was when 'shopping' occurred. *Scottish Star's* cargo included Australian Swan Lager, a highly prized item. Community spirit extended to monthly sailing regattas. An 'Olympiad', featuring a range of sports in the lake and on board, was organised to coincide with the 1968 Mexico Olympics. One of the most distinctive hobbies was the designing and making of postage stamps. Initially crudely made on gummed paper, they evolved into impressive, professional products. GBLA Postage stamps were even sought by philatelists worldwide.

The Canal was reopened eight years later, in 1975. Only two GBLA ships departed under their own power. Alas, *Scottish Star* wasn't one of them as she'd been declared a total constructive loss in September 1969 and her crew had been repatriated. She was towed to Port Said with her cargo of apples, bales of greasy wool, and jarrah timber, sold to Greek owners, towed to Piraeus in Greece, where she was laid up until June 1979, bought by Spanish shipbreakers and disposed of. A very sad end to a fine ship.

We popped out at Port Suez and continued south into the Red Sea towards our first port, Jeddah. It was nice to be in the desert climate of the Red Sea again. I loved working on deck in the sun, then the end-of-the-day beer with Bill and the engineer day-workers on the deck outside the aft end of the mess. The group was usually Paul Burgess (Engineer Cadet), Barry Murphy (3rd Engineer), Jeff Partridge (Fridgie), and Jim Harbot (Chief Lecky). We laughed and joked as both beer and sun went down, until it was time for a shower and dinner.

The approaches to Jeddah were tricky. The seabed shoaled, with the added hazard of innumerable underwater coral reefs and pinnacles parallel to the coast, on which to ground or at least scrape the hull. In the buoyed channel, depths increased until we entered the port itself on 29 May.

Fig 9.5 Suez Canal, looking for'ard.

Fig 9.6 Suez Canal, looking aft

Meanwhile, the Falklands War had hotted up and *HMS Antelope*, *HMS Coventry*, and *Atlantic Conveyor* were sunk. *Atlantic Conveyor* was a 14,950-ton, roll-on, roll-off container ship owned by Cunard and requisitioned by the Ministry of Defence. She carried an invaluable load of five Chinook and six Wessex helicopters, plus eight Fleet Air Arm Sea Harriers and six RAF Harriers loaded at Ascension Island. Of the 12 sailors killed, six were Merchant Navy (including the Master), three were Royal Fleet Auxiliary, and three Royal Navy – another example of the British Merchant Navy's contribution to supporting Britain's armed forces in time of war. The battle of Goose Green was won, and our Paras and Marines made significant progress yomping and fighting their way across the island towards Port Stanley.

Jeddah was Saudi Arabia's second-largest city and commercial capital, its King Abdullah Port served the holy cities of Mecca and Medina. The Saudis had clearly spent a huge sum in building a modern port with all facilities. There were wide expanses of shiny white concrete wharf and brand-new kit: portainer cranes, straddle-carriers, and so on. Typical of most Middle Eastern oil-rich nations, there was barely a Saudi to be seen. The wharfies were all migrant workers from the Indian subcontinent or the Philippines, with a few South Koreans. They were all bussed in to work from their 'simple' accommodation outside the port. On board security was an issue. We locked our cabins and only one external door to the deck remained unlocked but manned by an AB.

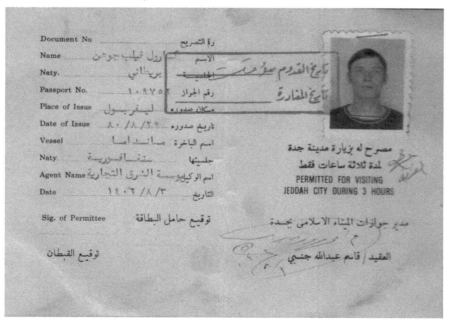

Fig 9.7 Jeddah shore pass

We required permission from the authorities to go up the road. No-one else was interested, but I applied and was eventually issued with a pass. Conditions were strict. A bus did a tour of the ships to collect those lucky individuals like me, and then drove us into town. We were dropped off at some notable point and had to be back there at a certain time for the trip back to port. My pass showed the total time permitted was three hours, so I had just enough time to wander around the new bits of Jeddah, including a souk. But it was all immaculate terracotta rendering everywhere so I had no idea what the old Jeddah was like. There was clearly much money around, as every Saudi man was immaculately dressed in white robes with his wife/wives trailing astern at the correct distance and dressed in full black abaya. I felt a little uncomfortable but not in danger. It was worth the effort but I wouldn't bother again.

Minus a few hundred tons of frozen chicken, we sailed from Jeddah and continued south along the Arabian coast. *Mandama* berthed in Hodeidah on 2 June, after negotiating a tricky entry from the north between two sand spits, into a more open sandy bay, and finally squeezing between another pair of low headlands to reach the port. Yemen's principal Red Sea port had been developed by the Ottomans and was one of its largest cities. But, crikey, what a dump! When we were there, the port was in an undeveloped, ramshackle state, with too few berths, so we were alongside some interconnected pontoons with a short bridge to shore. The wharfies were all Yemeni in traditional clothes, including the usual 'safety' flip-flops. The trucks to transport our frozen chickens ashore were decrepit and mostly didn't seem to be refrigerated. Goodness knows what state our chickens were in on arrival at a warehouse or cold store.

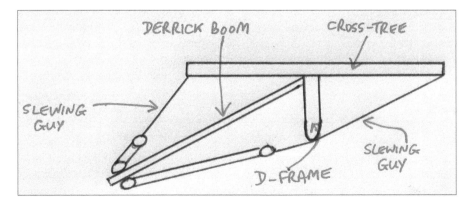

Fig 9.8 Hallen swinging derrick, plan view

There was no dockside cranage so our Hallen swinging derricks were used to unload the chickens. With the unmistakeable profile of the D-frame, a large steel bracket welded to the mast on the centre line. The guy wires were attached to heavy, sprung pendants, which bore against the D-frame when the derrick was swung to 75° from the centre line, and permitted efficient working at only 15° above the horizontal. The D-frame maintained a good controlling angle on the guy-wires, which carried 75% of the load. The guys also doubled as topping lifts so if both were hauled or slackened together, the derrick topped (rose) or lowered. Three winches were required – one each for the guys and one for the lifting wire – all operated by a single joystick control. Limit switches prevented over-topping and over-swinging. Hallen derricks did the job of a crane, but with lower capital expenditure and a higher SWL compared with ship cranes of this era

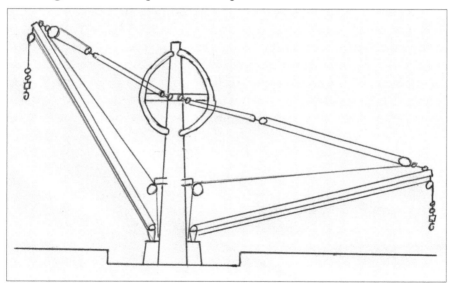

Fig 9.9 Hallen swinging derrick, side elevation

The ship's agent organised a minibus tour into Hodeidah. A few of us went, including Keith and Bill. It was quite an eye-opener as the decrepitude of virtually all the buildings, combined with the utter poverty of the people, was inescapable and shocking in many ways. The kids seemed happy enough, making the most of what little they had. The adults looked hard-pressed, struggling with every aspect of daily life. It was all very sad and depressing that people had to live in this way. I felt incredibly fortunate to be British.

A couple of other ships were in Hodeidah at the same time as *Mandama*. A stone's throw away was a Danish Lauritzen reefer of a similar size to us. Their officers invited us over for a beer or two. It was interesting to visit a foreign company's ship in the same trade, but I didn't detect any meaningful difference in the way we operated. We staggered back late that night. This was the sum total of going up the road in Hodeidah. Another destination I have no desire to revisit.

Mandama continued south in the Red Sea and passed through the Bab el-Mandeb, the strait between Yemen on the Arabian Peninsula, and Djibouti and Eritrea in the Horn of Africa. It connected the Red Sea to the Gulf of Aden and then to the Indian Ocean. Its width was about 20 miles (30 km), from Ras Menheli in Yemen to Ras Siyyan in Djibouti, with Perim Island dividing the strait into two channels. The narrower eastern Bab Iskender (Alexander's Strait) was 2 miles (3 km) wide and 98.4 feet (30 m) deep, while the western (Dact-el-Mayun) was about 16 miles (25 km) long with depths up to 1,017 feet (310 m). During my transits of the strait, there was little piracy.

Turning to port on exiting Bab el-Mandeb, *Mandama* steamed northeast and I observed the striking rocky cliffs along this length of the Arabian coastline. Yemen was left astern as we entered Omani waters. We rounded Ras al-Hadd, the north-eastern tip of Oman, and headed north-west to Muscat. On the approach to the port, old Muscat was hidden behind the island of al-Jazirah. We picked up the pilot and passed the Old Watch Tower at the entrance to Mutrah Bay. This was undoubtedly the most spectacular port entry I had done to date.

The reigning Sultan Qaboos had built a new port in the bay, including an expanse of breakwater and several wharves. The recently built Corniche around Mutrah Bay formed the main coastal route to old Muscat and the Sultan's al-Alam Palace. Along the Corniche a string of interconnected old buildings (residences, shops, cafes) thronged with people, particularly in the evenings when the souk was the main attraction. Behind the Corniche and these buildings, arose a striking, almost vertical, rockface of hills. The gullies and ridges changed colour, as did the length and angle of the shadows across the precipices as the sun passed overhead and slowly set. Tucked in the north-west corner was Mutrah Fish Market. Some of the port's berths were allocated to vessels of the Royal Yacht Squadron. There were a couple of portainer cranes at the container terminal but our Hallen derricks were needed to resume the unloading of frozen chickens.

Fig 9.10 Mina Sultan Qaboos, Muscat

I savoured every moment on deck as I was completely captivated by the truly magnificent panorama. I had no idea that 15 years later I would actually live in Muscat for three years while on Loan Service to the Royal Navy of Oman. My wife and I (together with hundreds of the Sultan's Armed Forces' officers) enjoyed dinner in the garden of al-Alam Palace in the presence of Sultan Qaboos to celebrate Armed Forces Day in 1999. Our whole 'living in Oman' experience was, for me, a dream come true.

Regrettably, this was a short visit and I never managed to get ashore. The voyage continued north-west in the Gulf of Oman and through the Strait of Hormuz into the Persian Gulf. As the seaway narrowed, we followed the traffic separation scheme as it wound its way between the northern tip of the Musandam Peninsula and the Iranian coast and fully into the Gulf itself.

The Strait of Hormuz was one of the busiest seaways in the world, particularly for the oil tanker trade. The traffic was certainly heavier than we'd been used to so far, but not as frenetic or multi-directional as the Dover Strait, with its cross-Channel ferries speeding across at 90° to the merchant ships, plus innumerable fishing vessels. Nevertheless, you had to keep your wits about you in case a dhow simply got in the way due to a lack of ROR awareness. I noticed Bandar Abbas on the chart – the very port at which I'd almost joined *Mandama* nearly 18 months ago, thwarted by the US hostage crisis in revolutionary Iran.

We berthed in Dubai on 9 June, the day after the Argentinian attack on Royal Fleet Auxiliary ships *Sir Galahad* and *Sir Tristram*, which caused so many killed and wounded. Dubai's skyline in the 1980s was impressive but not so absolutely dominating as it is today. Port Rashid dated back to the 1960s and, by mid-1982, it had 35 berths, including a container terminal. We managed to go up the road a couple of times, shopping in the ubiquitous malls, which have since evolved into monstrous enterprises. I bought some polo shirts with fake designer logos, of course. Compared to Muscat, there was money around of a significantly greater magnitude, ostentatious commercialism reigned. A hint of Dubai's future.

Mandama resumed her voyage deeper into the Gulf, steering as directly north-west as practicable, given the series of fields of oil and gas platforms to be avoided. They were all marked on the chart by a black square with a magenta plume, denoting its particular flashing light. They were easily detected by radar and visually both day and night. By day, there was frequently a heat haze through which their legs and platform were visible. Nights offered clearer visibility and the flares of burning waste gas from each platform gave the immediate vicinity a reddish/orange glow.

En route to Kuwait, the Falklands War reached its climax, with a British victory and an Argentinian surrender in Port Stanley. It was all over by the time we arrived in Kuwait on 20 June. Even General Galtieri, the military junta's leader, had resigned. This was our last port and the remaining chickens were unloaded. I didn't get up the road here as it was a short visit. From Shuwaikh Port, I saw the skyline of Kuwait City but there didn't appear to be too much of interest to see, so I wasn't disappointed.

Now empty of cargo, *Mandama* sailed back down the Gulf, transited the Strait of Hormuz, on 'the other side of the road' this time, closer to Oman than Iran. Ships 'drive' on the right-hand side of the 'road', passing each other port-to-port, or red-to-red. As we cleared the Strait, the Gulf of Oman opened up before us. Traffic density decreased significantly as we steered south-south-east across the Arabian Sea towards the southern end of India. The sea state was calm with a gentle low swell, the days were hot and sunny, the evenings and nights warm and balmy. What wasn't to like about day-work on deck (shorts, T-shirt and Doc Martens), culminating in a few beers with shipmates on the 'terrace' outside the mess as tropical dusk fell before dinner? What a life!

Mandama cut across the Laccadive Sea and rounded the southernmost point of Sri Lanka. From there, a more easterly course took us well south of the Andaman Islands and passed We Island off the northern tip of Sumatra at Banda Aceh, scene of the terrible tsunami at Christmas 2004. With Sumatra to starboard and Malaysia to port, *Mandama* headed south-south-east again, down the Malacca Strait. This 580-mile (930 km) stretch of water was the main shipping channel between the Indian and Pacific Oceans, narrowing to a width of 40 miles (64 km) and increasingly congested as Singapore approached.

Fig 9.11 *Mandama's* bow, anchor cable ranged on dock bottom

We embarked the pilot and anchored the rest of the day and overnight in Singapore Roads. Next day (29 June), a docking pilot, assisted by a couple of tugs, guided *Mandama* into the vast Hitachi Zosen Robin dry dock. The caisson closed behind us and, after the dockyard maties had completed their preparations, the dry dock was gradually pumped out. This took hours due to the dock's enormous water capacity so the work package only started the next day.

In addition to an engineering work package, this docking was primarily to inspect the hull and its intakes, and to remove, inspect, maintain, and refit the rudder and propeller. Her hull was also repainted with red anti-fouling, bright blue boot-topping, clean light grey sides topped off with brilliant white around the gunwales, fo'c'sle, and stern.

Of course, I couldn't resist a stroll around the dock and then down the steep concrete staircase to the dock bottom to get a close look at *Mandama*. I 'inspected' her keel, rudder, and propeller, admired her sleek lines, the flare of her bow, and her rounded cruiser stern. She was just as beautiful and graceful when naked and fully exposed in the vast dry dock as she was at sea or alongside. I felt privileged to call *Mandama* home for a few months. I was in love with her!

Fig 9.12 Propeller and rudder removed for inspection

There wasn't much work for the deck officers to do, so I certainly took the opportunity to get ashore. I enjoyed several day trips, either solo or with Keith, Nick, and Bill.

We had a great day in the Tiger Balm Gardens, created by the Aw family in 1937 to promote their Tiger Balm products. The gardens contained statues and dioramas depicting scenes from Chinese folklore, legends, history, and illustrations of various aspects of Confucianism. I felt compelled to visit these gardens because I recalled my father's photos during his National Service in Singapore, which included his own visit to the Tiger Balm Gardens. There was one photo of him outside the main entrance. I recreated that photo during my own visit. Dad was pleased as his own memories of Singapore flooded back.

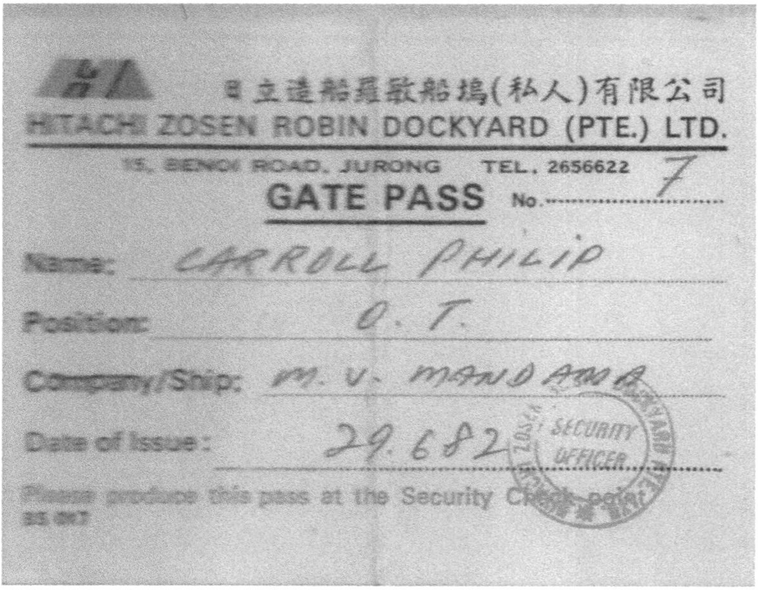

日立造船羅敏船塢(私人)有限公司
HITACHI ZOSEN ROBIN DOCKYARD (PTE.) LTD.
15, BENOI ROAD, JURONG TEL. 2656622
GATE PASS No. 7
Name: CARROLL PHILIP
Position: O.T.
Company/Ship: M.V. MANDAMA
Date of Issue: 29.6.82
SECURITY OFFICER
Please produce this pass at the Security Check-point

Fig 9.13 Hitachi Dockyard gate pass, Jurong

One day, Keith and I ended up at the north end of Singapore, overlooking the causeway across to Jahor Bahru in Malaysia. We must have used Singapore's extensive and efficient public transport system to get there. I think we visited the famous zoo. We ended up at Old Admiralty House, built in 1939 for the Commodore Superintendent of the Royal Naval Dockyard at Sembawang. Re-named Admiralty House in 1958, it was the home of the Commander of the Far East Fleet until 1 November 1971. Those were the days, when Britain had a Navy! It was called ANZUK House for the following three years, when the Australian, New Zealand, and United Kingdom tripartite force was responsible for Singapore's military defence until 1974. After the departure of the ANZUK force, the building became Sembawang Shipyard's recreational club. When we got there, it was a recreational facility (dining, bar, gardens) open to the public. Naturally, we enjoyed a couple of Tiger beers before returning to the ship.

I spent some hours wandering around the city, including Singapore Cricket Club, founded in 1853 and located in front of the Supreme Court Building and City Hall. It was so quintessentially English, yet in an equatorial climate. Nearby was the famous Merlion statue, a 28 feet (8.5 m) statue with the body of a fish and the head of a lion, and a water-fountain spouting from its mouth. Located at the mouth of the Singapore River, it became Singapore's national mascot from 15 September 1972, when Prime Minister Lee Kuan Yew officiated at its installation ceremony.

Fig 9.14 Nick, me, Barry and Bill, with *Mandama* in background

No visit to Singapore was complete without a few expensive drinks at Raffles Hotel. Naturally, we enjoyed Singapore Gin Slings in the Long Bar, shelled the gratis peanuts, and customarily strewed the husks on the floor.

Solo, I went to the Commonwealth War Graves Cemetery at Changi. I knew my paternal grandmother's brother-in-law had served in the Manchester Regiment but had escaped at the fall of Singapore in February 1942. I've always been impressed and moved by these immaculate cemeteries, with their countless rows of brilliant white headstones in beautifully tended, irrigated green lawns.

I'd first seen such cemeteries on a school History/French trip to Normandy as a second-year pupil. We toured several D-Day battlefields (including Arromanches and St Lo) but it the war cemeteries had equally impressed me. That was my first overseas trip and I'd been awarded the history prize, a beautiful folded booklet of the Bayeux Tapestry.

I strolled all over Changi cemetery and, in the shade of the columns of the roll of honour, I found the tabulated dead of the Manchester Regiment. I took a couple of photos to pass on to Uncle Bob and Aunt Sheila. It was all quite emotional.

Being well-rounded merchant seamen, we felt obligated to spend evenings in Bugis Street and at Clifford Pier. The former had a long history of ill-repute, with prostitutes and brothels combined with sailors drinking themselves into oblivion. Post-World War II, hawkers set up stalls to sell food and goods, followed by the establishment of street bars beside rat-infested drains. Transvestites (kai-tais) started to meet in the area, which inevitably attracted tourists and seamen to experience the scene. Bugis Street evolved into a thriving, bustling area.

A tradition founded by sojourning sailors was the ritualistic 'dance of the flaming arseholes'. Shipmates chanted the signature, 'Haul 'em down, you Zulu warrior' song, while sailors performed their bent over waddle between two arbitrary points, with pants around the ankles and a lit, rolled-up piece of newspaper wedged between their buttocks. Much mirth for the onlookers. Alas, by the mid-1980s, the authorities frowned on this 'ancient' custom and it gradually faded as the area was redeveloped and became a typically antiseptic tourist shopping area. Dreadful!

Clifford Pier was an equally humming but more civilised location. We ate from a range of satay stalls offering extraordinarily delicious dishes washed down with a few Tiger beers while we chatted and looked out at the ferry movements and the twinkling lights of ships and junks offshore.

Barry the Mate tasked Bill and I to cement-wash one of *Mandama's* fresh-water tanks. The tank lids were removed and the space was ventilated for a calculated suitable period to ensure we wouldn't succumb to noxious fumes. Bill and I clambered into the tank. A portable light was clipped to one of the baffles inside so we could see what we were doing. Although it was quite a small tank, it took us a couple of days to chip off the old cement-wash lining. We collected the debris in buckets, passed them through the access, to be taken up on deck and ashore to a skip. A long, laborious process. Barry inspected our work and deemed it satisfactory.

On the third day, we were shown how to make up the cement-wash, an emulsion-like mix of cement and water applied with an emulsion brush. Each clutching a paint brush and a bucket of cement-wash, Bill and I climbed back into the tank. Another couple of days were consumed by 'painting' the tank walls with the grey, paste-like substance. I was surprised that it adhered quite easily to the tank surfaces (sides, top, and bottom). When we'd finished, Barry inspected our handiwork and pronounced it satisfactory. Undoubtedly, good 'cadet training'!

There were a few changes to the crew towards the end of the dry docking. Notably, Barry the Mate was relieved by George Rawding, a decent, competent young Chief Mate from Yorkshire. That was the last I saw of Barry. It was only via the Blue Star Facebook site that I sadly learnt that Barry had been tragically lost overboard while Master of a Turkish cargo ship sailing down the North Sea only a few years later. His body was never recovered. Awful! I don't know the circumstances but what a terrible fate, highlighting just one of the many hazards to which seafarers are constantly exposed. RIP, Barry, a true gentleman.

Mandama completed her dry docking, exited the dock, and departed Singapore on 19 July, her holds empty again for the trip to New Zealand to load frozen lamb. The Java Sea was a tricky and busy passage from Singapore to Sunda Strait, with Sumatra and a string of Indonesian islands close to starboard and Borneo to port over the horizon. Myriad small local fishing boats cluttered the route.

Fig 9.15 In the bar: Jim the Lecky, me, Paul (Engineer cadet), Nick, Keith (3rd Engineer)

Sunda Strait, orientated north-east/south-west, with a minimum width (15 miles/24 km) and depth (65 feet/20 m) at its northeast end, was the primary route into the Indian Ocean and separated Sumatra from Java. It had been an important trade route for centuries, not least for the Dutch East India Company's access to the Spice Islands. Navigation was awkward due to its shallowness, strong tidal streams, numerous sandbanks, and many oil rigs. The Strait was also littered with volcanic islands, most notably Krakatoa, which had spectacularly and destructively erupted in 1883. We passed Krakatoa to starboard, but too far offshore to discern any evidence of its famous eruption.

Onwards we steamed, south-south-east, to the west coast of Australia. En route was my first distant encounter with Christmas Island. I didn't know then that over a quarter of a century later, I'd spend much sea-time in its vicinity, intercepting and boarding Indonesian fishing boats carrying illegal immigrants to the promised land of Oz. We transferred the immigrants to HMAS *Melville* or *Leeuwin* and disembarked them at Christmas Island for processing.

Somewhere off Australia's north-west shelf, *Mandama's* engine suffered a defect in one of its cylinder heads. We sought shelter to allow the engineers to replace the defective component. The nearest port was Geraldton, about halfway down the west coast of Western Australia. As berthing attracted fees, we anchored off the port for a couple of days while the engineers did their thing. The bay was quite open so *Mandama* was subjected to periods of heavy rolling, which hampered the engineers' work. Despite being robust metal pieces, there was a delicate side to engineering, which meant almost surgical precision was necessary. Still, the 'dings' (engineers) completed the job and we resumed passage to New Zealand.

I'd sailed across the Great Australian Bight on *ACT 5*, but the contrast in sea and weather conditions on this occasion was dramatic. The wind blew a right hooley. Sea state and swell increased to Force 11 at best. Just shy of reaching Force 12 'hurricane' on the Beaufort Scale, it was a 'violent storm', defined by wind speeds of 56–63 knots (64–72 mph/103–116 kmph) and 'exceptionally high waves' of 37–52 feet (11–16 m). Life was uncomfortable. In such seas, small and medium sized ships disappear behind the waves for lengthy periods, before reappearing. The wind blew across the wave crests, covering the sea with foam, and white parallel streaks on the sea surface denoted the wind direction, all of which reduced visibility.

Table 9.1 Beaufort wind scale

Force	Term	Wind speed knots (km/h)	Deep sea criterion	Mean wave height ft (m)
0	Calm	1 (1.8)	Sea like a mirror	0 (0)
1	Light airs	1–3 (1.8–5.5)	Ripples with appearance of scales are formed, but without foam crests	0.3 (0.1)
2	Light breeze	4–6 (7.4–11.1)	Small wavelets, short but more pronounced; crests have glassy appearance and do not break	0.7 (0.2)
3	Gentle breeze	7–10 (12.9–18.5)	Large wavelets; crests begin to break; foam of glassy appearance; perhaps scattered white horses	2.0 (0.6)
4	Moderate breeze	11–16 (20.4–29.6)	Small waves, becoming longer; frequent white horses	3.3 (1.0)
5	Fresh breeze	17–21 (31.5–38.9)	Moderate waves of more pronounced long form; many white horses formed; chance of some spray	6.6 (2.0)
6	Strong breeze	22–27 (40.7–50.0)	Large waves begin to form; white foam crests more extensive everywhere; probably some spray	9.9 (3.0)
7	Near gale	28–33 (51.9–61.1)	Sea heaps up and white foam from breaking waves begins to be blown in streaks along the wind direction	13.1 (4.0)
8	Gale	34–40 (63.0–74.1)	Moderately high waves of greater length; edges of crests begin to break into spindrift; foam blown in well-marked streaks along wind direction	18.0 (5.5)
9	Strong gale	41–47 (75.9–87.0)	High waves; dense streaks of foam along wind direction; wave crests begin to topple, tumble and roll over; spray may affect visibility	23.0 (7.0)
10	Storm	48–55 (88.9–101.9)	Very high waves with long overhanging crests; resultant foam is blown in dense white streaks along wind direction; sea surface takes a white appearance; tumbling of the sea becomes heavy and shock-like; visibility affected	30.0 (9.0)
11	Violent storm	56–63 (103.7–116.7)	Exceptionally high waves; sea completely covered with long white patches of foam lying along wind direction; everywhere the edges of wave crests blown into froth; visibility affected	37.7 (11.5)
12	Hurricane	>64 (>118.5)	Air filled with foam and spray; sea completely white with driving spray; visibility very seriously affected	46.0 (14.0)

With little else to do, I made frequent visits to the bridge. Visibility through the bridge windows was severely affected by the huge volume of spray and rain that filled the air. The poor old windscreen wipers, a bit more rugged than those fitted to road vehicles, were totally ineffectual. The Kent clear view screen, an electric motor-driven, rotating circle of toughened glass, which threw off rain and spray via centrifugal force, created a clear, if limited, view over the forward hatches and mast-houses towards the bow.

I was fascinated to witness the sea at (almost) her worst. The ship's bow pitched up and down through a considerable arc. *Mandama* plunged into the troughs, then climbed a seemingly vertical green wall of water to surmount each crest before she dived down the other side of the green slope of sea. At times, it was difficult to gauge what our fate would be when we hit the trough. *Mandama* shuddered. Then she climbed up the green wall, marbled with wind-created white streaks, through blinding sea and spray. To survive each of these short episodes seemed like a triumph.

The elements 'pushed' us along, rather than coming at us from ahead, nevertheless *Mandama* was tossed about with incessant heavy pitching and rolling. It wasn't just the rollicking seascape and the ship's sometimes violent movement. The ambient cacophony was astonishingly loud and penetrated the whole ship. The wind whistled wildly through the derricks, the wires and standing rigging 'sang' in an endless series of banshee wails and added to nature's symphony. If caught right, *Mandama's* entire being shook and trembled with terrifying ferocity, then stabilised to her almost rhythmic heavy pitching and scary rolling.

The weather deck was out of bounds. We hunkered down in the mess to ride out the storm. The cooks provided sandwiches, and the bar was open – it was a pretty sociable period. Anyone not on watch was there. Perhaps it was some sort of group mutual safety and security thing? I certainly didn't fancy a beer in case of an untoward outcome. Throughout, I never felt seasick, but didn't want to tempt fate. I also wanted to stay as alert as possible in case of an emergency.

It was somewhat hard work to get to sleep in my cabin. I propped my orange life jacket along the side of the mattress. I also used the lee board, a piece of wood with a couple of metal tongues that fitted into matching recesses in the side of your bunk. This combination helped keep me in my bunk and reduced my sympathetic rolling from side to side. Once settled and stable, I was quite comfortable and fell asleep satisfactorily. It was interesting to use the heads or take a shower. Sitting on the loo was the safest method for a pee. Showering was hard work, braced against the sides of the cubicle while trying to shampoo your hair and wash your body. Still, I survived unscathed.

We laboriously continued east-south-east across the Bight to Bass Strait. This weather seemed endless and, although frightening, I didn't feel endangered as such. Rather, I was wary throughout the prolonged experience, acutely aware that it could all go horribly wrong in an instant if we were unlucky.

As we neared Tasmania, the 'violent storm' waned and eased to more clement conditions. We altered to a more southerly course to pass down the west coast of the island and rounded its southernmost point. We altered again to an east-south-east course. *Mandama* headed for the southern tip of South Island, New Zealand. During this passage, although the weather had abated, residual effects of the Force 11 meant there was still a heavy sea, large swell, high winds. But at least the gloomy overcast cleared to reveal intermittent bright sunshine.

An unusual incident occurred one night as we crossed the Tasman Sea. The on-watch engineer officer pumped fuel oil up from a double-bottom fuel tank to a settling tank. The tank level alarm failed, which resulted in about three tonnes of fuel oil spilling out of the tank's gooseneck vent onto the poop deck. The ship's motion caused this oil to slosh about the poop deck and also swill over the side through the scuppers. It wasn't pretty to see a black slick of fuel oil spread over the deck and starboard side with a coat of the black stuff down to the waterline. Captain Igoe notified the relevant authorities and headed to Bluff, New Zealand's southernmost port for an assessment and decision on remedial action to clear up the mess.

By the time we transited Foveaux Strait, between Stewart Island and Bluff itself, the oil had largely solidified on deck and on the ship's side. An article about the incident and *Mandama's* arrival appeared in *The Southland Times*, including a not very flattering picture.

> Bluff is the oldest European settlement in New Zealand and just about its southernmost town. It is famed for its oysters, reputed to be the best in the world, it was also a commercial port frequented on occasions by Blue Star ships to load frozen lamb. From Bluff, a ferry served Stewart Island and Rakiura National Park, an hour-long trip across the Foveaux Strait. With a population of some 1,800, there's not much more to say about Bluff.

The authorities in Timaru wouldn't permit *Mandama* to enter the port until the oil was cleaned up. Solvents were delivered and we all turned-to in boiler suits and wellies to scrub my beautiful ship. It took a few days, as the starboard side was the most difficult and awkward to reach from the deck, over the bulwark, and from one of our lifeboats. This Herculean group effort paid off and *Mandama* was restored to an acceptable state of cleanliness. The authorities were assured she wasn't leaking oil.

Fig 9.16 Dried coat of fuel oil on poop deck

To assist the cleaning effort, *Timaru Star's* O/Ts were transferred to *Mandama*. They remained on board until we were all paid off in the Gulf. Sam Davies joined BSSM with me, Tim Moore was one of Bill's contemporaries – four O/Ts on one ship, a rare event indeed! Teamwork matured during the cleaning operation and we enjoyed a few nights in the nearby pub where I experienced my first Kiwi lock-in. In small isolated towns, with little police or regulatory presence, it was common practice for a pub landlord to lock the doors and draw the curtains at closing time to camouflage uninterrupted beer-drinking into the small hours. Luckily, we didn't have anything other than cleaning up the oil spill each day.

From Bluff, it was a short trip to Timaru. We rounded Slope Point, New Zealand's southernmost mainland extremity. North-north-east along the coast, past the rump of Otago Peninsula, near Dunedin, protruding into the Pacific Ocean, and arrived in Timaru on 15 August.

Timaru was about halfway up the east coast of South Island, 98 miles (158 km) south-west of Canterbury. It began as a whaling station in 1839 but few Europeans lived there until 1859 when 120 immigrants arrived. Thereafter, Timaru slowly grew into one of South Island's major cargo ports, focused on processing, packing, and exporting meat, dairy and other agricultural produce. It was a popular port for Blue Star ships, given the Vesteys' interests in the cattle and dairy trade. Not surprisingly, there were two incarnations of *Timaru Star*, the first built in 1945, the second (from which Sam and Tim had transferred) built in 1967 and fitted with a 150-tonne Stülcken heavy-lift derrick. More about this impressive bit of kit in the next chapter.

Timaru's No. 1 Wharf was characterised by its four all-weather mechanical meat-loaders, opened in 1966. Faster meat-loading rates to reduce ships' idle time in port to a minimum were needed. This led the ports of Bluff and Timaru to install this equipment during the mid-1960s.

Fig 9.17 Lamb carcasses stowed in a hold

The loading system comprised a transfer shed, with one line of rail track for each of the four horizontal conveyor belts. The shed's roof hatches allowed the loading belts of the meat-loaders to be lowered to take lamb carcasses off the conveyor belt. The loading belts had a continuous apron so the carcasses were carried from the conveyor belts, through the roof hatches, across the gantries and luffing booms, and down into the ship's hold. There, the carcasses were deposited onto a fan-shaped tray for the wharfies to stow and stack them in the hold. The loaders carried whole lamb and mutton carcasses weighing 60 lbs (27 kg) each at a rate of 2,100 carcasses per hour per meat loader. The entire system – from freezer works direct to transit shed, without shunting delays or effects of extreme weather, then to the ship's hold – was conducted under cover. As a result, meat-loading rates at both ports substantially increased.

Fig 9.18 Dusk in Timaru

I enjoyed Timaru. The port's working hours were civilised, as the wharfies knocked off about 1700, leaving us lads free evenings to go up the road to the pub, where we played pool, talked rubbish, and drank beer.

It was in Timaru that I learnt of the 'six o'clock swill'. Introduced as a temporary wartime efficiency measure in December 1917, 6pm closing was made permanent in 1918 and continued for nearly 50 years. The 'six o'clock swill' became part of Kiwi life. That one hour between the end of the working day and closing time meant the men crowded together to drink as much beer as possible before the pubs shut. Mounting

pressure from the people and the restaurant and tourism industries led
the government to hold a national referendum on 23 September 1967.
Nearly two-thirds of the electorate supported 'later closing'. Most local
authorities opted for pubs to open from 11am to 10pm. The last 'six
o'clock swill' occurred on 7 October 1967.

It was also in Timaru that I learnt of the 'jellybean' cocktail. Its ingredients
were all clear spirits (well, at least ouzo, vodka, and white rum), with
lemonade, and some grenadine (or raspberry cordial) for a bit of colour. It
was ordered by the jug and was also known as an 'adult's milkshake'. I didn't
like clear spirits, so I avoided sampling this lethal blend.

Fig 9.19 George's four O/Ts: me, Bill, Sam, Tim

There were a couple of crew changes in Timaru, most notably Nick paid
off and Dave Fotheringham signed on as Third Mate. Harry Curry joined
as Chief Engineer and Ian Hunter as Fridgie. Keith Eade replaced Jim as
Chief Lecky. Engineer Cadet Paul also paid off and replaced by two blokes
– Ted Gyseman from Saundersfoot near Tenby, and Tom Devereaux. All
except lean, tanned, clean-shaven Harry Curry were wild-looking blokes
with moustaches, beards, and unruly mops of hair. Despite their ragged,
scruffy appearance, they were all great fun, with genuine hearts of gold. We
all got on famously. In fact, our sundowners outside the mess were brilliant

social affairs at the end of the working-day, clad in our grubby boiler suits or shorts and T-shirts.

Sadly, all good things come to an end. *Mandama* departed Timaru on 20 August, fully loaded with 4,500 tons of frozen lamb carcasses, bound for Bandar Abbas, Iran. It looked like I would finally get there. Captain Igoe set our speed at 20 knots for the voyage of 19 days across 9,000 miles (14,500 km) of the Southern and Indian Oceans. We reversed our course to pass Tasmania and cross the Great Australian Bight. Fortunately, the weather had improved and it was a far more comfortable trip. We made landfall at the south-west coast of Australia, near Albany and hugged the coast past Windy Harbour, Augusta, Margaret River, and left Yallingup astern as a north-north-west course was set towards the Gulf.

George the Mate considered how best to employ his four O/Ts for the next three weeks. At 0740 daily, as senior O/T, I visited him on the bridge to get our tasks for the day. Armed with this, I gathered the others at 0800 to start work. The 4–8 watchkeeper always had an afternoon nap before going on watch at 1600. To avoid having his nap disturbed, George gave us 'job-and-knock' each day. This meant that when we'd completed the allotted tasks/jobs he gave me each morning, we knocked off. It was a great incentive to work as efficiently and swiftly as practicable to maximise the opportunity for an early finish. The four of us got stuck in, had shorter smokos and usually cleared away at least a half-hour or even an hour before 1600. Great!

The focus was on chipping and painting. We used pneumatic chipping hammers for vast swathes of the weather deck and handheld chipping hammers for more confined, awkward areas. The bare patches of steel were red-leaded, then primed. The entire weather deck and mast-house roofs, and the spaces between the hatch coamings and mast-houses, were painted with a topcoat of standard bright green using paint rollers, cutting in with paint brushes. They looked like a croquet lawn or a snooker-table.

We repeated the process on the hatch coamings and mast-houses and completed the job with a brilliant white topcoat.

I found it peculiarly satisfying using a chipping hammer to pierce a bulbous area of rusty paintwork. A decent strike resulted in chips and large flakes of several layers of old paint and rust skittering away. Sometimes a small amount of water was retained in these bubbles. It dribbled out when released by a chipping hammer. A concession to health and safety was the wearing of goggles, as chipped paint or rust debris could damage our seaman's perfect eyesight. Your career as a deck officer would be finished.

The pneumatic chipping hammers achieved the same result but were used on large patches of deck. The noise of their hammering was intense. Ear defenders and safety goggles were obligatory. At the end of a day, we were grubby with rust dust but noted, with satisfaction, the acreage of newly red-leaded deck.

Primer and top coats followed. It was oddly rewarding to see the result of our endeavours. The weather deck beautifully clean and sharp bright green, hatch coamings, hatch covers and mast-houses in brilliant white.

Timing was crucial in our 'job-and-knock' routine. We didn't want to work beyond 1600, so we ensured that our chipping ended with sufficient time to red lead the patches of bare metal we'd created that day. Besides, the day-work engineers expected us to join them shortly after 1600 for a customary couple of pre-dinner sherbets. The late afternoon warmth of the sun in the middle of the Indian Ocean was perfect for sitting on the 'patio' outside the officers' mess, quaffing a cool beer, talking rubbish, and having a laugh. I don't know about other companies, but 'cabin drinking' in Blue Star was strictly forbidden. Quite right, too.

Fig 9.20 Sundowners with Tom, Tim, Ian the Fridgie, Ted

George was impressed with our work ethic and standard of chipping and painting. The last gasp was to chip and paint the cargo hooks and swivels with bright 'international orange'. This required rather more delicate and dainty preparation and painting but we got the job done. George was thrilled but exasperated by our energy, drive, and efficiency. For our last few days in the Indian Ocean we dismantled, cleaned, greased, and reassembled the dogs on the hatches and mast-houses.

My *Mandama* time was nearing its conclusion. Entry to Bandar Abbas was delayed a few days. Until a berth became available, the ship anchored off Khor Fakkan (nicknamed cool for cats). This port city was an exclave of the Emirate of Sharjah, one of the seven in the United Arab Emirates (UAE), surrounded by Fujairah, another Emirate. Khor Fakkan was located on the east coast of UAE on the Gulf of Oman, just shy of the Strait of Hormuz. The city sat on the bay of Khor Fakkan (Creek of Two Jaws) and was the region's only natural deep water port. Its container terminal was opened only in 1979.

We anchored in the bay, late afternoon on 8 September. We enjoyed a bit of a 'Channel night' as a large crew change was planned for the next day. Reliefs embarked from a tug the following afternoon. Handovers were conducted and those paying-off gathered at the top of the gangway. George's four O/Ts were ready to go after many a goodbye and good luck. We collected our Discharge Books from Captain Igoe, bid a final farewell to George and down the gangway we clattered to the waiting tug. An AB lowered our luggage by heaving-line. Dusk had been and gone, it was now a dark but cloudless, starlit night, about 2100.

The tug made its way into the port. The shore lights of port and city loomed larger and brighter. At the wharf, we clambered ashore to the minibus and driver that BSSM had arranged. We settled in for the ride across the desert to Sharjah. I had no idea of direction or duration for this journey. Neither did anyone else as far as I could tell. It was rather mysterious, if perhaps worrying too. We'd landed on a strange shore at night, got in a minibus with a local driver, and set off along unknown roads to an airport somewhere in the desert. Still, we arrived at Sharjah Airport without incident two or three hours later. We unfolded ourselves as we tumbled out of the minibus and collected our baggage.

In the mid-1980s, the Gulf was still a bit off the beaten track compared to today. The airport was brightly lit and shiningly new and modern, completed in 1976. The vast concourse of polished marble was almost empty of passengers, another indication that UAE hadn't yet attained its anticipated zenith of popularity. There was no crush of bodies queueing at check-in or at passport control and a largely cursory security.

We flew Gulf Air, formed in Bahrain in 1950. The Middle East's two largest and well-known airlines, Emirates and Etihad, weren't founded until 1985 and 2003 respectively. It was good to touch down at Heathrow the next morning. After passport control, baggage reclaim and customs, we said cheerio and went our separate ways. I caught the road-rail coach service to Reading, the train to Pompey Harbour, and home.

Another great trip. I'd seen more places on the Arabian Peninsula and visited New Zealand's South Island. I enjoyed being on a reefer, carting frozen meat to the Gulf from France and from Kiwi. A second dry docking, in Singapore, was an added bonus. Best of all, my shipmates were great fun and we'd had so many great times. All capped off by being on *Mandama*, the most beautiful ship in the world. I loved everything about the trip. Where would Mr Burke send me next?

Fig 9.21 *Mandama* under Timaru's meat-loaders

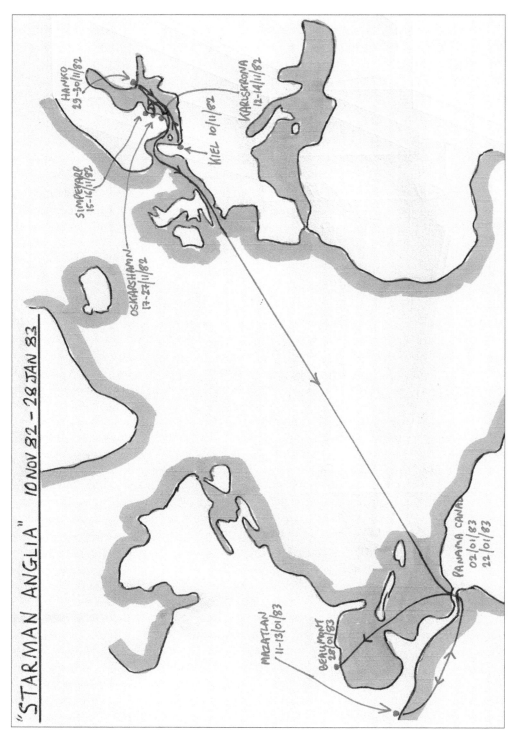

Fig 10.1 *Starman Anglia* voyage

10 Heavy Lift with *Starman*

Fig 10.2 *Starman Anglia* battling the elements in the English Channel (Fotoflite)

I packed my kit and flew to Hamburg on a dreary, damp, cold November day. Brian Ross (an AB) and I were met by a driver whose Mercedes took us to Kiel to join *Starman Anglia* during her transit of the Kiel Canal.

Officially the Nord-Ostesee-Kanal, the Kiel Canal is 61 miles (98 km) long and is the world's busiest artificial waterway. It cuts across Schleswig-Holstein, northern Germany, to link the North Sea at Brunsbüttel, at the mouth of the Elbe, to the Baltic Sea at Kiel. This route by-passes Denmark's Jutland Peninsula and therefore saves about

250 miles (460 km) of sea passage. It was completed in 1895 and has a lock at each end, although the difference in water-level between the two seas is very little. It was widened to accommodate ships with maximum dimensions of 772 feet (235.5 m) length, 106.6 feet (32.5 m) beam, 23 feet (7 m) draught. The permanent fixed bridges across the canal give a clearance of 138 feet (42 m).

Starman Ltd was formed jointly by BSSM and Sloman Neptun Schiffahrts-Aktiengesellschaft to compete in the global heavy-lift trade with *Starman America* (BSSM) and *Starman Australia* (Sloman). These were joined by *Starman Africa* and *Starman Anglia* (both BSSM), sister-ships built in 1977 and 1978 respectively.

Fig 10.3 *Starman Anglia* transporting two dockside cranes from Finland to Mexico. Note stern door and Stülcken derrick (Fotoflite)

Starman Anglia was the smallest ship I sailed on at only 2,776 gross and 1,013 net tons, 308 feet (94 m) long, 52 feet (16 m) beam and a draught of 14½ feet (4.5 m). A pair of Klöckner-Humboldt-Deutz diesel engines drove her twin propellers to a maximum speed of 12 knots, a pedestrian pace compared to the 20-odd knots I was accustomed to.

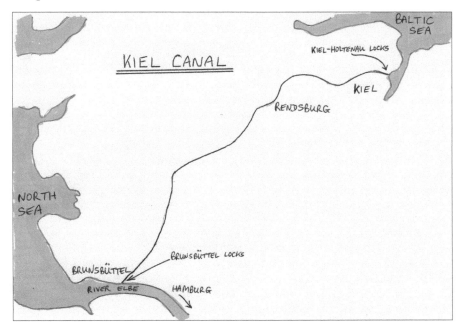

Fig 10.4 Kiel Canal

Unlike my previous ships, her accommodation was forward, which created a large weather deck area aft with a 36 feet (11 m) wide, hydraulically-operated stern door between twin funnels. Beneath the weather deck was a single cargo hold, 98 feet (30 m) long by 30 feet (9 m) deep, providing 60,000 cubic feet (1,700 cubic metres) of under-deck cargo stowage. The hatch covers, stern door and weather deck were strengthened to bear a hefty 30 tons per square metre. The roll-on/roll-off capability via the stern ramp was 1,016 tons. The ship's bottom frames and plating were strengthened to allow beaching to deliver cargo to undeveloped and isolated locations.

Brian and I stood on an empty quay with our bags, abandoned by the Mercedes driver. We got colder as late afternoon edged towards an increasingly damp dusk. There was no sign of our ship and no idea of her ETA. Brian was a tall, strapping Liverpudlian with a Mexican bandit moustache, a strong Scouse accent and a razor-sharp sense of humour.

Eventually, *Starman Anglia* appeared out of the gloom and berthed. It was impossible to miss, at the aft end of the accommodation, the ship's most striking feature: the twin king-posts and 108 feet (33 m) long derrick boom. Specifically designed for heavy lifts, this Stülcken jumbo derrick had an impressive SWL of 300 tons. More of this bit of kit later.

Brian and I clambered aboard to be greeted by the Mate, an amiable Australian named Graham Clarke, who sported a Graham Hill moustache. Moustaches were 'in' at the time. I was shown to my cabin, while Brian went below to the crew cabins. *Starman Anglia* resumed her transit of the Kiel Canal. I unpacked and slept soundly in my new home. In the morning, we were in the Baltic Sea.

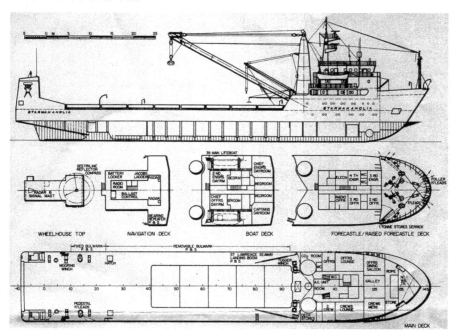

Fig 10.5 Deck plan. I occupied 3rd Officer's cabin. (Fraser Darragh Collection)

At breakfast, I met the Master, Peter Hutchinson. He soon departed to the bridge for the 8–12 watch. Graham came down from the bridge shortly after 0800. After his breakfast, he gave me a comprehensive ship's tour. *Starman Anglia* certainly was different to my previous ships. I realised I'd entered a unique sector of merchant shipping. Starman crews possessed a particular skill set, gained in the heavy lift trade. They loaded, secured, carried, and discharged a wide variety of awkward, outsized, heavy cargoes. There were apparently three each of Masters, Mates, Chief Engineers,

Second Engineers, Electricians, Bosuns, and Donkeymen, and a smattering of ABs who rotated through our *Starman* ships. Once folks had been on heavy lift, they liked to remain in that specialised environment.

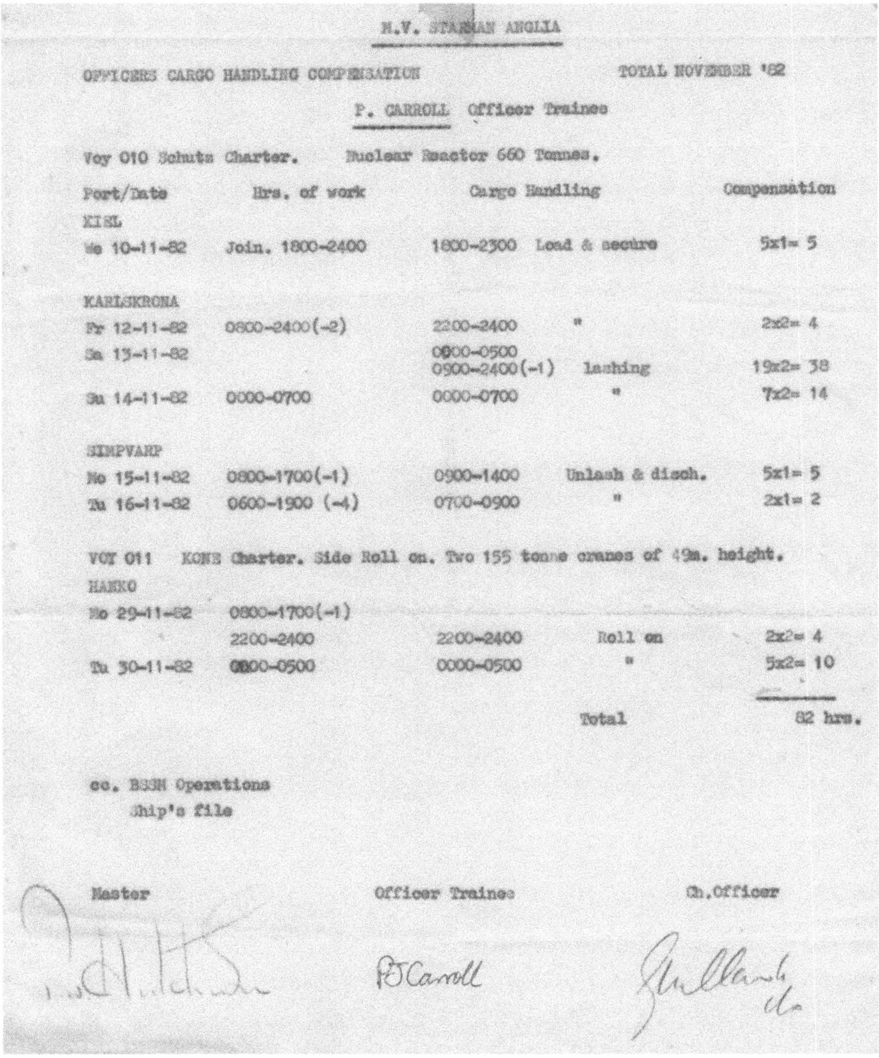

M.V. STARMAN ANGLIA

OFFICERS CARGO HANDLING COMPENSATION   TOTAL NOVEMBER '82

P. CARROLL Officer Trainee

Voy 010 Schutz Charter.   Nuclear Reactor 660 Tonnes.

Port/Date	Hrs. of work	Cargo Handling		Compensation
KISL				
We 10-11-82	Join. 1800-2400	1800-2300	Load & secure	5x1= 5
KARLSKRONA				
Fr 12-11-82	0800-2400 (-2)	2200-2400	"	2x2= 4
Sa 13-11-82		0800-0500		
		0900-2400 (-1)	lashing	19x2= 38
Su 14-11-82	0000-0700	0000-0700	"	7x2= 14
SIMPVARP				
Mo 15-11-82	0800-1700 (-1)	0900-1400	Unlash & disch.	5x1= 5
Tu 16-11-82	0600-1900 (-4)	0700-0900	"	2x1= 2

VOY 011 KONE Charter. Side Roll on. Two 155 tonne cranes of 49m. height.

HANKO				
Mo 29-11-82	0800-1700 (-1)			
	2200-2400	2200-2400	Roll on	2x2= 4
Tu 30-11-82	0000-0500	0000-0500	"	5x2= 10
			Total	82 hrs.

cc. BSSM Operations
    Ship's file

Master	Officer Trainee	Ch.Officer

Fig 10.6 Overtime chit: Karlskrona (loading), Simpvarp (unloading) and Hanko (loading)

Graham explained that since they were currently without a Third Mate, the Captain did the 8–12 watches, the Mate the 4–8s, and the Second Mate the 12–4s. As an experienced O/T, soon to be attending his final college phase and exams, I'd take the 8–12 watches, which released

Captain Hutchinson to focus on his duties as Master. I felt the weight of responsibility fall upon me.

Starman Anglia was in ballast en route to Karlskrona, Sweden, to load a cargo, take it 'round the corner', and unload it, then – after a couple of weeks in dry dock – head to Finland for the next cargo for delivery to the west coast of Mexico. This was typical of the heavy-lift trade: no rhythm or predictable routine to the jobs; no specific 'trade route'; no fixed schedule; no regular ports of call. This was the 'tramp trade' or 'tramping'. Even after only a few hours on board, it looked like a very interesting trip and a unique experience. Keeping my own bridge watches added to my excitement.

On 12 November 1982, we berthed near Karlskrona, at an isolated wharf backed by a huge building. This was, apparently, a nuclear reactor 'factory' and our job was to load a 660 ton nuclear reactor and ancillary parts and move it to an established nuclear power station at nearby Simpevarp.

Fig 10.7 Nuclear reactor on its trailer, ready for loading

The weather deck was completely cleared and the stern ramp lowered to the wharf in readiness. No lifting was required as the reactor was already secured to a long, low crawler-trailer, with 16 sets of 16 wheels along its length and width to spread the 660 tons evenly across the bed. Amazingly, a tractor unit manoeuvred the crawler-trailer up the ramp between the twin funnels and into position on the weather deck.

As the 830 tons (reactor plus crawler-trailer) rolled aboard, the weight was concentrated on the ship's stern. This affected the ship's trim and the stern was forced deeper, the bow rose up. However, *Starman Anglia's* super-responsive, counter-ballasting system was capable of pumping 1,000 tons of water per hour, so the water ballast in the aft-peak and fore-peak tanks was constantly adjusted to maintain perfect trim during the loading. The Master controlled the ballasting system from the bridge, in close walkie-talkie coordination with the Mate on deck.

The reactor's ancillary bits and pieces were loaded on to the for'ard end of the weather deck, using the Stülcken jumbo derrick. Although not as heavy as the reactor, the weight of these pieces still affected the ship's stability. With the jumbo derrick slewed over the wharf, as soon as the weight left the ground, physics dictated that the weight transferred instantly to the head of the derrick boom. This resulted in the ship heeling to that side, but *Starman Anglia's* ballasting system countered this motion as her ballast pumps almost simultaneously reacted to prevent any such heeling. Wondrous engineering!

After loading, the crew's task was to secure the cargo on deck. Lashing began immediately and continued through the night until it was completed and checked by Master and Mate. Starman was unique in BSSM as the only ships in the fleet where officers earned overtime. My 'overtime chit' showed we worked at Karlskrona from 0800 on 12 November through to 0700 on 14 November, with a four-hour rest-break early on the morning of 13 November.

Fig 10.8 Me, Neil and Brian in our grubby Starman overalls

We were lucky with the weather, which remained dry but chilly. I don't remember feeling cold at all as I was fully engaged the whole time: fetching and carrying; tightening-up lashings; coiling lashing wire. As a heavy-lift novice, I was used throughout as a dog's body and not involved in the technicalities of wire-rope lashing such a monstrous piece of cargo.

Nevertheless, it was a fascinating experience. The galley provided hot food and sandwiches throughout, supplemented with tea/coffee. We were all exhausted by the end and our smart orange Starman overalls were filthy.

Fig 10.9 Tractor attached to unload reactor

Captain Hutchinson was happy with the lashings. We sailed from Karlskrona after lunch. After dropping the pilot, there was a tricky exit through the Blekinge archipelago that guarded the approaches to Karlskrona. Second Mate Mike O'Keefe threaded *Starman Anglia* between Tjurkő and Aspő. About a year earlier, an 'international incident' had occurred when a Soviet Whiskey class submarine ran aground near the next island east, Sturkő. S-363 was conducting a covert mission and her grounding was allegedly due to the crew's inebriation. Who really knows?

Once clear of the archipelago, we headed south-west and rounded the southernmost island, Stenshamn. A north-north-east course paralleled the coast and led us to the Kalmar Strait, between the Swedish mainland and the island of Őland. Opposite and west of the northern tip of Őland was Simpevarp. *Starman Anglia* berthed at the wharf on 15 November.

This nuclear power station was one of three such facilities in Sweden. The plant was about 18 miles (30 km) north of Oskarshamn, the municipality's capital. The first and second reactors were commissioned in 1972 and 1975 respectively. Our delivery brought the third unit. All three were 'boiling water reactors'. At the same site, Oskarshamn OKG (the operating agency) managed Sweden's central interim storage facility for radioactive waste. I wondered if we'd glow in the dark when we departed!

Fig 10.10 Reactor pulled down stern ramp

We started unlashing the cargo that morning. A simpler and less time-consuming task than securing it. There was a mountain of wire to coil and stow. The following morning, the tractor unit reversed up the stern-ramp, connected up to the crawler-trailer, then gradually pulled the reactor off the ship. Meanwhile, the Stülcken jumbo derrick unloaded the ancillary items to the dockside. Some time was spent clearing up the deck before departure after lunch.

It was a short passage to Oskarshamn, on mainland Sweden, south-west of the north end of Öland, across the Kalmar Strait, to the shipyard founded in 1863. Ferries ran from the port to Gotland, Öland, and Blå Jungfrun, an island nature reserve in the Strait.

We arrived late afternoon on 16 November. The next day, the ship manoeuvred into the dry dock, which amply accommodated *Starman Anglia*, and the gate closed astern of us. I was accustomed to this procedure and appreciated how critical it was for the docking pilot to ensure the ship was positioned precisely. As water drained from the dry dock, *Starman Anglia* eventually settled on the dock-bottom blocks, critical in ensuring a safe dry docking. They took the ship's mass and distributed it among the line of blocks placed below the keel plates. Every ship had a docking manual with a guide 'block plan' approved by the ship's classification society (Lloyd's Register in our case). Blocks were constructed from one material (either timber or concrete with steel) so their 'stiffness' was uniform. If *Starman Anglia's* weight was unevenly spread it could damage the blocks or, worse, the hull itself. Side blocks were also arranged to support the ship and were a little taller than the keel blocks to account for the the hull's curving up from keel to the ship's vertical sides.

The 10-day work package started shortly after docking down was complete. This was my third dry docking, so I was used to the general content of a work package and the crew routine. I had little to do.

I took my customary wander along the dock edge. I noted the blunt shape of *Starman Anglia's* red hull. Certainly not as graceful as Blue Star's sleek box boats and reefers. She definitely looked workman-like. After a circuit of the dock, I clambered down the steps into it. Her bow was more rounded and the flare of the hull rising to the white of the fo'c'sle bulwarks was more convex. Below and abaft the hawse pipes for the anchor cable was the 550 horsepower, electrically powered Brunvoll bow-thruster.

Fig 10.11 Blunt bow, hawse pipes and bow-thruster tunnel

The hull flattened out, which allowed her to beach comfortably in isolated locations. From about midships, the hull gradually tapered towards the stern, to allow for the rudder/propeller assemblage. At the stern, the twin propellers were fitted so that the deepest part of their circumference didn't go below the flat of the hull. This avoided hull and keel damage during beaching operations. Two spade-shaped rudders were centrally positioned, relative to the propellers. Between the twin rudders and the propellers, a central hull fin supported *Starman Anglia* when she was beached.

Fig 10.12 Stern ramp between funnels, twin propellers and rudders below

Her red transom stern was quite petite, resembling two right-angled triangles with their bases abutting the centre line and apexes outboard. Twin propellers, twin rudders, and a bow thruster made *Starman Anglia* extremely manoeuvrable in confined waters. With a strengthened flat-bottom, she was designed to operate under exceptionally difficult conditions to deliver awkward, heavy cargo via lifting or roll-on/roll-off at shore sites.

Back on board, from the stern ramp looking forward, the weather deck was bare, revealing the large, unencumbered working deck.

At the far end, dominating the deck and superstructure was the Stülcken jumbo derrick. Its boom rose high above the accommodation and, from the sheaved block at its head, the 65 feet (20 m) long, eight-fold purchase and 7 ton ramshorn cargo hook hung down and was secured to the deck. The 108 feet (33 m) boom enabled the ship to lift 300 tonnes within a radius of 16½ feet (5 m) to both sides of the ship. Two additional 5 and 10 tonne derricks were fitted either side of the main boom for servicing and handling stores.

Fig 10.13 *Australia Star*, with her 300 ton Stülcken derrick (Rick Vince)

These jumbo derricks were designed by Willi Sprengel at shipbuilder HC Stülcken Sohn during the early-1950s. He'd spent much of World War II designing U-Boats. Until then, heavy-duty derricks had a traditional configuration with two problems: it took hours to set them ready to lift; and they lacked flexibility in some directions, especially when handling longer, heavier pieces of cargo. Sprengel's jumbo derrick was instantly recognisable with its V-form twin samson posts and derrick boom harnessed between. It had several advantages: ready for use in under 15 minutes; easy to operate; and highly manoeuvrable.

The first Stülcken jumbo derrick was fitted to DDG Hansa Line's *Weissenfels*, built in 1961. Stülcken continued to build these derricks until 1966 when the shipyard was acquired by Blohm & Voss. Eventually, advanced versions lifted over 350 tons. By the 1980s, alternative heavy-lift derricks had evolved. The last 'active' Stülcken derrick, built in 1979, was scrapped in 2020. So ended another important part of maritime history.

Blue Star Line had acquired good historical experience with Stülcken derricks, whose typical capacity was 150 tons, but the first 300-ton version was fitted to our own *Australia Star* in 1965. At the time it was the largest jumbo derrick on a merchant vessel. Its presence amidships, to serve both the hold immediately for'ard and the hold immediately aft, made *Australia Star* easily recognisable. She used her Stülcken to deliver heavy machinery for the hydroelectric Snowy

Mountains Scheme in Australia. In 1966–67, she carried parts for the Manapouri hydroelectric plant in Doubtful Sound, New Zealand. She was the only ship at that time with the capacity to lift these parts and enter the Sound. Several Starman regulars had spent time on *Australia Star*, picking up invaluable experience, which undoubtedly helped them become Starman continuity crews. *Australia Star* had been sold several years before I joined BSSM. She ended her life at a Shanghai ship-breakers in 1985. Sad.

The history of heavy-lift shipping dated back to the 1920s. The German shipping company DDG Hansa saw an increasing demand for shipments of assembled locomotives to British India. In 1929, *Lichtenfels* was the world's first heavy-lift vessel, with a 120-tonne derrick. After World War II, DDG Hansa became the world's largest heavy-lift shipping company, beginning with *Weissenfels* in 1961 and culminating in 1978 with refitting bulk carrier *Trifels* with two 320-tonne Stülcken derricks.

In 1980, DDG went bankrupt. The market opened up to Dutch heavy-lift specialist shipping companies – such as Jumbo, BigLift Shipping (formerly Mammoet Shipping) and SAL Heavy Lift – triggered by the rapid expansion of the deep-sea, offshore installation industry. Starman Shipping carved out a place in the trade with its compact but capable vessels. Two episodes of the Discovery channel's *Mighty Ships* illustrate today's impressive heavy-lift vessels: BigLift's *Happy Star* (Season 8, Episode 3) and Jumbo Shipping's *Fairplayer* (Season 2, Episode 6).

A Stülcken jumbo derrick operated with two cargo winches and two topping winches, that is, one winch on each topping lift purchase and two for the cargo purchase. This permitted the heavy boom to be raised or lowered quickly. The winches were housed within each of the derricks, giving protection from weather, seawater, and spray, therefore reducing their maintenance requirements, and extending the service life of the wires.

With such heavy lifting, the cargo hook had to be robust. On her maiden voyage, *Starman Anglia* carried three oil storage tanks (each of 90 tons, 55 feet (16.6 m) diameter, 48 feet (14.6 m) high) from Grangemouth to Sullom Voe. During the return trip to Grangemouth for another load, the cargo hook tore from its stowage in moderate weather. Imagine the danger of, and potential damage caused by, a 7 ton rams-horn hook and block flailing around on the end of the 66 feet

(20 m) eight-fold purchase. Frightening! Fortunately, no injuries or serious damage occurred.

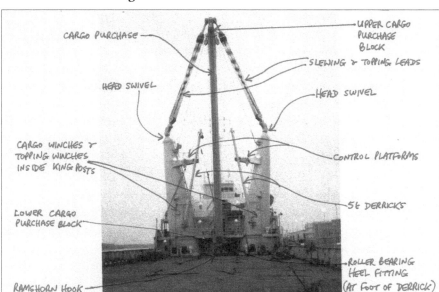

Fig 10.14 *Starman Anglia*'s Stülcken jumbo derrick

Her fully-laden maximum draught of 15 feet (4.5 m) allowed *Starman Anglia* to reach small ports or locations that otherwise might be inaccessible. The overall package was an impressive, capable, robust, multi-role vessel for a growing niche market. Heavy-lift shipping had begun to boom, in particular, carrying cargoes to developing nations.

I went up the road a couple of times to look around Oskarshamn, a small and unremarkable town. The wide streets gave it spaciousness. I spotted a couple of lovely churches set among trees and grass. The clapperboard houses were painted in pastel shades – nothing too bright or vibrant. Small sandy beaches nestled between low-lying rocky headlands. The weather was grey, overcast, cool with the constant threat of rain, which failed to materialise.

One day, Graham the Mate asked if I wanted a game of squash. He'd somehow heard that I played. I was delighted. We went to Oskarshamn's sports centre and had a great game, which I won. I felt grateful to my father for introducing me and my brother to badminton, then tennis and finally squash, which now paid dividends. It showed that playing a sport or two was a great outlet and served as a useful 'ice-breaker' in developing and expanding your social and sporting network at work and beyond. My ability and experience as a racquet player stood me in very good stead throughout my subsequent naval careers. Even in retirement I've taken up racketball at our local sports centre. It keeps me fit and active and I've made new acquaintances.

Starman Anglia departed Oskarshamn on my birthday, 27 November. It was a quiet two-day passage north-east to Hanko in Finland to load our next cargo. Despite it being winter, the weather was mild but perpetually overcast, and a slight sea with very little swell. There was only light shipping traffic in this part of the Baltic Sea.

The cargo was two 155 ton, 161 feet (49 m) tall dockside cranes. We berthed at Kone's wharf and preparations were made to load the cranes. The city of Hanko was located on its eponymous peninsula, the southernmost tip of mainland Finland, an area occupied by the Russians in the first years of World War II. In addition to its 80 miles (129 km) of coastline, of which 30 miles (48 km) were sandy beaches, the city's limits included an archipelago of over 90 islands and islets. Of course, being Starman, there was no chance to go up the road.

> Kone was founded in 1910, manufacturing elevators, at first under licence before they designed, built, and installed their own. As part of war reparations paid to the Soviet Union, the Finnish government required Kone to contribute elevators, electric hoists, and cranes. This forced Kone to expand capacity, rationalise production processes, and learn to meet strict manufacturing schedules. The acquisition of companies larger and older than Kone itself in the 1970s and 1980s brought the company respectability and a prominent position in the market. Kone further expanded and became one of the world's largest manufacturers of hoists and cranes, as well as high-tech electronic hospital and laboratory equipment. Kone also bought International MacGregor, makers of the hatch covers most commonly found on merchant ships, which included many BSSM ships. The five flush-fitted 'pontoon' hatch covers that sealed the hold on *Starman Anglia*, and her stern ramp, were also MacGregor products.

A bit of a crew change occurred in Hanko. Captain Hutchinson and Graham Clarke were relieved by equally devoted Starmen, Captain 'Gas-Axe' Ganderton and Charlie Brown.

The weather deck was cleared completely and the starboard bulwark removed. The cranes were to be side-loaded. Preparations included welding two pairs of rails athwartships upon which the cranes sat when loaded and to which they were secured for the passage to Mexico. The cranes, with their bright red legs and jibs sandwiching an orange cab and their yellow motors at the foot of each leg, awaited us on the wharf. It was a lengthy process to complete the preparations for loading. A set of rail tracks on the wharf were fixed to bridge the gap between the shore and *Starman Anglia's* deck.

The slow task of hauling each crane on board began. As a crane transited from wharf to ship's side and on to the deck, so *Starman Anglia's* super-responsive counter-ballast system operated to prevent her heeling, as it had when we loaded the nuclear reactor. The most dangerous part was when a crane's weight first impacted on the ship. Thereafter, careful communication between Master (on the bridge) and Mate (on deck) ensured that the pumping of water ballast effectively countered the onset of the crane's full weight and its slow transit across the deck to exactly straddle the ship's centre line. The process was repeated to load the second crane.

Fig 10.15 Cranes loaded and strapped down, our seven ton rams-horn hook in foreground

When loading was complete, lashing began. This meant welding a large number of steel strips along the underside of each crane's cabin and then welding their ends to the deck diagonally opposite. This braced the cranes against lateral movement athwartships to prevent them 'falling over'. My overtime chit showed we worked overnight, finishing at 0500 on 30 November.

Fig 10.16 Cargo dominated *Starman Anglia*

In the grey dawn, the cranes dominated the ship, even towering over the Stülcken derrick. They resembled two red, long-necked dinosaurs poised to devour anything in the vicinity – or a pair of Meccano aliens from HG Wells' *War of the Worlds*.

Starman Anglia sailed from Hanko later that morning, bound for Mazatlán on the west coast of Mexico. An 8,000-mile (12,900 km) voyage to the Panama Canal, a day's transit and a further 2,400 miles (3,900 km) to Mazatlán. At 10½ knots, to allow for inclement sea and weather conditions during the voyage, it was planned as a 36-day trip, door-to-door.

I took the watch after disembarking the pilot and set a south-south-west course through the Baltic. The weather remained overcast, with light winds and good visibility. Traffic was sparse as we left Finland's mainland astern. Comfortable with my solo watch, I settled into a routine: constant visual lookout; frequent checks of the radar for new contacts; plotting our position using the Decca Navigator System (DNS) as land was beyond visual and radar range.

Ships and aircraft use the DNS electronic navigation system to determine their position by receiving radio signals from fixed navigational beacons. The system was invented in the US but developed by Decca in the UK. It was first deployed by the Royal Navy during World War II for the vital task of clearing minefields prior to the D-Day landings.

Post-war, Decca proposed, developed, designed, promulgated, manufactured, sold, operated, maintained, and supported DNS for its entire 50 years of life. At its peak popularity and usage, there were over 50 chains covering the UK and northern Europe, the west and east coasts of North America, Australia, India, Japan, Vietnam, and the Persian Gulf.

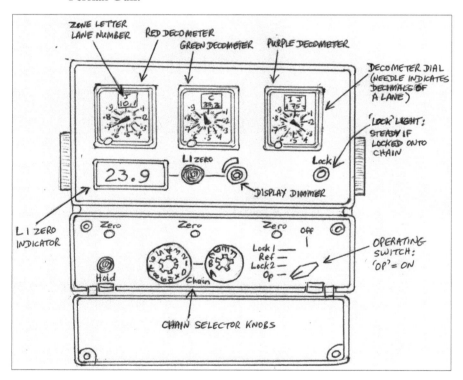

Fig 10.17 Decca Navigator receiver

Decca's land-based radio beacons were arranged in 'chains' and deployed primarily for ship navigation in coastal waters, to about 240 miles (387 km) offshore. Each chain consisted of three slave stations (red, green and purple) positioned at the vertices of an equilateral triangle, with the master station at the centre. Red, green and purple patterns formed a printed lattice, criss-crossing the affected nautical charts. Each coloured pattern was divided into lanes, grouped into zones: 24 Red (numbered 0 to 23), 18 Green (numbered 30 to 47), or 30 Purple (numbered 50 to 79) lanes in each zone. The zones were labelled A to J. If more than ten zones occurred, then labelling resumed again at A, B, C, etc.

Position is determined by reading each of the three rotating 'decometers' on the receiver. The two lines that intersected at between 30° and 90° were used to determine the ship's position. They were plotted using the simple, yet effective, 'Decca interpolating ruler'. This looked like a rather cheap, long, rectangular bit of transparent plastic with its centre cut out. The variety of gradations in sixths (on its inside edges) and tenths (on its outside lengths) allowed any lane width to be accommodated when plotting a position line on the chart. Brilliant! I've still got mine. Like my *Norie's Tables*, I'm loath to discard it as it's an important memory of my working life at sea.

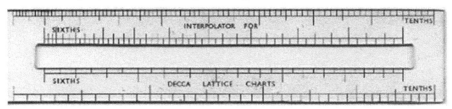

Fig 10.18 Decca interpolating ruler

I enjoyed using DNS at sea as it was easy to use the receiver, to read its decometers, and to change from one chain to another during, say, an English Channel transit. If you were sufficiently competent, you could do inter-chain fixing during the transition from one chain to another. With an operating range of about 240 miles (387 km), it was excellent for confirming your expected landfall after an ocean voyage before radar detected land and certainly prior to the loom of any lighthouse. Similarly, it was useful as your last known accurate position when you commenced an ocean voyage after land fell beyond radar range.

Its series of interconnected chains of a 'master' and three 'slave' stations greatly assisted navigation and the position yielded by Decca's Chain 6E

(Gulf of Finland) showed whether I needed to adjust the 'course-to-steer' to maintain Mike O'Keefe's nav-track.

As the whole crew had worked overnight, the engineer on watch and I were the only folks awake this morning. I handed over the watch to Mike at noon and went below for lunch. The night's work and the bridge watch caught up with me. I enjoyed a deep slumber in my bunk that afternoon!

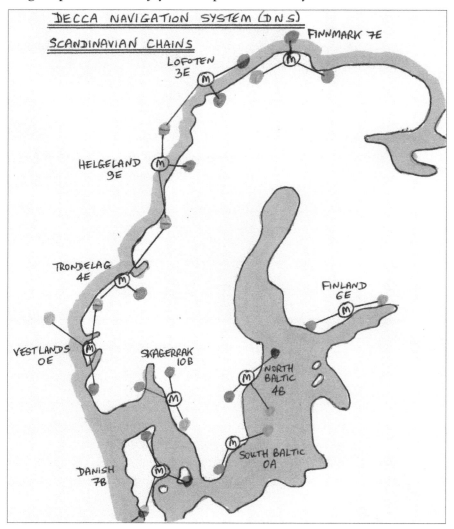

Fig 10.19 Decca Navigation System chains: Scandinavia

We changed Decca chains en route, to 4B (North Baltic) and then 0A (South Baltic). At the south end of the Baltic, we altered to a more westerly course, rounded the southern tip of Sweden and switched to Chain 7B (Danish). There followed a tight northbound passage through Øresund, between Scandinavia and Danish Zeeland. One of five Danish Straits or 'Belts', Øresund was 73 miles (118 km) long, with a width that varied from 2½ miles (4 km) to 17 miles (28 km). At its south end, we passed Copenhagen to port and Malmo to starboard. There was heavy traffic in this constrained area, particularly with ferries crossing. We popped out between Danish Helsingør and Swedish Helsingborg at the north end, Øresund's narrowest part, into the Kattegat. Although a larger open area, the Kattegat is a shallow sea, difficult and dangerous to navigate because of its mobile sand waves, stony reefs and tricky currents. Shipping traffic decreased in volume.

Passing between Skagen, the very northern tip of Jutland, and Gothenburg in Sweden, we switched to Decca Chain 10B (Skagerrak) and entered the Skagerrak itself. Using Skagen as a pivot point, *Starman Anglia* altered from her north-west course to a south-west one. The Skagerrak was 150 miles (240 km) long and 50–87 miles (80–140 km) wide, deepening to over 2,300 feet (700 m) in the Norwegian Trench. The area was busy with fishing boats and recreational sailing.

At last, we were in the North Sea, passing along the coasts of Denmark and Germany towards the English Channel. The weather slowly deteriorated as wind and sea state increased. British winter weather was characterised by 'families' of depressions crossing the Atlantic to dump rain in the south-west, with strong winds associated everywhere. *Starman Anglia*'s top speed of 12 knots was reduced significantly by strong headwinds and increased sea state.

Rain made visibility difficult but, like many ships, *Starman Anglia* had a Kent Clearview Screen mounted in one of the bridge windows. This glass disk rotated to disperse rain, spray, and snow. It was driven by an electric motor at its centre, and was heated to prevent condensation or icing. This 'rotating windshield wiper' spun so fast that all precipitation was flung off by centrifugal force and provided a clear view. Patented in 1917, it was a brilliant invention.

It was a very pedestrian transit of the Dover Strait. We were overtaken by almost every vessel headed south-west. 'Speed made good' decreased to a miserable 1 knot as we crawled along the Channel. Captain Ganderton decided this was just no good at all. We anchored in Torbay to await a break in the weather. Nearly 72 hours later, we weighed anchor and resumed the voyage. *Starman Anglia* plodded on, rounded Start Point to re-enter the

Channel, onwards to the Celtic Sea and the South West Approaches. Progress remained slow, nowhere near our top, or even planned, speed. The British Isles eventually disappeared astern, beyond the effective range of the DNS. Ahead was the vast emptiness and raging ferment of the Atlantic Ocean.

Ships pitch and roll in any sort of sea state; flat-bottomed, shallow-draught vessels even more so. With the added height of our crane cargo, ship stability was affected. The top-heavy effect of the cranes exaggerated the ship's pitching and, particularly, rolling. Those clever naval architects had taken account of both factors. *Starman Anglia* had a high in-built stability factor to allow very tall cargoes to be transported safely.

Meanwhile, rolling and pitching forces and movement in a seaway were reduced by a special flume reduction tank across the full breadth of the vessel, situated between the cargo hold (aft) and the bow-thruster (for'ard) and below the accommodation. Partially water-filled, its shape, size, and internal baffles allowed the liquid inside to slosh from side to side in response to the ship's roll motion. The phasing of the roll moments acting on the ship and the resultant liquid motion dampened and reduced roll motion. Ship motion was considerably more comfortable than expected. A great relief!

I enjoyed being on watch solo. After all, this was the main role for which I was being trained. The time and experience I'd accrued when doubled-up with a deck officer on previous trips proved invaluable. The responsibility was no different than on any other merchant ship. I was charged with safe navigation, obeying the ROR, determining if risk of collision with any other vessels existed, and then to take correct and timely action to avoid collision. I was ultimately responsible for ship and crew safety during my four-hour watches.

In daylight watches, the deck officer manned the bridge alone. The ABs were all employed on deck. If necessary, I could call my nominated AB to come to the bridge. Ordinarily, this only occurred in 'restricted visibility' (usually fog) as an especially vigilant visual lookout was required to supplement my own visual lookout and monitoring of the radar picture. His extra pair of ears listened out for other ships' fog signals.

At night, the AB kept lookout on either of the bridge-wings, usually the leeside, sheltered from the wind. Throughout my Blue Star experience, it was unusual for the AB to be allowed inside the bridge, except in horrendous weather, such as heavy rain or sub-zero temperatures. Union-agreed working practices allowed the AB to go below for a half-hour smoko during a night watch, leaving the deck officer alone in the dark from about 2200 to 2230, 0200 to 0230, and 0600 to 0630.

I busied myself throughout the watch, day or night. Being new to the game, I wanted to prove competent, knowledgeable, and professional to the Master, Charlie, and Mike. It may sound dull to be bimbling along at an absolute maximum of 12 knots in an empty ocean for days on end, with very few other ships observed by radar, never mind seen by naked eye or binoculars. But I developed a routine that kept me occupied throughout every watch – and I rather enjoyed the role. Every watch was different in some minor way.

Early in my time with Blue Star, someone told me to never sit down on watch. Why? I do not know. Sitting down on watch wasn't expressly forbidden in company policy. It was one of those unwritten rules, I supposed. So I was on my feet for the entire four hours. Between various regular tasks, I strolled back and forth across the width of the bridge. This non-stop activity and movement meant I never fell asleep on watch, a heinous crime, even in the middle of nowhere. If the Old Man came to the bridge during my forenoon watches, I never had to leap out of the chair, red-faced, embarrassed, and ashamed. I continued this non-seated regime on watch during my subsequent career in the Royal Navy. Old habits die hard and I never fell asleep on watch slumped in the Captain's chair.

Visitors to the bridge were rare. Neither the deck crowd nor the engineers had any interest and were busy with their respective departmental tasks. Occasionally, Charlie Brown visited briefly. Captain Ganderton appeared daily during each watch. Every morning, Mike came to take his sextant observations and plot the results to derive the ship's position. The longest and most involved interaction occurred at watch handovers.

Deep sea, Mike and I took a morning sun sight by sextant between 0900 and 0930 daily. At noon, we shot the sun at its zenith (its highest altitude, or angle above the horizon) to determine the ship's position at 1200. I had my own 'sight book', an A4, hard-covered, lined notebook, wherein I scribed my observations and calculations.

I used my observed times and altitudes, plus figures and tables extracted from the *Nautical Almanac* and *Norie's Tables*. Care was essential in the interpolation of several of the tables. Neatness was vital, too, as it was very easy to misread your figures or do a bit of simple arithmetic in a blasé manner. A gross error can quickly evolve and often remain undetected until you plot the result. There then follows a laborious re-checking of the whole calculation as it is difficult to spot where the error occurred. Being a naturally cautious chap, I scrupulously wrote clear numbers and logical little steps at each stage.

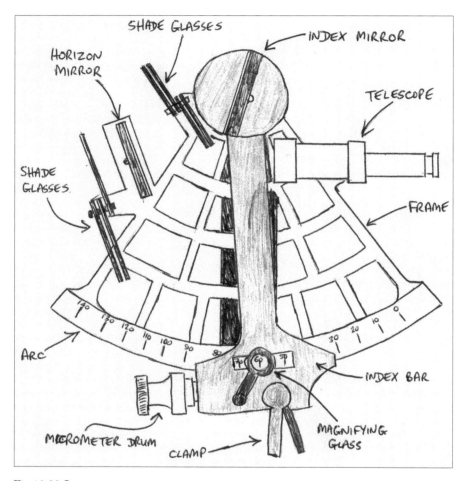

Fig 10.20 Sextant

It was on *Starman Anglia* that I learnt the intricacies of the sextant. This fabled instrument was used in various forms for centuries by a long list of famous navigators on worldwide expeditions: Cook, Magellan, Vasco da Gama, Flinders, Bligh to name only a few. Of course, the ordinary everyday deck officer used, checked, and adjusted his sextant with equal aplomb.

A sextant is a precision instrument to measure the angle a heavenly body (star, planet, sun, moon) made with the visible horizon, or the vertical or horizontal angle between two terrestrial objects. The sextant consists of a telescope, a half-silvered horizontal mirror which the telescope 'looks' through, and a moving arm on which the index mirror is fixed. By manipulating the arm, a star or other celestial body is made to appear on the horizon. Accurate adjustments are made with a micrometer knob. The angle (altitude) is read from the arc and micrometer. Shades are used when observing a bright object, usually the sun.

There can be several errors in a sextant. Some are adjustable by the operator, others aren't and can only be rectified by the manufacturer, if at all.

Adjustable errors, checked before each use of a sextant, are: perpendicularity, where the index glass isn't perpendicular to the plane of the instrument; side error, where the horizon glass isn't perpendicular to the plane of the instrument; index error, caused by the index glass and the horizon glass not being parallel to each other when the index bar is set at zero; and collimation, due to the axis of the telescope not being parallel to the plane of the instrument. With a small screwdriver, kept in its little slot in the sextant box, a deck officer can make tiny adjustments to the mirrors to nullify these observed errors.

Non-adjustable errors include: graduation error, due to the inaccurate graduation of the main scale on or off the micrometer; shade error, where the two surfaces of the coloured shades aren't exactly parallel to each other; centring error, caused by the pivot of the index arm not being coincident with the centre of the circle of which the arc is a part; optical errors, prismatic errors of the mirrors or aberrations in the telescope lenses; and 'wear on the rack and worm', which 'drive' the micrometer movement, and cause a backlash and inconsistent errors.

Sextants are delicate instruments which require careful handling. For a start, they are kept in their own lovely, varnished wooden box in a cupboard beside the chart table. A sextant is taken from its box in the left hand by the frame and transferred to the right hand, which grasps the handle.

To take a 'sight' or 'shoot up' the sun/star/planet/moon, a firm, braced stance on the bridge wing is necessary. The right hand firmly grasps the sextant's handle, while the left hand lightly holds the clamp on the arc. In the relative wind on the bridge wing, you can detect the sextant's movement, despite a stable stance with legs astride. This light movement is negated when you firmly tuck both elbows into your sides. Although it is a little uncomfortable after some minutes, this technique does the trick and the sextant is as steady as a rock.

Then, the sextant's telescope is focused on the horizon, the selected celestial body found and the sextant aimed at it. The body is brought down to the horizon by moving the arm along the arc, then clamped. Use the micrometer knob to make small adjustments of the angle (altitude) while gently swaying the sextant in a tiny arc until the observed body's lower limb brushes the horizon. Immediately note the time, seconds first, then minutes and hours, then the name of the body and its observed altitude. Every second of time counts. As a general rule, an error of four seconds equates to an error of one nautical mile in the calculated position. Make a mad dash into the bridge to read the chronometer's time, while seconds are counted (a slow 'and one, and two, and three, and …') and then subtract them from the observed chronometer time.

Ship's chronometers are also old-fashioned things of beauty. Housed in their own wooden compartment with a glass top, they adjoined the chart table. Every ship usually had two. They always remained on Greenwich Mean Time (GMT) and daily, at a specified time, were each wound the same precise number of turns. Their accuracy was checked against the BBC's Greenwich time signal. Any error was logged in the Chronometer Log, as was the winding time. In the old days, chronometers were critical for astronomical navigation calculations. In the 1980s, new fangled, highly accurate, quartz watches became more widespread. Ship's chronometers eventually fell into disuse, particularly with the introduction and universal use of satellite navigation systems.

It's sad that these traditional, old-fashioned, but effective bits of kit are no longer relevant. I doubt today's ships are fitted with chronometers. Likewise, the art and skill in using a sextant seem to be no longer taught to deck officers or naval officers. GPS (Global Positioning System) made both chronometer and sextant redundant.

When our observations were completed, Mike and I occupied the chart table to do our respective calculations. I was most satisfied to get solutions and positions similar to, and even the same as, Mike's.

I didn't snack during the watch as I ate a decent breakfast, lunch, and dinner daily. I always had three courses for dinner. If I didn't fancy the dessert on the menu, I ate a generous portion of ice cream instead. My weakness was tea. On watch, an hourly mug of the hot stuff was unbeatable. A characteristic of my entire working life!

Overall, being on watch was a rather solitary existence, particularly when deep sea. Off-watch time was very much my own as I had no deck commitments. Lazy afternoons were spent reading, either books I'd brought with me or books borrowed from the ship's library. The Marine Society was established to increase seafarers' knowledge and qualifications and it generously provided fiction and non-fiction titles to all British merchantmen. Sometimes a port visit included a delivery of new books from the Marine Society. Those interested in reading scrambled among the new arrivals and swiftly stole away with a couple of books.

I had a small 'ghetto-blaster', bought during *Mandama's* dry docking in Singapore, and some music cassettes, also bought cheap in Singapore. My abiding musical memory was of the Australian band Men at Work's album *Business as Usual*, which included 'Who Can It Be Now' and 'Down Under' – excellent and 'of the time'.

To landlubbers, it may seem a strange solitary existence, but I enjoyed it.

Starman Anglia defied foul north Atlantic weather and transitioned to warmer, calmer, tropical waters. It was my third consecutive Christmas at sea. Nothing special happened except that I finished my watch at noon and stuffed myself with an excellent Christmas dinner, courtesy of our cook.

We passed through the Mona Passage and were in the Caribbean for New Year's Eve. I came down from the bridge at midnight but no-one was around. I didn't even bother with a lonely celebratory beer to welcome 1983. Such was life in a small-crewed merchant ship.

Starman Anglia anchored in the roads off Colon and its port of Cristobal, waiting to join the convoy for the southbound transit of the Panama Canal on 2 January. Instead of a 28-day voyage at 12 knots, bad weather had prolonged it to 33 days. It took the usual day to complete the 'PanCan' transit – almost exactly two years after my first one on *ACT 5*, Christmas Day 1980. Crikey, I'd certainly seen and done so much since then. I thought, for the umpteenth time, what a lucky bloke I was!

After Panama, it was a more pleasant eight-day passage along the coasts of Central America and Mexico. Nothing noteworthy occurred. It was nice to enjoy sunshine on the bridge wing and a calmer sea.

> **Mazatlán is a provincial city in the Mexican state of Sinaloa, some 190 miles (306 km) directly east across the Gulf of California from Baja California Sur. It is a popular tourist destination, due to its extensive sandy beaches, served by a car ferry to La Paz on Baja. Tourism and fishing dominate the city's economy.**
>
> **For the mariner, the most significant feature is the El Faro lighthouse on the peak of Cerro del Creston, at the southern end of Mazatlán's peninsula. The lighthouse was built in 1879 on an island 700**

yards (640 m) long by 350 yards (320 m) wide and a peak of 515 feet
(157 m). This made it the highest natural lighthouse in the Americas,
and one of the highest operating lighthouses in the world.

Fig 10.21 In the locks at Panama Canal

The peak and El Faro were unmissable during the approach to Mazatlán,
observed in the distance, it gradually increased in size until we steamed past
and it overshadowed us to port. After a fairly short stand-by, we were soon
alongside, early on 12 January 1983.

Fig 10.22 Miraflores Locks with mule

Preparations were made to discharge our cargo. The starboard side bulwark was removed. Sets of rails were already in place on the wharf. *Starman Anglia* was aligned with the rails ashore and bridging pieces were welded to connect the ship's rails to the wharf's rails. Shoreside workers cut all the welded steel lashing bands which had proved a great success in holding the cargo securely in place on the long transatlantic trip from Hanko.

When the port authorities, Captain Ganderton, and Charlie Brown were ready, the process of trundling the cranes from the deck, across the bridging pieces, to the wharf began. Again, close coordination between Master (on the bridge) and Mate (on deck) ensured that counter-ballasting prevented *Starman Anglia* from heeling dangerously, or even capsizing, to port or starboard. The aft-most crane was discharged first. The bridging pieces were removed while the ship was warped astern along the wharf until the forward crane's rails aligned with the wharf rails. The bridging pieces reconnected ship to wharf and the second crane was eased ashore. It was a long, slow procedure. My overtime chit shows we were on deck from 0600, all day and overnight, until 1400 the next afternoon.

Fig 10.23 Cranes unloaded to wharf, weather deck empty again

m.v.Starman Anglia

Officers Cargo Handling Compensation   Total January 1983

P.CARROLL Officer Trainee UK063656

voy 011 Side roll off.Two 155tonne dockyard cranes.

Port/Date	Hrs of Work	Cargo Handling	Compensation	
Mazatlan				
12-1-83 Wed	0600-1100			
	1800-2400	1900-2400	5 x 1	= 5
13-1-83 Thurs	0000-0500	0000-0500	5 x 2	= 10
	1300-1500	1300-1400	1 x 1	= 1
	2300-2400			
		Total		16 hrs

D.A.Ganderton,Master   P.J.Carroll,O.T.   C.D.Brown,Chief Officer

No news within a month, contact Howard Baker at Officer's Salary.

Fig 10.24 Overtime chit, Mazatlán unloading

Cargo delivered, we squeezed in a few hours' sleep before tidying up the mess on the weather deck. *Starman Anglia* sailed from Mazatlán late afternoon on 13 January. No chance to go up the road. I'd learnt this was typical in our Starman heavy-lift world. Astern of us, silhouetted against a pale overcast sky, the swanky new dockside cranes stood proud and tall over the docks.

Fig 10.25 Cranes silhouetted at Mazatlán

The passage south to Panama was as uneventful as that northbound, with similar weather conditions and sea state. During my day watches, I spent time on either bridge wing and, looking aft, it was unusual to see the weather deck empty of cargo and completely uncluttered. The deck crowd were down there, though, doing some chipping and painting.

On 22 January, *Starman Anglia* made the return northbound 'PanCan' transit. This was my seventh and, although I didn't know it, final Panama Canal experience. The locks (Gatun, Pedro Miguel, Miraflores), Culebra Cut, and the lakes (Gatun and Miraflores) were old friends. The 'mules' guided and hauled us into and through the locks without a hitch. I knew the procedure, the kinks and quirks of the canal, the dangers of interaction between ships passing close by in confined waters. I observed the southbound convoy at anchor in Gatun Lake as our convoy continued uninterrupted to Gatun Locks and exited into the Caribbean.

Starman Anglia's next cargo was to be loaded in Beaumont, Texas, a passage of about 2,000 miles (3,220 km). One week at a maximum speed of 12 knots. It was a north-north-west course from Panama, through the Caribbean, to the gap between Cuba and Mexico's Yucatán Peninsula, where we altered course to a more north-westerly one across the Gulf of Mexico. It was pleasant to be steaming at a gentle pace through calm water, under bright sunshine and blue sky. I was truly enjoying being on watch solo. Life was good.

It was a straightforward approach to the Port of Beaumont at the mouth of the Neches River. The topography was very low-lying, only a few feet above sea level. Pilot embarked, *Starman Anglia* headed a few miles upriver into Sabine Lake. A further 10 miles (16 km) later, she turned to port and soon berthed at the wharf on 27 January.

Fig 10.26 *Starman Anglia* at Beaumont, Texas

Although it is not one of America's largest or best-known cities, Beaumont was the US's fourth-busiest port, largely due to its deep water harbour. It was also the busiest military port in the world for processing US military equipment. It served as headquarters to the US Army's 842nd Transportation Battalion, specialists in port logistics operations. Beaumont was close to the state border between Texas and Louisiana, approximately 84 miles (135 km) east of Houston, 270 miles (435 km) west of New Orleans, and about 42 miles (68 km) inland from the Gulf of Mexico along the Sabine-Neches Waterway.

There wasn't much for me to do, except 'suitcase trials', as I was paying off. No concerns about my luggage allowance as I hadn't had an opportunity to buy souvenirs and had actually reduced my baggage weight by using four months' worth of toiletries!

The next day, I collected my Discharge Book from Captain Ganderton. I was delighted he was pleased with my performance and competence as a Third Mate. This augured well for my career as a deck officer. I bade farewell to Charlie Brown and Mike O'Keefe and, lastly, to Brian and Neil, the two Abs with whom I'd spent so much time on deck and then on watch. I don't recall the journey home, but guess the ship's agent drove me to Houston Airport for a direct transatlantic flight to Heathrow, then the rail-air coach service to Reading, and train to Pompey Harbour.

Starman Anglia had certainly been an interesting, terrific, and novel experience. Grubbing around on deck, lashing and unlashing cargo throughout long hours and overnight was brilliant. But I wasn't a 'convert' to the heavy-lift environment, and was not desperate to return. I hadn't been up the road at all, save for my couple of strolls around Oskarshamn, and that had been because we were in dry dock. On previous trips, I always made the most of seeing as much as I could. Nevertheless, it was a great opportunity to serve as Third Mate before completing my ticket. According to the Old Man, I'd turned in a good solid performance, and proved competent, reliable, and professional.

There were about three months until the final college phase started in May 1983. Insufficient for another proper trip so Mr Burke engineered some short 'coasting' trips to accrue more sea-time during what would otherwise have been 'dead time'.

I joined *California Star* in Felixstowe on 18 February for a tour of European ports, paying off a week later at Felixstowe. Three days later, four days on *Boniface, Benedict's* sister ship, going from Heysham to Liverpool via Dublin. I don't remember anything of these short stints, but they were detailed in my Discharge Book and boosted my total sea time.

I had nearly a month's leave before joining *Benedict* on 5 April in Heysham. It was pleasant to sail with Captain John 'Flash' Harris again. He hadn't changed at all. He still switched off the radar as soon as land disappeared astern, and conducted walkie-talkie 'comms' with the Mate while having a pee in the bridge heads. *Benedict* sailed from Heysham to Dublin to load more cargo, then set off across the Atlantic. We arrived in Bridgetown on 27 April after an uneventful voyage. It was a short stop, as usual, before departing for Trinidad. I paid off from *Benedict* on 30 April in Port of Spain and flew direct to Heathrow, courtesy of British West Indies Airways (nicknamed Bee-Wee).

With this extra sea time logged, I was on leave for a few days until my peers and I reconvened at the Bel in New Brighton for our final college phase at Liverpool Polytechnic.

11 Examinations Loom

We returned to the Bel in May 1983 for the final college phase at Liverpool Polytechnic. This culminated in the shuddering climax of written examinations and the frightening ordeal of the oral exam by the Principal Examiner of Masters and Mates. The latter was the defining moment of our cadetship, our seafaring career in the balance.

On several weekends, I drove south to see Sue, who was teaching at a school in Eastbourne. Crikey, that was a long flog of 325 miles (523 km) each way. Motorway from New Brighton to Junction 11A on the M5, then the A417 and A419 to Swindon to join the M4, round a bit of the M25 to the M23 to Brighton, and finishing with the A27 into Eastbourne. This exhausting journey took about six hours, as did the reciprocal on Sunday. Hardly a restful, romantic weekend, but needs must.

During other weekends, our quintet (Nigel, Sam, Tom, Mick, and I), unless one of us had gone away, went into Liverpool for a night out. The city centre was always lively, the pubs full, the nightclubs (or were they still discos?) throbbed loudly.

On Sunday afternoons I liked to take a stroll along the riverside promenade. It ran from Seacombe, where you caught the Mersey ferry to Pierhead near the famous Liver Building, north past Wallasey, and all the way to the very tip of The Wirral at New Brighton Beach. There was always activity to watch on the river: merchant ships arriving or departing; the Mersey ferry perpetually crossing; plus fellow strollers, families and joggers along the route. It was refreshing after a week cooped up in 'school'.

New Brighton was in a sorry state of decay and economic strife. The old town hadn't changed much since its heyday, but now about a third of the shops in the high street were empty, abandoned, or derelict. Very sad for this once thriving suburban community and popular destination for Scousers taking the ferry 'cross the Mersey for a day on The Wirral.

We'd all passed the sight test as part of the job application process. Now, after resuming college two-and-a-half years later, we were required to get our eyesight tested again. Our future career in Blue Star, and indeed the merchant navy, depended on showing no deficiency. We took a day out of college to attend at the registered optician and successfully passed the test. A huge relief and another milestone.

An essential certificate was 'First Aid at Sea', a four-day course in our classroom at the Poly. The source reference was *The Ship Captain's Medical Guide*, deliberately intended for use in ships that didn't carry a qualified doctor. This applied to all cargo ships and tankers. Whereas passenger cruise liners (or 'fanny freighters', as we deep sea, rufty-tufty merchantmen called them) had doctors embarked to deal with elderly passengers' heart attacks. One of the Master's roles was 'ship's doctor'. He had access to the drugs in the medical safe in his day cabin. Clearly a weighty responsibility should an accident occur on board, deep sea, hundreds of miles from the nearest port.

The *Guide* described the treatment and prevention measures that could be reasonably expected of non-medically qualified crewmen. It outlined the general principles of first aid on board ship and how to assess a medical situation. The course syllabus explained: how to give immediate first aid; actions on discovering a casualty; cardiopulmonary resuscitation (CPR); scene management; unconscious casualty; casualty examination; recovery position; shock; bleeding wounds and injuries; burns; head injuries; fractures and dislocation; soft tissue injuries; spinal injuries; poisoning; temperature extremes; and care of the rescued casualty.

We practised and demonstrated our skills by bandaging and dressing wounds, applying splints, conducting CPR – the usual topics covered in every first aid course. I'd never had any interest in 'medical stuff', so first aid courses were torturous necessities throughout my working life. I've only had to deal with one real incident, thank goodness! I passed all such courses but they were always hard work.

Within the classroom timetable was another prerequisite, the 'Electronic Navigation Systems' certificate. Captain Bole was our instructor. The syllabus covered: operational use of radar; automatic radar plotting aids (ARPA); radio direction finders; echo sounders; electronic navigation systems; gyro compasses; and 'Transit' satellite navigation system.

Radar (RAdio Detection And Ranging) used radio waves to determine the range, bearing, and velocity of objects, particularly ships, in our maritime environment. The system comprised a transmitter emitting radio waves, via a wave guide (conduit) to a transmitting antenna (which doubled as a receiving antenna), a receiver, and a processor that determined the properties of detected objects. The transmitter's radio waves reflected off the object, returned to the receiver, and were displayed on the radar screen with information about the object's location and speed.

Captain Bole explained the principles of radar in some detail. The strength of the returned signal from the detected object or target depended on five factors: material, aspect, shape, texture, size (mnemonic MASTS). Four decades later, I still recall the mnemonic and what it represents.

We learnt that radar was not infallible and that it was susceptible to several limiting factors. Signal noise was an internal source of random variations in the signal, generated by all electronic components. Clutter concerned echoes returned from 'targets' such as the sea, precipitation, sandstorms, flocks of birds, atmospheric turbulence, and other atmospheric effects. Clutter was reduced or eliminated during our setting up of the radar system. Two control knobs were manually tweaked in combination to decrease levels of clutter from sea and rain. It was a fine art, as too much anti-clutter meant that small surface objects (yachts, dinghies, buoys) may not be detected as their echoes would be masked out.

Captain Bole painstakingly described the exhaustive procedure for switching on and setting up the radar. This was a certain topic in the Electronic Navigation Aids practical examination. We practised this routine many times as it was vital to follow it exactly, step-by-step. We'd all used radar at sea. Now we knew how to set it up correctly and use it properly.

Captain Bole introduced us to the black art of automatic radar plotting aids (ARPA), a relatively new computerised feature to basic radar. It took data of one's own ship's course and speed, the target's course and speed, and calculated collision avoidance data. This obviated the use of chinagraph pencils on screen to manually plot targets and to calculate their course, speed, and closest point of approach (CPA). ARPA's collision avoidance and detection data was instantly available to the officer-of-the-watch by clicking on the target. None of my BSSM ships were fitted with this new-fangled technology.

As part of the examinable radar syllabus, Captain Bole taught us radar plotting. We took a series of radar ranges and bearings of a target and drew them on a plotting sheet that represented a radar screen. The target's course and speed were calculated. Importantly, extrapolating the plot showed the target's CPA, if it (and one's own ship) maintained the present course and speed. We practised more complex examples, such as, if a target changed course and speed and the effect of 'own ship' altering course and speed. When I got the hang of it, I enjoyed these graphical exercises, using my neat hand and accuracy in plotting.

We spent much time on hyperbolic radio navigation systems. Captain Bole taught us about the DNS system, used by ships and aircraft to determine their position by receiving radio signals from fixed navigational beacons. This consolidated my recent practical experience on *Starman Anglia* where, as solo officer-of-the-watch, I'd used it to steam through the Baltic, around Jutland, into the North Sea, and along the English Channel.

Captain Bole introduced us to two other hyperbolic position fixing systems: LORAN-C and Omega. They used similar principles to that of the Decca Navigator. The classroom was my only contact with both as I never saw them used in BSSM ships – I'm not even sure they were actually fitted with one or other. LORAN-C had an air of black-box mystery to me, so I neither understood it nor got the hang of it in practice, despite Captain Bole's expert instruction. Captain Bole touched briefly on GPS, which was in its infancy but destined to revolutionise navigation and position-fixing.

> LORAN (LOng RAnge Navigation) used accurately timed, low frequency (100 Hz) transmissions from three or more transmitting stations to compute a position. It had a typical range of 620–1,240 miles (1,000–2,000 km), several times that of DNS. LORAN-C had become largely redundant by 2000 due to GPS.
>
> Omega was the first worldwide, ground-based radio navigation system operated by the United States Coast Guard from the early 1970s until 1997. Using very low frequencies (VLF) (10–14 kHz), it provided a continuous, medium accuracy aid to navigation. Eight transmitting stations around the world and a ship's receiver determined position from range measurements based on the phase of the received signals from two or more Omega stations.
>
> DNS, LORAN-C and Omega were all susceptible to the effects of daily changes in the ionosphere, making positional accuracy a bit dodgy, particularly at dawn and dusk.
>
> At sea, we'd all used the Transit (NAVSAT) satellite navigation system, the first such system to be used operationally. Transit provided a continuous navigation satellite service from 1964, initially for Polaris submarines and from 1967 for civilian use. Transit's 'constellation' of satellites provided reasonable global coverage. As only one satellite was usually visible at any given time, a valid fix occurred only when a satellite was above the horizon. At the equator the delay between fixes was several hours but decreased to about 90 minutes in mid-latitudes. Transit lacked the ability to provide high-speed, real-time position measurements, but its computed position was accurate to within 220

yards (200 m). Plenty good enough when deep sea. Transit ceased
service in 1996, superseded by GPS, Global Positioning System.

We were all delighted to pass the written and practical exams and get our
Electronic Navigation Aids certificate. Another prerequisite on the road to
the Second Mate's ticket.

Finally, there was General Ship Knowledge (GSK), the catch-all
subject that swept up anything else to do with ships not covered in the other
examination subjects. We were physically familiar with components of ship
construction, having been all over each of our ships, such as: longitudinal
and transverse framing, beams and beam knees, watertight bulkheads,
cofferdams, hatchways, rudders, steering gear, shell and deck plating, double
bottoms and peak tanks, bilges, side and wing tanks, stern frames, propellers
and propeller shafts, stern tubes, goosenecks, sounding pipes, air pipes, and
general pumping arrangements.

I'd always spent some time looking at the 'general arrangement' plans
on display in each of my ships. They were usually framed on the bulkhead,
in the alleyway containing the duty mess, deck office, engineers' office, and
accesses to the weather deck. After a tour of the ship on joining, they
certainly helped with getting familiar with the ship's geography. Captain
Watson took us for most of this interesting, but very broad, subject.

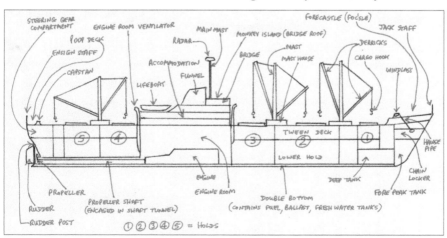

Fig 11.1 Main parts of a merchant ship

In ship construction, we were aware of stiffening to resist panting,
pounding, and longitudinal stresses, and the cause of, and simple methods

to prevent, corrosion. Instruction continued with the laws of a floating body, displacement, and tonnes per centimetre (TPC) immersion.

> Panting is the tendency for ship's plating to work 'in' and 'out' like a bellows, due to pressures on the hull at each end when the ship ploughs through waves. It is most severe when running into waves and pitching heavily. Pounding describes severe local stresses in the ship's bottom shell and forward framing when driving into head seas. To counter both effects, additional strengthening was built into the hull.
>
> TPC is defined as the mass loaded or discharged that changes a ship's mean draught in salt water by one centimetre. It varies with draught and water density, because changes in draught (during cargo loading and discharging operations) cause a change in displacement.

We gained a general understanding of centre of gravity (G), centre of buoyancy (B), metacentre (M), metacentric height (GM), and righting levers and moments, and how adding and removing cargo/fuel/ballast affects each of these factors. Captain Watson explained that GM (metacentric height) had a direct relationship with a ship's rolling period. A ship with a small GM was 'tender' and had a long roll period. A greater GM made a vessel 'stiff' and more responsive to the sea as it attempted to assume the slope of the wave. A 'fanny freighter' (passenger ship) typically had a long roll period (12 seconds) for comfort, but a cargo ship usually had a shorter roll period of six to eight seconds.

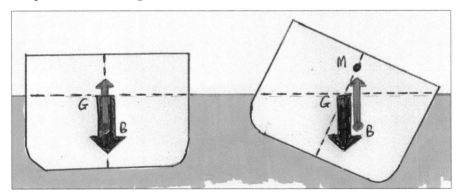

Fig 11.2 Relative positions of G, B, M

> The weight of a ship acts through G but is counteracted by buoyancy (the force of displaced water) acting upward through B. When a ship

is upright, the forces are in direct opposition. When the ship heels, B shifts to the low side. Buoyancy then acts through the metacentre (M), a point on the ship's centre line above G. The UK's legal minimum GM was merely 6 inches (0.15 m), which seemed to me an incredibly small distance of such critical importance, especially to the largest of ships. Regardless of ship dimensions, G, B, M, and GM were always present, it was just a question of scale.

We were introduced to the danger of slack tanks (a tank that isn't full – a full tank is pressed up) introduced and the 'free surface effect'.

> The free surface effect is the dangerous tendency of liquids to move in response to sea state. Interestingly, loose cargoes (such as seeds, gravel, grain, coal, ore) behave similarly to liquids. If tanks or spaces partially filled with a fluid or semi-fluid (fish, ice, grain) are inclined, the surface of the fluid/semi-fluid, stays horizontal. Similar to the effect of carrying a large, flat tray of water: when an edge is tipped, the water rushes to that side, which exacerbates the tipping . Breaking up the free surface by fitting baffles (low mini-bulkheads) in tanks significantly reduces the effect. In the flooded, or partially flooded, compartments of damaged ships, free surface isn't broken up, so the ship's rolling increases in magnitude until the ship capsizes. This occurred in the cross-Channel ferry *Herald of Free Enterprise* in 1987, when she departed Zeebrugge with her bow door open. The sea flooded her car decks, and she capsized in minutes, killing 193 passengers and crew.

Although they had been covered in our EDH ticket, rigging a ship for loading and discharging cargo, and the use of derricks, winches and cranes, were explained theoretically and mathematically. The stowage separation and dunnaging of cargoes in the hold was described. We learnt the causes of cargo 'sweating' and the importance of ventilation in the hold before, during, and after stowing to prevent damage to cargo.

BSSM didn't operate tankers. Nevertheless, a basic knowledge of tankers was required. This covered safety precautions during loading and discharging bulk oil, chemicals, and other inflammable cargoes; gas detection and methods of gas-freeing large tanks; danger of explosions in tankers due to residual gas vapours; and hazards arising from static electricity in tankers. The more I learnt about this subject, the more pleased I was that I wasn't a 'tanker-man'. It seemed an extremely hazardous occupation.

Precautions to be taken before entering cargo and ballast tanks and void spaces was a hot topic as a disproportionate number of merchant navy casualties were due to deaths in confined spaces. It was absolutely critical to ensure that the correct procedures were conducted. You can't simply open a tank lid and climb in to inspect or clean the tank. The accumulated toxic fumes take a certain period to egress before entry can be considered safe. There were numerous examples of a seaman being overcome by fumes, and a succession of his mates also dying in attempted rescues. Frightening.

Noting the many hazards on board a merchantman (being crushed by heavy weights, struck by swinging cargo hooks, cut in half by parting ropes or wires, poisoned by deadly vapours in an empty tank, falling overboard or from a mast, lead poisoning from painting – the list is endless), certainly increased your awareness of our working environment. It instilled a keen eye for spotting and preventing a potential accident.

Nautical physics, nautical mathematics, and meteorology rounded off the syllabus.

> Nautical physics involves simple calculations based on the fundamental relationship and practical application of physical laws and principles. The syllabus covered a broad range: statics, which explains the composition and resolution of forces; principle of moments; stress, strain, shear forces and bending moments; centre of gravity; types of equilibrium (stable, unstable, neutral); and simple machines, including pulley systems, mechanical advantage (MA), velocity ratio (VR) and efficiency; pressure in liquids; density and relative density. All relevant because ships were constantly subjected to force and stress from external and internal forces.
>
> Heat covers: temperature, thermometers, and thermocouples; transfer of heat (conduction, convection and radiation); coefficients of expansion; specific and latent heat; and properties of gases, including principles of refrigeration, which are particularly relevant to the variety of cargoes a ship might carry.
>
> The topic of light embraces laws of reflection and refraction, and their application to instruments used at sea, particularly the sextant.
>
> Also covered are the theory and laws of magnetism, pole and field strength, magnetic induction, deflection of a magnetised needle, and terrestrial magnetism – in particular in their guise as deviation and variation, to account for the difference between a compass and true direction or course.

The principles of electricity and nature of electric current include potential, resistance, current, capacitance, insulators, electric and magnetic fields.

We delved into the functions and uses of electrical measuring instruments, then of batteries and cells, and culminated in a bit of applied chemistry with corrosion, oxidisation, and extinguishing fire by foam and inert gas. JH Clough-Smith's *Applied Physics for Students of Nautical Science* proved an excellent text book.

I recognised the importance of mathematics at sea when following the procedure for calculating position lines from sun and star sights. The Nautical Mathematics syllabus covered algebra, logarithms, and basic calculus. Geometry was more comprehensive and delved into co-ordinate systems; equations of a circle, parabola, ellipse, hyperbola and straight lines. All had properties that applied to navigation. There was a deep focus on trigonometry, essential in traditional astronomical navigation calculations. The crucial importance of the haversine formula to determine the great circle distance between two points on a sphere given their latitudes and longitudes was explained. It was a special case of a more general formula in spherical trigonometry.

We revisited school trigonometry with basic sine, cosine, tangent exercises, moved on to compound angles, then to the application of the properties of a spherical triangle. Another of JH Clough-Smith's text books was absolutely invaluable, *An Introduction to Spherical Trigonometry*. We had to solve a spherical triangle by haversine formulae and *Norie's Tables* included a table of haversines. In fact, *Norie's Tables* was absolutely indispensable in the pre-satellite navigation and pre-programmable calculator eras. My own copy was well-thumbed in college, and certainly the ship's copy was used daily.

Weather was of immense importance to seafarers so knowledge of the basics of meteorology was essential. At sea, we used several instruments: the aneroid barometer showed air pressure, which the barograph recorded on a chart fixed to a rotating clockwork drum to show trends in air pressure. This helped the mariner to determine the approach of a depression or anticyclone, and to forecast associated weather affecting sea state and swell.

Wet and dry bulb thermometers were housed in a small version of a Stephenson screen. This white box with wooden latticed sides allowed free air flow but prevented penetration by direct sunlight. There was one sited on each bridge wing. Dew point temperature and the hygrometer were covered, the latter calculated relative humidity and was used to determine the dew point. This led to general principles of water vapour in the atmosphere, evaporation, condensation, and precipitation.

We learnt about the formation and classification of clouds, fog, and mist. From there it was a short hop to the characteristics of, and weather associated with, pressure systems and the passage of fronts (cold, warm, occluded) and hence to daily and seasonal changes in atmospheric pressure, prevailing winds, and the local and regional effects of heating and cooling, land and sea breezes, monsoons, and anabatic and katabatic winds.

The Beaufort wind scale and means of estimating wind direction and force at sea were important to a mariner bobbing about in his ship. Some of BSSM's ships had an anemometer. When held at arm's length, its cups spun round and measured wind speed, read off from a scale.

The types of weather messages available to the seafarer from the World Meteorological Organisation (WMO) were explained. We practised coding ship's weather reports using WMO's standard formats and the 'weather facsimile' machine. The best reference was the Meteorological Office's *Marine Observer's Handbook*, packed with everything we needed to know about weather.

The final element, which I dreaded most, was Signals – reading Morse code from a flashing light at a speed of six words per minute.

The overall syllabus across the spectrum of written examinations was extensive, and I found it interesting and relevant to my job as a deck officer. As exams loomed, like a lighthouse beam over the horizon, I felt content and confident that I'd comfortably achieve a pass in all topics.

Suddenly, exam week occurred! There were seven written papers: Nautical Physics; Nautical Mathematics; General Ship Knowledge; Practical Navigation; Principles of Navigation; Chartwork; and Meteorology. The first four of three hours duration, the latter three of two hours. Thanks to the expert instruction and guidance from Captain Moore, Captain Watson, and Captain Bole throughout our college phases, we felt ready to go and launched into examinations with gusto.

I feared Signals. To stand any chance of reading Morse code flashing light at six words per minute required unparalleled levels of concentration for the short duration of the exam. Fortunately, I managed to pass. Much relief!

I think we were notified of our written results before the oral exam, otherwise it would have wasted the examiner's time. Despite years of revising for and sitting 'O'-level, 'A'-level, and university exams, I felt trepidation about this final hurdle, the oral examination by the Principal Examiner of Masters and Mates, a hard-bitten old Master Mariner with decades of seafaring experience and expertise. This was the climax of our cadetship and our future career hung upon it. Scary.

The syllabus was broad. We were expected to prove our understanding of all instruments and equipment fitted on the bridge. This included meteorological instruments; azimuth mirror and pelorus to take bearings; and the care, winding, rating, and comparing of ship's chronometers. There was a focus on the sextant, particularly observing vertical and horizontal angles; reading a sextant 'on' and 'off the arc'; correcting a sextant's errors. The examiner asked questions on the practical use of electronic navigation aids, gyro compass, auto pilot, course recorder, and echo sounder.

Despite being certified EDHs, he expected us to explain methods of ascertaining the proof and SWLs of natural and synthetic fibres and wire ropes, rig purchases and the power gained by their use. Our knowledge of practical seamanship was tested regarding usage of common knots, hitches and bends; seizings; rackings; rope and chain stoppers; splicing of plaited and multistrand manila and synthetic fibre rope and wire rope; slinging a stage, rigging a bosun's chair and a pilot ladder. The examiner had various 'props' with which we showed our skill while explaining it to him.

As deck officers, we impressed with our description of duties prior to proceeding to sea, making harbour, entering a dock, berthing alongside quays or other ships, and securing to buoys. A thorough understanding of helm orders, conning the ship, the effects of propellers on ship's steering, stopping, going astern, manoeuvring, turning a steam-ship 'short round' (a method of turning a big ship around in a confined waterway), emergency manoeuvres, bringing a ship to single anchor in an emergency, and man overboard. The duties of the officer of the watch at sea, at anchor, and in port were also fair game for interrogation.

Archaic equipment cropped up: marking and use of a lead line; use and care of mechanical logs and sounding appliances; and the use and care of rocket and line throwing apparatus. I'd seen lead lines on all my ships but they were never used. Mechanical logs and sounding appliances were definitely museum pieces. I was sure our ships weren't equipped with rocket and line throwing apparatus. Luckily, I was quizzed only on the markings of a lead line and 'taking a sounding'.

The Principal Examiner delved into the syllabus of our lifeboat certificate. I supposed that was a check on knowledge retention as it was over a year since we'd completed the lifeboat course.

It was vital to possess a knowledge of the contents of *Merchant Shipping Notices* (M Notices) and the use of Admiralty *Weekly Notices to Mariners* and

Annual Summary of Notices to Mariners. Our answers didn't require great detail, rather a grasp of their contents illustrated with examples. Naturally, accurate knowledge of the IALA buoyage system was necessary.

Without warning, he asked me to 'box the compass', a basic skill for any sailor, knowing all 32 points of the compass, a 'point' being 11¼°. When your lookout reported a contact at 'three points on the starboard bow', you had to instantly relate that to 33¾° measured from the ship's head and search in the correct direction. Likewise, when calling to the Master to report another ship that may cause a problem, you referred to how many points on the bow it was. In ROR, a vessel's masthead and port and starboard sidelights were also described as visible when 'coming up at two points abaft her beam', that is 22½°.

I started to 'box the compass' from 'north', all the way round to 'north by west' to complete the 'circle' back at 'north'. It was important to concentrate as it was easy to lose your way during this recitation. Luckily, I must have impressed him, because he stopped me when I reached 'south east by east' – phew!

Table 12.1 Boxing the compass

North	East	South	West
North by east	East by south	South by west	West by north
North north east	East south east	South south west	West north west
North east by north	South east by east	South west by south	North west by west
North east	South east	South west	North west
North east by east	South east by south	South west by west	North west by north
East north east	South south east	West south west	North north west
East by north	South by east	West by south	North by west

The modern compass in use is divided into 360°, commencing with 000° (representing North), through 090° (East), to 180° (South), then 270° (West), then back to 000°. North was never, ever called 360° or 0°. It was always 000°.

The most dreaded subject, packed full of pitfalls and self-inflicted traps, was ROR. A full knowledge of the content and application of the International Regulations for Preventing Collisions at Sea and its Annexes was essential. The rest of the oral exam's content allowed for the odd small inaccuracy and the examiner gave you the chance to redeem yourself if you showed an otherwise sound understanding and gave a comprehensive explanation. ROR, however, was the most difficult element, as there was zero leeway for error. The pass mark was 100% and passing or failing the oral exam in toto depended on achieving it! This was where Captain Moore's daily interrogation paid dividends. His methods proved a resounding success.

Finally, the examiner could ask us questions arising from the written examinations, if a particular weakness had been detected. Of course, you had no idea if this might occur!

I was thrilled beyond description when the gruff, salty, old seahorse of a master mariner informed me that I'd passed the oral examination. It was the most exhilarating and proudest moment of my life. Since September 1980 I'd been striving for this climax, mainly at sea, but importantly in college. It had borne a rather delicious fruit! Now all I needed was another trip to complete the stipulated 24-month sea service and to be awarded my Second Mate's (Foreign-Going) Certificate of Competency.

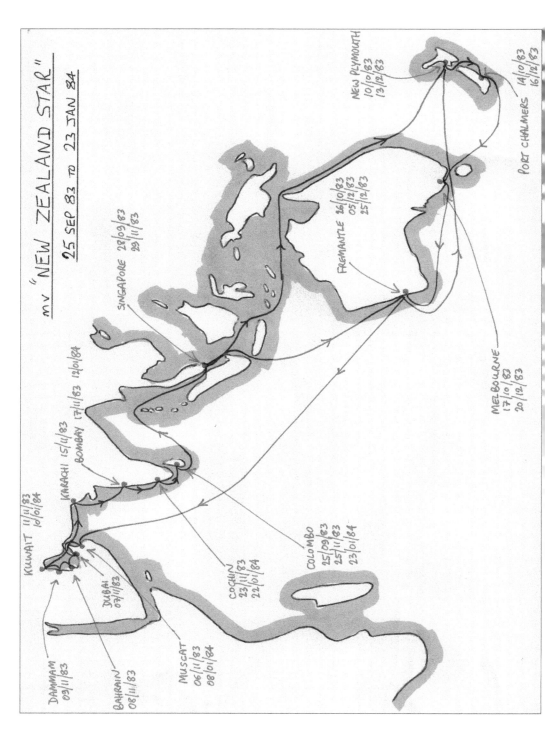

Fig 12.1 *New Zealand Star* voyage

12 Two Round Trips on *Kiwi Star*

Fig 12.2 *New Zealand Star*, aka *Kiwi Star* (Fotoflite)

Flushed with success in passing the written and oral exams, I now had to complete about four months to attain the required 24 months sea-time to gain my 2nd Mate's ticket.

After well-earned leave, I packed my bags and jetted off to Colombo, courtesy of Air Lanka It was an excellent flight and I was impressed with the Sri Lankan stewardesses' efficiency, attired in traditional brightly coloured, patterned sarees.

I was met and driven to Hotel Lanka Oberoi, a five-star hotel with 600 rooms, built in 1975. An enormous square atrium stretched high above me and immense 40-odd feet (12 m) long batiks hung from its upper reaches. A balcony around all four sides on each floor served the rooms. I was most impressed. It rather knocked the spots off the 'Bel' in New Brighton.

I spent the night in comfort and, after breakfast on 25 September 1983, the agent collected me and we drove to the port, a couple of miles (3.2 km) along Galle Road to the dock gates. Alongside was *New Zealand Star*. I gathered my luggage from the agent's car boot and clattered up the gangway. I was met by the Third Mate, Ian Dawson. He was on cargo watch on deck and spared a few minutes to welcome me and escort me up to my cabin. I was back on a big, fully refrigerated, cellular container ship.

Built and launched at Smith's Dock, Middlesbrough, in 1978, *New Zealand Star* joined the fleet in early 1979. She measured 554 feet (168.87 m) long, 82 feet (25.2 m) in the beam, with a draught of 31 feet (9.37 m), and weighed in at 17,082 gross and 8,930 net tons. In addition to her 721 container capacity, she had accommodation for up to six passengers, and was powered through the water by a Barclay Curle 6-cylinder Sulzer oil engine. She was also fitted with a 1,000 horsepower bow thruster, powered by its own diesel engine. This gave *New Zealand Star* an independent capability to manoeuvre in harbour and onto/from her berth without the assistance of tugs. Increasingly typical of new-builds, the engine room was designed to be unmanned overnight. The rostered Duty Engineer Officer was alerted to defects by an alarm panel fitted in his cabin.

Like all box boats, *New Zealand Star's* hatches were as wide as possible to maximise container capacity. Space between the holds' vertical bulkheads and ship's side contained ballast water tanks and an internal underdeck walkway (Burma Road). Similar to my previous box boats (*ACT 5* and *California Star*), this passageway ran right around the ship and doors and ladders provided access to the holds. The containers were inserted by crane into cell guides at the top of the hold. The crane continued to slide the container down the vertical rails of the cell guides deep down into the hold.

Refrigerated containers in the holds were kept at their required temperature when the Chief Refrigeration Engineer connected each box to the ship's cold-air system. The holds were also cooled to maintain a suitable ambient temperature. Reefer containers on deck were each fitted with a slimline clip-on fridge unit, powered by electrical cables connected to banks of sockets on deck.

New Zealand Star and her sister, the equally new *Australia Star*, were the third iteration of their names. Just as the Royal Navy had a history of same-named warships, so some shipping companies did similarly. The first *New Zealand Star* and *Australia Star* were built in 1935. I've previously mentioned the second *Australia Star* (1965) and its 300 ton Stülcken jumbo derrick. The second *New Zealand Star* was delivered in 1967 and, a decade later, was converted to a container ship, renamed *Wellington Star* and was still in service during my Blue Star era.

These two new vessels were self-discharging container ships built for the Australia–New Zealand–Persian Gulf service. Self-discharging meant they were equipped with three deck cranes to serve the five hatches forward of the accommodation and one crane for the two hatches aft. Each crane's 35 ton capacity was sufficient to lift-and-shift 20- and 40-foot containers.

In his second book of memoirs, *Away to Sea*, Captain Sandy Kinghorn described joining *New Zealand Star* as her first Master in late 1978. In the New Year, he took her on her maiden voyage from Teesside, transatlantic, through the Panama Canal, transpacific to New Plymouth. She was met by Edmund Vestey (Blue Star's owner) and Brian Muldoon (New Zealand's Prime Minister) and their wives. The Muldoons had launched the ship the previous year. Captain Kinghorn remained *New Zealand Star's* continuity Master for the next 2½ years.

After both ships entered service, the Iran–Iraq War broke out, which instantly halved their intended market in the Gulf. Nevertheless, trade continued throughout, with calls at Muscat, Dubai, Bahrain, Dammam (Saudi Arabia), and Kuwait. Passages to Kuwait occurred at night, at full speed, without navigation lights. The rumble of artillery fire between Iran and Iraq was heard in the port of Kuwait. *New Zealand Star's* maiden trade voyage yielded some firsts: first Blue Star ship into the port of Umm Qasr, Iraq; first ship to use the new portainer cranes in Bahrain; and first ship to resume delivery of refrigerated containers into Iranian ports since the political unrest began.

After unpacking my kit, I changed into uniform and introduced myself to the Mate. John Mockett was a senior Chief Mate and *Kiwi Star's* continuity Mate. He was most welcoming and explained that as an (almost) newly qualified Third Mate, I would be watchkeeping 8–12s for the duration. He arranged for John Tolman, an O/T a year junior to me, to show me the ship. I also met the Old Man in his cabin. Captain Paul Mathews was a senior Master who had commanded a variety of Blue Star and Booth Line ships. He was now *New Zealand Star's* continuity Master.

John Tolman was an engaging West Countryman. Well-spoken, with a marked Devonian accent, he hailed from Teignmouth. We instantly got on well as we toured from stem to stern. *Kiwi Star* had a similar lay-out to the other box boats in which I'd served: large accommodation block; engine room beneath; propeller shaft-tunnel through the aft holds; a 'Burma Road' along each side for access to the holds; and holds fitted with cell guides into which the containers were lowered and held during the voyage; deck hatches strengthened to carry up to three-high stacks of containers.

The superstructure's decks were: offices and duty mess on the main deck; crew cabins above; surmounted by the galley sandwiched between the crew mess (port side) and officers' mess (starboard side). Next deck were the officers' en-suite cabins, above which was the passenger cabins deck. We carried no passengers during my trip. Then the spacious accommodation for the Master and Chief Engineer of day cabin, night cabin, and en-suite bathroom. Finally, the bridge deck, which included the radio shack, occupied by the often rather odd folks trained as Radio Officers (Sparks). Topping the lot was the monkey island, a nice deck area for sunbathing provided you found a lee from the strong headwind created as the ship powered through the sea.

Tour complete, John and I went to the mess for lunch where I met most of the other officers. There were a couple of familiar faces: Steve Moore and Freddie Fox. I'd sailed on *California Star* with both and they had since been promoted to Third and Fourth Engineers respectively. It was always great to sail again with old shipmates, although it didn't happen to me too often.

Chief Engineer Salvatore Guiseppe 'Joe' Astorina was a big bear of a man with a thick, bushy, black beard. An Australian immensely proud of his Italian heritage, he took no bullshit from anyone and spoke in a very direct, commanding style. Once you got to know him, Joe was a likeable and humorous bloke, but beware his short-fused temper and prepare for his wrath.

New Zealand Star sailed from Colombo in the late afternoon. It was an easy departure, straight off the berth and exit between the breakwaters on either side. When clear and safe to do so, a sharp, nearly hairpin turn to port, to pick up an almost southerly course along the west coast of Sri Lanka. All along that coast were a myriad small fishing boats, almost dugout canoes, manned by one or two men. Our track took us offshore from this peril but it was a feature of every approach to, and departure from, Indian subcontinent ports.

That night, I took the watch from Pete Dixon, the Second Mate. Pete was a likeable Bristolian, tall, lanky, bearded. I soon realised that Pete, Ian, and I got on famously as bridge watchkeepers. Of course, it was a serious business to take over the responsibility for a 17,000 ton, 554 feet (168 m) long container ship. But there was usually an element of light-heartedness and humour at our watch handovers.

This first watch was quite different from my solo watches on *Starman Anglia*. It was a question of scale. *Kiwi Star* was a significantly larger, faster, heavier beast. The bridge was appreciably higher above the waterline and further aft. Visibility ahead was a little restricted due to the containers stacked on deck. The bridge was also a much larger 'room', with generous space across the front and the chart table set at the back. Equally, the bridge wings were more spacious. Once I got into my routine, I found my pacing athwartships was longer, especially with the bridge wing doors opened.

Pete guided me around the bridge before departure from Colombo so I knew where all the tools of my trade were located. I felt comfortable as the bridge equipment was virtually the same as that on my previous ships.

It was a moonlit night that first watch. The bridge (or wheelhouse) was in total darkness, other than the luminescent glow of equipment (gyro compass, helm, radar). This made it easier to keep a good visual lookout as there were no misleading reflections in the bridge windows or backscatter from our own lights. The AB on watch was on the port bridge wing. I re-established my routine of regularly fixing position by radar and visual bearings of lighthouses as we raced down the coast at 20 knots. I extrapolated our estimated position (EP) for the next two fixes. When plotted, it was pleasing that the process worked.

When *Kiwi Star* was affected by tidal stream or current, observed position differed from the EP. A bit of chartwork was required to determine the next EP more accurately by taking account of these effects. Course- and speed-made-good were calculated and applied. I had to tweak the autopilot a degree or two either side of the planned course to regain the track and then adjust again to remain on track. While all this was going on, I was conscious of maintaining a thorough lookout by radar and visually. It wasn't good practice to rely entirely on the AB lookout to detect and report surface contacts.

I was required to complete the Deck Log, a legal document for use in the event of an unfortunate incident. This entailed noting alterations of course/speed and anything else noteworthy. Once per watch a gyro error was calculated. This was important because the gyro fed the autopilot, the 'azimuth circles' on the bridge wings used to take visual bearings, and the radar. Any error had to be applied to your readings. The most commonly used was to compare an observed bearing of a celestial body with its calculated true bearing. Any difference (either high or low) was the gyro error and was noted in the Gyro Error Book. At the end of the watch, the Deck Log was compiled and included a record of: navigational and pilotage events; ship's position at regular intervals; behaviour of the vessel and effect of heavy seas; verification of compass error; and basic meteorological data.

For the meteorology, wind speed was noted using a handheld anemometer and wind direction by observing the waves, as wind direction was generally perpendicular to the wave front. Dry and wet bulb temperatures were taken from the Stephenson Screen on both bridge wings. The aneroid barometer, a neat little grey box fixed to the bulkhead near the chart table, showed air pressure. General weather and sea state observations were made. The most common description was 'slight sea, low swell, cloudy, fine and clear', often abbreviated to SS, LS, CFC.

In port, the Deck Log recorded inspections, visits of officials and authorities, cargo work, taking in bunkers (fuel), fresh water and stores.

For me, the last 20 minutes or so of a watch was the busiest time, with the Deck Log to complete, navigation, radar monitoring, keeping a good lookout, and preparing to handover to Ian.

In Blue Star, we were discouraged from idle chatter with the AB lookout. It was a distraction from maintaining your own constant lookout. I was inside the bridge, he was on either one of the bridge wings and disappeared below for the legally permitted half-hour smoko at night. During the day, my AB worked on deck and I was on my own, except for occasional visits by Mate or Master.

It was about three days to Singapore. After rounding the southern end of Sri Lanka, *Kiwi Star* headed east towards Sumatra, those pesky fishing boats increasingly astern of us. Leaving Banda Aceh to starboard, we entered the Malacca Strait. A south-south-east course took the ship through the Strait, similarly alive with small fishing boats which became even more troublesome as the Strait narrowed off Malacca itself.

New Zealand Star berthed at Singapore's container port on 28 September. We weren't going to remain for long as, at that time, Singapore was the fastest and most efficient container terminal in the world, with an hourly rate of some 50 or more container movements per hour. I'm sure that rate has been substantially overhauled in the four decades since, but to me it was an impressive speed. As Singapore operated portainer cranes, our own deck cranes were unlashed from their cradles and swung outboard, perpendicular to the ship. This gave the portainer drivers clear access to discharge and load containers in our holds. Depending on weather and sea state, the cranes were re-stowed in their cradles before departure or immediately after clearing the port.

Singapore Roads was invariably full of anchored merchantmen waiting to enter the port, with many small fishing boats and the constant movement of a variety of ships into, from, around, and through these confined waters.

You had to remain alert at all times as apparently harmless traffic suddenly caused a risk of collision. Prompt and decisive action could avoid a potential incident but may have caused another with a different vessel. It was a relief to escape the Roads and gain the relative quiet of the Java Sea.

We headed south-east and passed between Belitung (to port) and Borneo (to starboard), both well over the horizon. Indonesia's archipelago formed a barrier between the Java Sea and the Indian Ocean, although there were several 'gaps'. Those most used by merchantmen were the Sunda and Lombok Straits. I'd transited Sunda on *Mandama* about 15 months before. This time we used Lombok, which was about 37 miles (60 km) long, between Bali and Lombok Islands. At its northern end, it was 25 miles (40 km) across, but narrowed to 12 miles (20 km) at the southern end. Its minimum depth was 820 feet (250 m). Of course, there were more pesky little fishing boats in and around the Strait, but otherwise our transit was trouble free.

In the very north-east part of the Indian Ocean, we headed east-south-east until we passed between Timor and Ashmore Reef. There, we altered course to east-north-east into the Timor Sea. We skirted the Tiwi Islands (north of Darwin), and adjusted to an easterly course through the Arafura Sea.

New Zealand Star approached Booby Island, detected first by radar and later visually. So-named by several European explorers, including Captain Cook, for its large population of booby birds and its resultant widespread stain of glistening white guano, reflecting the tropical sunshine. This area was such a hazard to mariners in the 19th century that a store of provisions was established on Booby Island for shipwrecked sailors and in 1890 a lighthouse was built.

This was the entrance to Torres Strait, a particularly challenging passage between Cape York, the northernmost extremity of mainland Australia, and Papua New Guinea. Miles Hordern's excellent book, *Passage to Torres Strait*, describes its history and the navigators, mutineers, castaways, and beachcombers who've left their mark on the Strait.

> Torres Strait was named after the Spanish navigator Luís Vaz de Torres, who sailed through the strait in 1606. An important international sea lane, it links the Arafura Sea and Gulf of Carpentaria to the Coral Sea. Torres Strait is the interface between the diurnal (daily) tidal regime of the Indian Ocean and the semi-diurnal (twice-daily) regime of the Pacific. This produces a highly variable and complex

tidal system of strong tidal streams (up to eight knots in places) and rapidly changing tidal levels. The tide could be rising in one location yet be falling close by. Occasional local seasonal adverse weather conditions further complicate conditions. In addition, there are very shallow depths (23–49 feet, 7–15 m), a maze of about 580 coral reefs, and 274 islands, of which only 17 are permanently inhabited. Large submarine sand dunes constantly migrate across the seafloor.

Given its complexity, Torres Strait was hazardous to navigate and embarking a Torres Strait pilot was strongly recommended for all large vessels. In 1991, compulsory pilotage was introduced for vessels over 230 feet (70 m) in length and loaded tankers transiting Torres Strait and the Inner Route of the Great Barrier Reef (IRGBR).

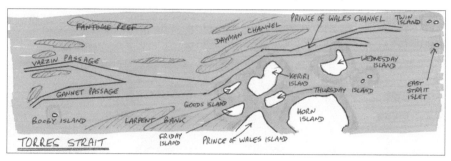

Fig 12.3 Torres Strait

We steamed through Varzin Passage, slightly deeper than the adjacent Gannet Passage. These two routes joined at the start of Prince of Wales Channel. The pilot boat came alongside at the pilot boarding station, off Goods Island. The pilot clambered up the ladder and was escorted to the bridge. He guided *New Zealand Star* through Prince of Wales Channel and on to Twin Island at the eastern end of Torres Strait, some 40 miles (64 km) from Booby Island. There, the pilot disembarked to be replaced by a Great Barrier Reef pilot.

I was fascinated to equate the chart, littered with hazards (shoals, reefs, islands, strong currents, and rips), with the reality viewed from the bridge. To the casual observer, the panorama bathed in the heat of a tropical sun seemed so benign: plenty of water for miles in all directions, interspersed with low-lying islands, and only a few fishing boats. Meanwhile, beneath lurked all those unseen dangers to the naïve mariner.

I hurriedly finished a letter to my parents for the Torres Strait pilot to post ashore, with its unique postmark.

Fig 12.4 Unique Torres Strait Pilots' post-mark

Our course was set to parallel the Queensland coast on the IRGBR. We took great care to navigate within the confines of this route to avoid not only the visible low-lying islands but also the invisible extent of the Reef.

The Great Barrier Reef, the world's largest living coral structure, stretches over 1,000 nautical miles (1,852 km) along Queensland's coastline. Almost its entire length is protected by the Great Barrier Reef Marine Park, established in 1975. The Inner Route passed between the mainland and all that delicate and highly sensitive mass of coral. It was extremely narrow in places, with reef edges only three cables (600 yards/556 m) from a vessel's track, but sometimes the nearest reef was several miles distant. Despite the complexity of the route, full sea speed was the norm, although it was wise to have an anchor ready to let go.

The route was well marked with lighthouses and beacons. Visual bearings were the priority for position fixing, sometimes combined with a radar range. I didn't find my watches particularly taxing as traffic was light compared to other major seaways I'd experienced. I was permanently aware of the close proximity of coral reef just below the surface, sometimes unnervingly close. The tidal stream wasn't significant and the weather, wind, and sea state were benign, as it wasn't yet cyclone season, so maintaining the ship's track on the chart was relatively easy.

It was rewarding to steam the reciprocal route taken by Captain James Cook in 1770. His influence was visible everywhere on the chart.

> Captain Cook observed and charted countless physical features: bays, headlands, points, peaks, islands, reefs. Some were named for their resemblance to a particular shape, others due to his circumstances at the time. Cook's *Endeavour* struck a reef, which he named Endeavour Reef. Badly damaged, the ship limped along the coast in search of a safe haven to effect repairs. Cook found the mouth of a river and named it Endeavour River. His crew spent seven weeks repairing *Endeavour* and replenishing their food and water. Years later, the coastal settlement of Cooktown was established there as a port for the nearby Palmer River goldfield. Mount Cook dominated the town, and the local authority was Shire of Cook. Other examples are Cape York (named for the Duke of York) and Cape Tribulation (where *Endeavour* scraped her hull on a reef a few hours before hitting Endeavour Reef).

It took a day's steaming to complete the 450 nautical miles (833 km) from exiting the Prince of Wales Channel to Cairns, where the pilot disembarked. I had no idea that, 26 years later, I would settle in Cairns, having been headhunted to transfer to the Royal Australian Navy – but that's another story.

New Zealand Star continued south, through Whitsunday Passage and Capricorn Channel, on the Tropic of Capricorn. Onwards past Coppersmith Reef and into the Coral Sea, from where it was an unremarkable three-day passage south-east across a benign Tasman Sea, direct to New Plymouth on North Island, New Zealand.

New Plymouth appeared on the horizon. Mount Taranaki, an 8,262 feet (2,518 m) conical volcano in Egmont National Park and the second-highest point on North Island, dominated the city and its surroundings. As we closed the coast, Mount Taranaki loomed ever higher in the background, while other features appeared in the foreground. I compared the chart with real life, married up Paritutu Rock (511 feet/156 m high), the remnants of a volcano's crater and, almost adjacent, a white chimney as tall as Paritutu. These were the most significant physical features of New Plymouth.

> New Plymouth wasn't well known to non-seafarers but it was the largest city in Taranaki province. It had been named after Plymouth in Devon, from whence the first English settlers had arrived. Richard

'Dicky' Barrett, a merchant seaman, set up a trading-post and, in 1828, he negotiated a treaty to purchase land from the local Maori to attract migrants from south-west England. It's tempting to claim that All Black Beauden Barrett and his brothers are the founder's descendants, as they all hail from New Plymouth. But my limited research revealed no such lineage.

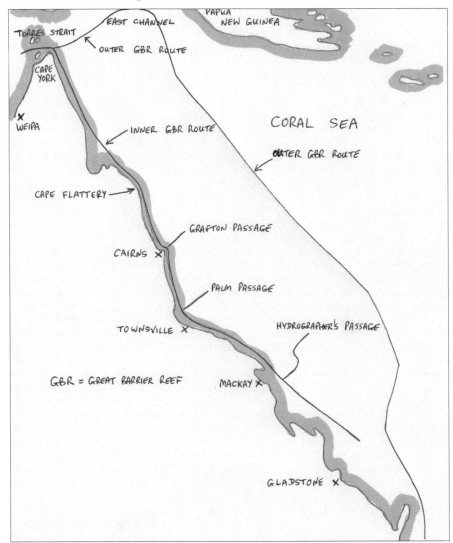

Fig 12.5 Inner and Outer Great Barrier Reef routes

The city was hardly picturesque. Its wide streets couldn't be described as smart boulevards. Houses were usually single storey, clapperboard or planked, occasionally brick-built. Ample shops supplied the population's requirements, but there was an overriding scruffy, industrial air. I bought a postcard which captured New Plymouth's essence: Paritutu Rock and the chimney dominating the skyline, the port, the adjacent industrial zone and, in the foreground, *New Zealand Star* departing. Blue Star ships featured on the odd postcard in New Zealand. I had previously bought one each of *Gladstone Star* and *Mandama* or *Mahsuri* under Timaru's meat-loaders.

Fig 12.6 Postcard showing *New Zealand Star* departing New Plymouth

New Plymouth's Port Taranaki was the only deep-sea port on New Zealand's west coast. It exported crude and petroleum products, methanol, liquefied petroleum gas, and logs; it imported grains, feed, fertiliser, and fuel. Approaches to the harbour were easy and accessed directly from seaward. No messing about with buoyed channels and turns. The roadstead was clear, the anchorage unoccupied. Inside the breakwaters, the pilot turned *Kiwi Star* around and comfortably positioned her on Blyde Wharf, ship's head (bow) towards the harbour entrance and the sea.

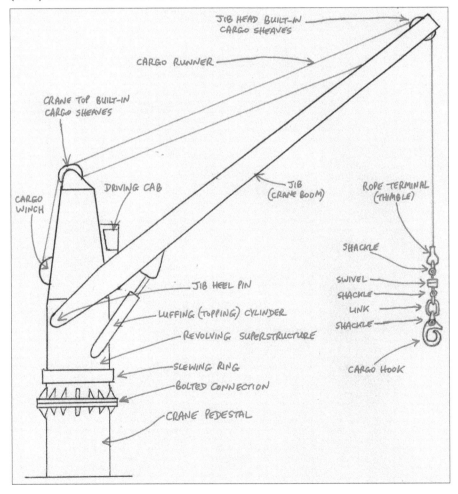

Fig 12.7 Deck crane

The port didn't have portainers, so the wharfies (dockers) used our deck cranes to work cargo. In the 1980s, wharfies rigidly adhered to their stipulated working hours of 0800–1700, with specified smokos and lunchbreaks. Our cargo watches, monitoring container movements on and off the ship, were therefore pretty easy and certainly not as challenging or hectic as in Singapore. It allowed us to go up the road in the evening to drink beer, shoot pool, and talk rubbish in several pubs. Kiwis were friendly talkative folks, certainly in the pubs, but their mangling of vowels concentrated the mind, especially as the evening wore on!

Fig 12.8 Our cranes used for loading cargo. John and Pete in white boilersuits on hatch cover

Fig 12.9 View into centre hold. Cell guides visible from top to bottom

We departed New Plymouth on 12 October. Hugging the coast to port, we rounded Mount Taranaki and entered South Taranaki Bight. The coast curved away from us as we steamed south-east to Cook Strait, which connects the Tasman Sea to the South Pacific Ocean. I'd transited the Strait on *ACT 5* three years before, stopping in Wellington. Not this time, though.

> Captain Cook was the first European to sail through the strait in 1770. Cook Strait is recognised as one of the most dangerous and unpredictable waters in the world, with a complex tidal flow. The main lunar tide component (about twice per day, or semi-diurnal) circulates anti-clockwise around New Zealand, and is out of phase at each end of the Strait. On the Pacific Ocean side, high tide occurs five hours before that on the Tasman Sea side. So, one side is at high tide, while the other is at low tide. This difference in sea level yields tidal currents up to five knots across Cook Strait. Both coasts were steep cliffs, with South Island's more cluttered with islands, underwater rocks, and entrances to the sounds, which makes the bottom topography quite irregular and creates violent eddies.

New Zealand Star survived unscathed and she was also unhampered by the cross-strait ferry traffic between Wellington (North Island) and Picton

(South Island). She rounded Cape Campbell and headed south-south-west along the coast of South Island. We passed Christchurch and its port, Lyttelton, tucked away in Pegasus Bay and hidden by Banks Peninsula, both of which had an historic involvement in Antarctic exploration. In central Christchurch stood a statue of Captain Scott sculpted by his widow, Kathleen. Scott and Shackleton used Lyttelton as the departure point for their respective expeditions. Lyttelton was also historically a port frequented by Blue Star Line ships.

Progressing down the coast, Timaru was at the south end of Canterbury Bight. Now in my fourth year with BSSM, I was revisiting ports and coastlines I'd seen before. Comfortably familiar. I was becoming an 'old hand' in my own way.

Now, however, I entered new territory. We closed the coast to approach Otago Harbour. Leaving the breakwater/mole to starboard, *New Zealand Star* rounded the spit which encroached the harbour at Aramoana, forcing her to pass close to the Harrington Point gun emplacements, built in the 1890s against a backdrop of panic that the Russian Empire might choose to invade New Zealand.

Fig 12.10 At Port Chalmers, looking for'ard down Otago Harbour

Otago Harbour was a beautiful stretch of water, culminating in Dunedin at its distant south-western end. It was generally navigable water, with numerous small bays and coves, which separated Otago Peninsula from the mainland. It was created from the drowned remnants of the giant Dunedin Volcano, which last erupted 10 million years ago. Both sides of the harbour rose from the water's edge as verdant hill ranges. After the narrows at Harrington Point, the channel followed the western side of the harbour, as the opposite side was too shallow due to sandbanks (exposed at low water). It was a delight to glide through this lovely scene under blue sky and sunshine on a merchantman.

Fig 12.11 Looking aft down George Street, Port Chalmers towards Dunedin in the distance

Port Chalmers was 5 miles (8 km) along this natural harbour, as further progress for large vessels was barred by two islands (Goat and Quarantine) on a line between Port Chalmers and Portobello. Seven miles (11 km) beyond lay Dunedin. Like most people, I believed it was a corruption of Dundee and Edinburgh. Not so. Rather, it derived from the Gaelic name for Edinburgh, and had been founded by the Lay Association of the Free Church of Scotland in 1848. After it had been designated as a city, many Scots emigrated to it, compounded by the Otago gold rush of the 1860s. It was home to the University of Otago, New Zealand's oldest university. Port Chalmers was established at a similar time.

On 14 October, *Kiwi Star* berthed at the Port of Otago, the primary exporting port of southern South Island. The old wharves were redeveloped into container wharves in 1971. The pilot turned the ship through 180° and berthed her so the stern pointed directly along Port Chalmers' main street, while the view from the bridge was back down Otago Harbour. It was truly picturesque. One of the most beautiful ports I'd visited.

Even though we berthed almost in the high street, there was insufficient time to go up the road as we sailed after a handful of hours. Retracing our track through Otago Harbour was enchanting, with the same wonderful weather. Exiting into the Pacific Ocean, *New Zealand Star* turned hard to starboard and headed south-west along the coast, rounded the southern tip of South Island and passed through Foveaux Strait between Bluff (to starboard) and Stewart Island (to port). From there, it was almost a west-north-west course across the Tasman Sea under benign weather and sea state conditions.

With mainland Australia over the visual and radar horizon, we rounded the Furneaux Group, islands off Tasmania's north-east coast, and entered Bass Strait. On making landfall at Wilson's Promontory, our course was adjusted towards the pilot station off the entrance to Port Phillip Bay. The pilot guided the ship through the tricky entrance, with its hazardous tidal streams and rips, and into the Bay itself. We followed the buoyed channel to Melbourne's container wharves in the mouth of the River Yarra.

Hard to believe that it was almost exactly three years ago since my first visit to Melbourne on my first trip to sea on *ACT 5*. This time, a longer stay in port enabled me to take a taxi up the road and to stroll around the beautiful city of Melbourne astride the banks of the Yarra. Bourke Street and the city centre were alive with shoppers and office workers on another lovely summer's day. The wide boulevards had tramway tracks down the centre. Melbourne's tramway system opened in 1885 and by 1890 was the world's most extensive.

Flinders Street Station, on the corner of Flinders and Swanston Streets, was as impressive as ever. The row of indicator clocks above the main entrance showed the next departure for each line. Below them, the wide staircase led up to the station entrance. A couple of Melbourne sayings referred to these features – meet you 'under the clocks' or 'on the steps'.

Between the Station and Federation Square, I crossed the Yarra via Princes Bridge and strolled along the riverbank's wide promenade, the river to my left and the many rowing clubhouses to my right. There always seemed to be folks rowing on the Yarra.

On the opposite bank loomed Melbourne Cricket Ground (the famous MCG) and the adjacent venue for tennis' Australian Open. Leaving the river behind me, I walked in King's Domain, part of the vast parkland on the Yarra's west bank with Alexandra Gardens to the north and the Royal Botanic Gardens to the south. After passing Government House (official residence of the Governor of Victoria), I found myself in the Botanic Gardens. My fetish for such beautiful, tranquil venues was renewed. I made my way to the totemic Shrine of Remembrance, the magnificent stone edifice originally built to honour Victoria's men and women who served in World War I. Officially dedicated in 1934, it now functions as a memorial to all Australians who serve in any war and is Australia's largest war memorial.

After a couple of days in Melbourne, *New Zealand Star* steamed through Port Phillip Bay and exited between Point Lonsdale and Portsea into Bass Strait. After disembarking the pilot, the ship headed south-west along Victoria's coast, rounded Cape Otway and I braced myself for the Great Australian Bight. I recalled the tumultuous violent storm of the eastbound passage on *Mandama* about 18 months before. Fortunately, weather, sea, and swell were kinder as we went west-north-west across the Bight.

It was a long haul from Melbourne to Muscat, some 7,600 nautical miles (1,4075 km) at 20 knots meant about 16 days at sea. After rounding the south-west corner of Western Australia, *Kiwi Star* struck out north-west across the Indian Ocean to make landfall at Ras al-Hadd, the easternmost point of Oman.

My 8–12 watches settled into their, now customary, routine. Apart from the short coastal passage around south-west Australia, it was all open ocean and largely devoid of traffic. I became more comfortable with watchkeeping, but wary of becoming complacent. The novelty hadn't waned.

Pete and I became proficient with a sextant. We took morning sun-sights, then used *Norie's Tables* and the *Nautical Almanac* to calculate our longitude. Noon was calculated exactly. This 'meridian passage' occurred when the sun's bearing was directly north (or south, depending on your latitude), therefore at its zenith (greatest altitude (angle above the horizon) for that day. Shortly before meridian passage, Pete and I continually monitored the sun's altitude by sextant. With practice, I learnt to judge when it had attained its zenith, recorded the time and the sextant altitude. The calculations that followed yielded our latitude at noon. The longitude position line from earlier that morning was then transferred, using our run (ship's course and speed) to where it crossed our calculated latitude. This yielded our true position at noon. This method of calculating an observer's position on earth (the Marcq Saint-Hilaire, after the French admiral who first proposed it in 1875) was adopted by all navigators and seafarers.

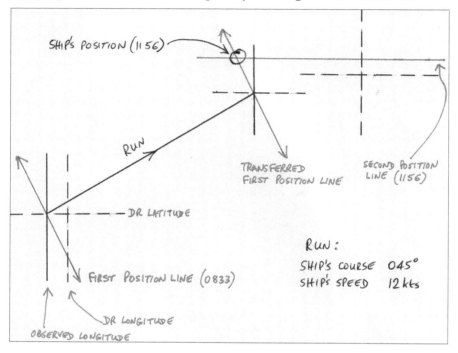

Fig 12.12 Marcq Saint-Hilaire method

Figure 12.12 shows the morning sight at 0833, for the sextant altitude of the sun to calculate the first position line. The second position line results from the sextant altitude of the sun exactly at the time of its meridian passage (Mer-Pass) at 1156. The morning (0833) position line is transferred to the same time as the Mer-Pass (1156) position line using ship's run (course 045°, speed 12 kts from 0833 to 1156). The intersection of the two position lines yields the ship's position at the time of Mer-Pass (1156). To get the 1200 (noon) position, a 4-minute run is applied. For greater detail than in my grossly simplified explanation, see *Munro's Navigation* or any comparable textbook. It was gratifying to do 'real navigation' by sextant at sea and prove that the method taught and practised at Liverpool Polytechnic worked.

Using today's noon position and yesterday's noon position, Pete calculated the day's run (mileage and average speed over the previous 24 hours) and created the 'noon chit'. This also included fuel consumption and fuel remaining, courtesy of the engineers, and the ETA at our next port. Pete then delivered the noon chit to Captain Mathews.

As I was at a bit of a loose end in the afternoons, John and I helped out with Ian's 3rd Mate responsibilities for lifeboats, life rafts, safety equipment, lifejackets, and associated kit. Ian's 12–4 watches were not very harmonious for tending to these important items. Ian and John worked together during the morning. When I joined John after lunch, he explained our tasks.

We emptied and scrubbed out the lifeboats, checked that their complement of rations and equipment were correct, in good condition, and in date. We applied similar diligence to checking the life rafts, albeit limited as they were cocooned in their protective shell until launched in an emergency. There were sundry other tasks, so we were fairly busy most afternoons. It was good to work on deck in shorts and T-shirt, in the sunshine, under blue sky, in the middle of the Indian Ocean. Life really was peachy.

One of the 8–12 watchkeeper's perks was 'meal relief' for the 4–8 watchkeeper in the evening. Usually, the Mate was 4–8 and the Third Mate 8–12. As a senior and highly qualified officer, the Mate had dinner at the correct time, which meant the Third Mate popped up to the bridge for a half-hour to allow the Mate to go below. Continuing this tradition, I did meal reliefs for Pete throughout the trip. It wasn't too onerous, but it meant my own dinner was a little more hurried than I'd have liked before going up for that evening's 8–12. Such was life.

My proficiency in using radar increased with each watch. No digital, LED, or colour displays in my day. Radar was basically an analogue cathode ray tube (like the old television sets), with an orange 'picture' on a black background. It didn't interface with other electronic systems, except for the gyro compass and the ship's log (speedometer). There was a certain quaint charm in painstakingly tweaking control knobs manually, eyes glued to the hood covering the display screen, gradually adjusting the radar picture to achieve the optimum.

The radar hood was used during daylight as it was impossible to see anything on the screen in natural light. A wide ring was clipped to the top of the display, with a pair of holes with rubber flaps for your hands to fit through. This was necessary to plot a target with a chinagraph pencil, a pencil with a hardened wax core rather than the lead found in ordinary pencils. In order to see your little line of 'x's, the hood also had a light ring to illuminate your chinagraph marks. The chinagraph plot was used to calculate and determine the target's course, speed, and, critically, its CPA. Fixed to the ring was the rubber hood itself, its top shaped to accommodate the average-sized nose and to enable your eyes to focus on the display during daylight, otherwise the screen was unintelligible. Those were the days! Radar technology and sophistication have evolved immensely since the 1980s.

As we continued north-westwards, we crossed the Tropic of Capricorn and the Equator in turn. The Indian Ocean became the Arabian Sea and then Gulf of Oman as *Kiwi Star* closed the Strait of Hormuz, gateway to the Persian Gulf. Ras al-Hadd marked the narrowing of the seaway. Traffic density increased as merchantmen, particularly oil tankers, and dhows approached or departed the Gulf.

We maintained a north-west track along the Omani coast, rounded the island of al-Jazirah, and adjusted to a westerly course. The entrance to Muscat, more correctly Mina Sultan Qaboos (Port Sultan Qaboos) at Mutrah, was as spectacularly beautiful as on my previous visits. The Corniche, backed by old buildings, shops, and the Souk, was constantly thronged with traffic. Rocky hills rose up behind, with shadows emphasising the deep crevices in the precipitous rock face, all under brilliant sunshine and blue sky. The Corniche wound its way to the east and then north, past al-Riyam Park, a favourite picnic place for Muscat families. Just visible at the tip of the peninsula was Muscat's Old Watch Tower.

On 6 November we spent only about four hours in Muscat, then departed for the hectic schedule of ports around the Gulf. We headed north-north-west and I was lucky enough to 'drive' solo at night through the Strait of Hormuz, one of the busiest shipping lanes in the world. The traffic separation scheme meant that as we rounded the northern tip of Musandam Peninsula (Oman), we were on the Iranian side, belting along at 20 knots. Merchant shipping traffic was sparse but I was wary of ill-lit dhows plying their trade, crossing willy-nilly in any direction, unaware of and oblivious to the ROR.

At the apex of Hormuz, *Kiwi Star* was overtaken by a faster container ship. The speed difference wasn't great, so it was a lengthy process as she hauled out and overtook me on my starboard side. I knew my ROR: Rule 13 applied to 'vessels in sight of one another' and stated, 'any vessel overtaking any other shall keep out of the way of the vessel being overtaken', so she was obliged to give way to me throughout overtaking; as also dictated by Rule 16 (action by give-way vessel); and, according to Rule 17 (action by stand-on vessel), I continued to stand on and maintain course and speed.

I monitored her approach on the radar and by taking compass bearings from the bridge wing. I knew she was coming up on me 'from a direction more than 22½° (or two points) abaft my beam', so she could see only my white stern light. I was on my mettle throughout as a moment's lapse could prove disastrous when complicated by those pesky dhows. It made the watch go quicker as I constantly monitored the situation. She overhauled us at about 300 yards (275 m) off my starboard side.

As she drew ahead, her aspect changed such that I lost sight of her red port sidelight, replaced by a view of her white stern light because I had fallen astern of her to more than 22½° abaft her beam. This 22½° marked the boundary of the arc of visibility between sidelights (and her masthead light) and stern light, specified in Rule 21 which defined the arcs of visibility of a ship's navigation lights.

When she was at a safe distance ahead, probably about 400 yards (365 m), she adjusted her course to port to regain her nav-track directly in front of me. I happily observed her white stern-light amid her illuminated poop deck and accommodation. This ensemble of lights gradually faded as she pulled clear over the next couple of hours. I was pretty busy and pleased to hand over an uncluttered visual and radar picture to Ian. I went below quite tired but adrenalin still coursed through me so it took a while to fall asleep in my comfy bunk.

Fig 12.13 *New Zealand Star* berthed at Port Rashid, Dubai

The next few days were a whirlwind of bridge watches in heavy traffic, entering and leaving ports, cargo watches on deck, and limited sleep. Our stops in port were exceedingly brief, four hours each or eight at most.

We knocked off Dubai, Manama, Dammam, and finally Kuwait on 11 November. Of course, there were no opportunities to go up the road in any of these ports. Although Port Rashid (Dubai) was almost adjacent to the city centre, time was just too short for a visit.

Bahrain was a flat, arid archipelago about 15 miles (25 km) off the coast of Saudi Arabia. A causeway was under construction to connect this island nation to Saudi Arabia. The port was in Manama, the capital. Dammam was a swanky, relatively new, Saudi Arabian port that, like most in the Gulf, was miles from the city itself – not that I fancied visiting it after the rigmarole of my Jeddah experience on *Mandama*. Finally, it was another short hop to the north end of the Gulf for Kuwait.

All these Gulf ports were of relatively new construction, largely on reclaimed land. Brilliant white concrete expanses dazzled in the piercing hot sunshine. All the wharfies were migrant labour from the Indian subcontinent (usually the foot soldiers), the Philippines and South Korea. The Filipinos and Koreans were in supervisory posts or straddle-carrier drivers and portainer-crane operators. I think they all lived in somewhat squalid camp/dormitory conditions either within or immediately adjacent to the port and were bussed in and out for their shifts.

On the chart, every Emirate had its own port and airport, to emphasise its emerging oil-driven economy and thriving independence, I supposed. Hence, there were extremely short hops between each of them, until the longer passage around the north tip of Qatar to Bahrain and Dammam.

The Gulf itself was shallow, with a maximum depth of 295 feet (90 m) and an average depth 164 feet (50 m). Given the increasing size of oil tankers in particular, and the volume of such traffic, there was plenty of scope for collisions. Various small islands helped complicate navigation. The Persian Gulf and its coastal areas were the world's largest single source of petroleum, including the world's largest offshore oilfield. Large gas reserves had also been discovered and developed, so innumerable rigs (gas or oil) cluttered the Gulf, and created a further hazard to navigation.

When previously in the Gulf on *Mandama*, I spent limited time doubled-up on the bridge. As 8–12 watchkeeper on *New Zealand Star*, I took an acute interest in studying the charts. Pete Dixon's nav-track negotiated the passages between ports the length and breadth of the Gulf, wove among clusters of rigs and avoided treacherous shoals. These dangers were clearly marked on Admiralty charts and I found it was easy to relate the 'real world' beyond the bridge windows to the chart and the radar picture.

In daylight, the rigs were distinct black structures on 'legs'. At night these platforms were visible because their constant burning-off of waste gas produced an easily visible orange flare. In addition, some had flashing lights emitting a letter in Morse code and others were fitted with radar beacons (racons) which showed on the radar screen as a Morse code letter.

The traffic was widely dispersed and encounters with other merchantmen were civilised as they all adhered to the ROR, particularly in the traffic separation schemes that guided us around dense rig areas, shoals, and port approaches.

Among the regular traffic of dhows, container ships, general cargo ships, oil tankers, and rig supply ships, it was impossible not to notice the livestock carriers. These were usually rather old and grubby cargo ships converted to carry large numbers of animals. There was obviously a lucrative trade into the Gulf, particularly of sheep, a staple food in Arabic countries. The ship conversions were pretty basic as they were merely extra decks atop the weather deck, between the fo'c'sle and the accommodation block. These decks were railed along their lengths to provide natural ventilation for the sheep, kept in pens. I assumed there was a mechanical ventilation system for the beasts in the holds.

Livestock carriers were pretty unsightly ships, as ugly as the shoebox-like car carriers I'd seen on my voyages. You knew when you were downwind of a livestock carrier as the stink was diabolical. I felt sorry for the animals. But what was it like on board as crew? I dreaded to think. Fancy living with that constant, penetrating stench on a long voyage from Australia or New Zealand, through the tropics to the Gulf? No thanks.

> Blue Star had a connection to the livestock trade. The old *Wellington Star* (built 1952) was sold to Middle East Express Line in 1976, renamed *Hawkes Bay*, and converted into a livestock carrier. She carried live sheep above and frozen mutton below, until she went for scrap in 1979. Booth Line's *Hubert* was transferred to Austasia Line and renamed *Malaysia* in 1964. She was sold in 1976, renamed *Khalij Express*, and converted into a cattle carrier. Her capacity was 20,000 cattle. She went to the shipbreakers in 1984. I was shocked that such lovely classic old ships, with their graceful lines, were reduced to such an ignominious end, reeking of sheep or cattle poo and urine. So sad and tragic.

We maintained a listening watch on VHF Channel 16, used for distress calls, for making initial contact with other ships, or for calling up a port or pilot station. I'd noticed there was more traffic on Channel 16 than I'd been used to. This was due to the peculiar atmospheric conditions 'up the Gulf', which meant you heard communications between ships and ports hundreds of miles away. This 'tropospheric ducting' was radio propagation during periods of stable, anticyclonic weather. When a radio signal encountered a rise in temperature in the atmosphere, instead of the expected temperature decrease, the signal was 'bent' and contained within this conduit. Therefore, it was heard at a much greater range. Maximum range for VHF was line of sight but under these conditions, a decent VHF signal could be picked up the entire length and breadth of the Gulf. As well as ships, pilots, and ports liaising with each other, you often heard miscellaneous chatter – sometimes national insults being hurled between watchkeepers on different ships.

A big danger in this peculiar environment was 'VHF-assisted collision'. Instead of strictly adhering to the ROR, ships sometimes called each other up to arrange mutual action to avoid collision. While this could be achieved under normal conditions, the atmospheric peculiarities of the Gulf made it a bit dangerous. It's all very well calling up a ship, including her course and speed and relative position to your own ship, but when ducting occurred a ship at the other end of the Gulf could easily misinterpret the communication and suddenly make a completely unexpected manoeuvre, leading to a 'risk of collision' when none had existed a few minutes prior. On Pete and Ian's advice, I completely ignored such VHF chatter.

Each watch was busy throughout. After handing over and scuttling down the ladders to my cabin, I was still 'high' as my brain ticked over and adrenalin continued to pump. I can sleep anywhere in an instant, but the Gulf experience ensured it took a little while to fully unwind. Still, each watch whizzed by. I liked being busy, and my expertise, competence, and confidence greatly increased with the responsibility.

Kiwi Star sailed from Kuwait on 11 November. It was an uninterrupted passage to and through Hormuz, into the Gulf of Oman. A welcome respite from the seemingly non-stop action of five ports in as many days, with watchkeeping on the bridge and on deck and participation in stand-by for each port entry and exit. Sleep was at a premium. From the Strait, we headed east along the coast, first Iran, then Pakistan. Fewer merchantmen were seen, but the proportion of dhows went up.

As we approached Karachi, the density of tiny fishing boats increased significantly. It was futile to monitor or plot them on radar. They were just too small and didn't always 'paint' on the screen. Far better to rely on visual monitoring and to tweak the course slightly to pass around individual boats or small clusters. Easier to do in daylight, far more testing at night as very few were lit.

Rounding Keamari Peninsula, we crossed Hawke's Bay to the roads to embark the pilot, continually dodging tiny fishing boats. He guided the ship around the breakwater and into the channel between Manora Beach and the industrial zone on the opposite (eastern) bank. A short time later, *Kiwi Star* turned to starboard and berthed at the container terminal, directly opposite Karachi Dockyard and Naval Base. It looked to me like the Pakistani Navy had a fleet of tired old second-hand American and British frigates and destroyers.

In the early hours of 16 November, cargo operations completed and another pilot guided the ship out of Karachi. Again, those fishermen made our clearance from the pilot station more difficult. Southwards, *New Zealand Star* maintained sufficient distance offshore not to be bothered by fishermen.

A day or so later, the ship passed the mouth of the Gulf of Khambhat and closed the Konkan coast. Again, we were besieged and surrounded by myriad fishermen in their dugout canoes. This was becoming a habit on the subcontinent coast. A constant keen eye was necessary to avoid colliding with or running over these blokes. As you got closer to singletons, duos, or trios of canoes and tweaked the autopilot, they were lost from view due to ship's hull and bow. From the bridge wing, it was a relief to see them reappear to one side of the ship, no wreckage or heads bobbing about in the sea.

With pilot on board (noted in the Deck Log as POB, with a time), *Kiwi Star* rounded Colaba Fort, guarding the entrance to Bombay's natural harbour. A tight, almost hairpin, turn to port around Colaba Point gave onto the wide expanse of the harbour itself. The water was brown, as in Karachi, due to the volume of sediment. Colaba Shoals extended half a mile (nearly 1 km) or so into the harbour from the western shore. Oyster Rock protruded from the centre of these shoals and, further along, you could see Middle Ground Coastal Battery atop another isolated rock.

Bombay's skyline was behind these features and, with binoculars, I espied the Gateway of India, the impressive arch that commemorated the landing of King-Emperor George V, the first British monarch to visit India, in December 1911. Adjacent was the Naval Base, full of frigates and destroyers (a mixture of second-hand British and Indian new-build) and the headquarters of Western Naval Command.

Due to the Colaba Shoals, the pilot guided *New Zealand Star* through the dredged channel to the lock entrance for the port itself. We squeezed inside, the gate closed astern, and we secured to the bollards on the lock side. When the water level was the same as that inside the port, the gate opened ahead and the pilot used a couple of tugs to manoeuvre *Kiwi Star* on to Number 1 Berth, Indira Dock.

The wharfies swarmed on board, hundreds of them. The stevedoring was labour-intensive compared to that in Antipodean and European ports. The sound of 'safety flip-flops' slapped along the deck and an incessant hubbub of chatter. There were no portainers, so our deck cranes were used to work cargo. I was on deck for 8–12 that evening and in the morning.

After lunch, I took a taxi to the Gateway of India. It certainly was an impressive monument but its surroundings were sadly neglected: worn-out 'lawn', untended bushes, pavements in disrepair, litter everywhere. This 85 feet (26 m) high, triumphal basalt arch was used as a symbolic ceremonial entrance to India for important colonial personnel. It was the point from where the last British troops left India in 1948, following Indian independence.

Adjacent was the statue of Swami Vivekananda, the Hindu monk who introduced Hinduism to the western world and who promoted interfaith understanding between the world's major religions.

A short walk away was Prince of Wales Museum, another magnificent building, dedicated to the history of India, from prehistoric times to the present. Its foundation stone was laid by the Prince of Wales on 11 November 1905. It was completed in 1915, but became a children's welfare centre and military hospital during World War I. It was inaugurated as a museum on 10 January 1922 and was renamed Chhatrapati Shivaji Maharaj Vastu

Fig 12.14 Cochin's Chinese fishing nets

Sangrahalaya in the 1990s, when Bombay reverted to its original name, Mumbai.

This part of Bombay was chock-full of historic picturesque buildings, monuments, and statues. My meandering took me past Rajabai Clock Tower, Flora Fountain, and Victoria Terminus (today, Chhatrapati Shivaji Maharaj Terminus). The Terminus is one of the busiest railway stations in India, serving long-distance and suburban trains. In exuberant Italian Gothic style, its construction began in 1878, and was completed in 1887 to mark Queen Victoria's golden jubilee.

I returned to the docks by taxi and was back on board for dinner before my evening 8–12 cargo watch. There were a large number of container movements (on and off) so we didn't sail until 21 November. I was used to 'dicing with death' among fishermen as the ship progressed further south to Cochin. We were too far off the coast to distinguish any features visually or through binoculars, but could discern a lush, forest-fringed shoreline. The radar picture showed alternating little bays and small headlands.

Halfway along, we passed Goa, the former Portuguese colony renowned for its sandy beaches and imported Western hippy lifestyle. Far over the horizon and paralleling the coast, lay the Maldives, a rather more up-market holiday destination.

We toiled with yet more local fishermen in dugout canoes on approaching the pilot station. This stretch of Kerala's Malabar coast was low-lying, forested with mangroves. With the pilot on board, *New Zealand Star* entered the channel between Vypeen peninsula to port and Fort Cochin opposite. Contrary to its name, the latter was a quaint old suburb of Cochin city.

As the ship progressed through the harbour, you could see plenty of Portuguese, Dutch, and British architecture dating back to the 16th century. Prior to that, China had exerted some influence, evidenced by 'Chinese fishing nets' on the shore. These were huge mechanical structures, about 30 feet (9 m) high, comprising a cantilever with an outstretched net about 60 feet (20 m) wide, suspended over the sea. Large stones suspended from ropes acted as counterweights. They were operated by a team of six fishermen. Introduced by Chinese explorers in the 14th century, this fishing method was almost unique to Cochin.

We rounded the north end of Willingdon Island and berthed at Ernakulam Wharf. Further along was the home of the Indian Navy's Southern Command, another base and dockyard with several warships berthed. At the port, our cranes were used to load and unload containers for the few hours alongside. Sadly, even during the limited time between cargo watches, it proved impractical to see anything more of Cochin itself.

After departing Cochin, *New Zealand Star* continued southwards to the southern tip of India and crossed the Laccadive Sea to Colombo. It was just over a day's run at 18 knots, and we arrived on 25 November, exactly two months since I'd joined the ship in Colombo.

We only had a handful of hours in Colombo before heading out to commence my second round trip. Three and a half days to Singapore, including another birthday at sea for me, for another speedy turnaround of containers. On 29 November, the ship transited through the ever-crowded Singapore Roads and headed south-west to the Java Sea. We retraced *Mandama's* track to Sunda Strait, as our next port was Fremantle.

Exiting Sunda Strait, *New Zealand Star* turned to port around the westernmost islands off Java, steered south-south-west direct to Fremantle, and arrived on 5 December. A slightly longer stop allowed me to go up the road one afternoon. It was great to step out on terra firma again. It seemed a long time since Bombay.

Freo was bathed in warm summer sunshine. I was fond of its quaint, small town-ish ambience, I imagined it quieter and more relaxed than the bustle and business of Perth, the state capital further up the Swan River.

It took nearly a week to round the south-west point of Australia and cross the Great Australian Bight and Tasman Sea again to New Plymouth, where we spent a short time. I was fond of this place, like Freo, despite its scruffy, shabby, and industrial focus. Through Cook Strait we went and back down to Port Chalmers for another brief stop. Otago Harbour was as scenic as on my first trip, blessed with glorious weather again.

From there, we resumed the trade route: Melbourne (20 December), Fremantle (Christmas Day), across the Indian Ocean to the Gulf. Another New Year at sea. Being absent from home for my birthday and the entire festive season was my norm in BSSM for four consecutive years.

Another hectic tour of Gulf ports (Muscat, Dubai, Dammam, Kuwait) followed by respite and recovery during the passage to Bombay, no stop in Karachi this trip. Onwards to Cochin and finally Colombo, where I paid off on 23 January 1984, virtually four months on my two round trips.

The limited narrative for the second round trip was because nothing particularly noteworthy occurred. The landlubber may think it a dull, repetitive life, away from home for months, missing Christmases, birthdays, and sundry family events. However, I and countless shipmates thoroughly enjoyed our life and times with BSSM. It was an enjoyable and satisfying novelty to be a bridge watchkeeper for the duration, never straying from my twice daily, 8–12 watches, at sea and in port. Sure, free time and opportunities to go up the road (which I loved to do) were markedly reduced in this role, but that was what a deck officer's job entailed. No good whining about it.

Like all my trips, I greatly enjoyed my time on *New Zealand Star* and the company of the blokes with whom I sailed. There were plenty of laughs. I also added several new places and countries to my growing list. I was, truly, fortunate.

I flew home from Colombo via Air Lanka (today, SriLankan Airlines), landed at Heathrow and coached/trained down to Portsmouth Harbour station. Home was this sailor, home from the sea.

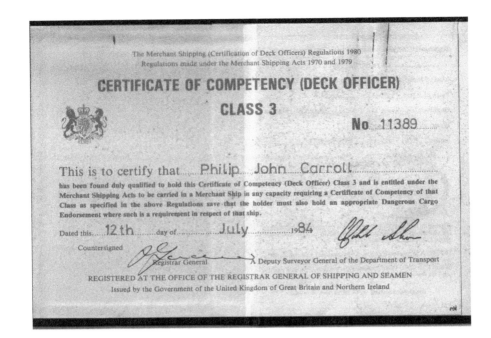

The Merchant Shipping (Certification of Deck Officers) Regulations 1980
Regulations made under the Merchant Shipping Acts 1970 and 1979

CERTIFICATE OF COMPETENCY (DECK OFFICER)

CLASS 3

No 11389

This is to certify that Philip John Carroll

has been found duly qualified to hold this Certificate of Competency (Deck Officer) Class 3 and is entitled under the Merchant Shipping Acts to be carried in a Merchant Ship in any capacity requiring a Certificate of Competency of that Class as specified in the above Regulations save that the holder must also hold an appropriate Dangerous Cargo Endorsement where such is a requirement in respect of that ship.

Dated this 12th day of July 1984

Countersigned

Registrar General   A Deputy Surveyor General of the Department of Transport

REGISTERED AT THE OFFICE OF THE REGISTRAR GENERAL OF SHIPPING AND SEAMEN
Issued by the Government of the United Kingdom of Great Britain and Northern Ireland

Fig 13.1 My Second Mate's ticket

13 A Big Decision

I don't recall when I decided to resign from BSSM. A combination of factors conspired in this decision. By the mid-1980s, the British merchant navy was in deep malaise. British companies switched their registry from the UK to foreign flags of convenience to reduce costs and the burdensome, expensive compliance with rigorous British certification requirements for ships and crews. It was cheaper and easier to ditch British officers and crews and to replace them with 'cheapo' Filipinos and others. If Brits were retained, their terms and conditions of service likely changed for the worse. Concomitant was the rapid collapse of the British shipbuilding industry. Ships were built more quickly and cheaply abroad, particularly in Asia. Foreign ship repair facilities were increasingly more competitive.

In BSSM, I heard anecdotal tales of newly-qualified engineer and deck cadets in UK Nautical Colleges being congratulated on passing their tickets by their employer and, in the same breath, receiving their redundancy notices.

BSSM seemed to be selling older ships but not replacing them with new builds. We looked to be in an increasingly sorry and potentially perilous state.

I attained the requisite 24 months sea time to marry up with my exam success. I clutched my 2nd Mate's Foreign-Going Certificate of Competency (Deck Officer) with great pride. I'd worked and studied hard for four years to earn this professional qualification. It was more rewarding and satisfying than gaining my honours degree!

As born and raised in a naval town, across Portsmouth harbour from the Dockyard, the Royal Navy had influenced me subliminally and was ingrained in my subconscious. I decided to apply to join. It was now or never, as the upper age limit for graduate seaman officer entry was 26, which I would attain in late November 1984.

So I sent in my application and was invited to attend the Admiralty Interview Board at HMS Sultan, in my home town of Gosport. I passed and was accepted to join in April 1984. With much regret and sadness, I submitted my resignation to Mr Burke at BSSM.

When I'd joined BSSM in September 1980, the fleet contained 34 ships under several house flags: Blue Star, Lamport & Holt (Lean & Hungry), Booth, Austasia, ACT, Starman. By autumn 1984, there were only 21 ships listed in *Gangway*, the company's quarterly magazine. Starman had gone and L&H had reduced from four hulls to a single vessel.

The rapid demise of BSSM began in the 1980s. Old ships were disposed of during my time. All famous traditional names steeped in Blue Star history: *Canterbury Star, Halifax Star, Montreal Star, New York Star, Timaru Star, Trojan Star, Tuscan Star, Gladstone Star, Rockhampton Star*. In 1975–76 Blue Star built six lovely-looking, five-hatch, refrigerated cargo ships with 'banana doors' fitted in the ship's sides. These new 'A'-boats (named after Blue Star's classic 'A'-boats of the mid-1920s) worked the lucrative fruit and banana trade from Central and South America to the USA and Europe. They were all sold off after about a decade's service.

L&H's swanky SD-14 (shelter-deck 14,000 tons) general cargo ships built by Austin-Pickersgill, Sunderland, in 1979 (*Belloc, Bronte, Browning, Boswell*) were all gone by 1983. My *New Zealand Star*, renamed *Churchill* in 1986, became the last L&H ship. 1986 marked the disappearance of Booth Line when *Benedict* and *Boniface* were sold. In 1993, Austasia Line became defunct when it was subsumed into the Blue Star Line. *Wellington Star* and *Southland Star*, container ships on the Australasia/Fiji/North American west coast Crusader Service, were scrapped in 1993.

Despite all this gloom, four versatile new reefers (*English Star, Scottish Star, Auckland Star, Canterbury Star*), built at Harland & Wolf in 1986, came into service. They were the last of a long succession of Blue Star Line ships. They had four fully refrigerated holds with banana doors in the sides and a fully automated machinery space. All four suffered the same fate in 2011: being run up the beach at Alang, India, to be scrapped. A short, heart-wrenching YouTube video shows *Scottish Star* steaming straight towards the shore, aiming for the gap between the remnants of two other hulls. She rode up onto the beach and stopped among the junk. About two minutes of awful viewing.

By 1990, the Vestey empire's debts had increased to £420 million. Many of the tax loopholes the family had used for decades were closed by the UK government in 1991. More than 50 banks were owed money. A consortium of banks called a halt to their spending and demanded cutbacks and economies. The supply-chain business was changing as supermarkets developed their own wholesaling operations, including specialist butchery sections, with the advantages of economies of scale in purchasing across a spectrum of goods.

Union International, Vestey's vast global cold storage company, was placed in administrative receivership in 1995. Blue Star Line's shipping interests were sold to P&O Nedlloyd in 1998. The Vestey organisation retained their refrigerated ships via ownership of Albion Reefers, operated by Star Reefers, a merger of Hamburg Sud and Albion Reefers. Star Reefers (24 ships) was sold in July 2001 to Norwegian interests, who later formed NYK Star Reefers with NYK Line (making a 74-ship fleet). Not only did this end the Vestey family's 90-year involvement with shipping, but it also closed a significant chapter of British merchant shipping. So many other famous British shipping names also disappeared: Port Line, Clan Line, Elder Dempster, Furness-Withy, Shaw, Savill and Albion Line, Blue Funnel Line (aka Blue Flue), Harrison Line, Palm Line. Very sad and tragic in so many ways.

BSSM's ACT container ships were sold to P&O Nedlloyd and traded until February 2003 between the west coast of North America and Australia/New Zealand, still with Blue Star funnels: *America Star* (ex-*ACT 3*), *Melbourne Star* (ex-*ACT 4*), *Sydney Star* (ex-*ACT 5*) and *Queensland Star* (ex-*ACT 6*). *ACT 7* was renamed *Palliser Bay* when she was taken over by P&O in 1991 but was scrapped in 2002. The last vessel to trade thus was *America Star*, but she was handed over to the breakers at Shanghai on 19 February 2003.

During my research for this book, I was deeply saddened to discover those famous shipping lines were consigned to history less than 20 years after I left. The glorious interwar years of Blue Star with its magnificent first-generation 'A'-boats (*Arandora Star, Almeda Star, Andalucia Star, Avelona Star, Avila Star*) trading between Europe and South America with passengers accommodated in luxurious cabins were gone forever. As were the trades between Australasia and North America.

No more trips up the Amazon to Manaus or Iquitos on a Booth boat.

The increased domination of containerisation destroyed typical merchant navy life as described in Sandy Kinghorn's *Before the Box Boats*, like *Tasmania Star* in 1973. En route to New Zealand, she spent a couple of hours off Pitcairn Island, where the *Bounty* mutineers had settled, collected their mail and posted it from Auckland. Three months in New Zealand was split into a month each in Auckland and Wellington, two weeks in Lyttelton, nine days in Bluff, and two weeks in Timaru.

Similarly, it wasn't unusual for two, three or even four Blue Star Line reefers to be in the same port simultaneously. Captain Kinghorn on *Saxon Star* in Melbourne's Victoria Dock saw *Wellington Star* and *Tasmania Star* berthed nearby, joined later by *Trojan Star*. Such heady days!

All terribly sad but reflected the sad demise of Britain's 'Red Duster' merchant navy fleet.

What became of my old ships? They were all sold off to other companies and ultimately scrapped and demolished.

My first ship, *ACT 5*, was re-engined as a motor ship in Yokohama in 1987, transferred to Blue Star Line and renamed *Sydney Star*. She was sold to P&O Nedlloyd in 1998, but retained her name until her demolition in Shanghai in May 2003.

Poor *Benedict* had a chequered life. In 1986, she was sold to Venisol Shipping Corporation and renamed *Zamet*. Cool Wind Navigation Corporation bought her in 1993 but she collided with a bulk carrier off Madagascar eight years later. In 2005, she was sold again and renamed *Ismail Prince*. The following year she suffered engine failure in the Dardanelles and was repaired in Turkey. Next, she was managed by Tomeh Shipping Company, Tarsus, Syria, and was involved in another collision off Istanbul in 2008. She had two further owners, based in the Gulf, before being scrapped in Mumbai in 2011. What a sad and sorry tale.

California Star remained with BSSM with a couple of name changes (as Austasia's *Mulbera*, then transferred back to Blue Star Line as *Fremantle Star*) until her scrapping at Alang, a few hundred miles north of Mumbai.

Rockhampton Star was scrapped before I left BSSM. After my trip on her, she was laid up at Falmouth before being sold and renamed *Golden Lady*. She was broken up at Chittagong, Bangladesh, in mid-1983.

What of my beautiful *Mandama*? She, too, was scrapped at Chittagong in May 1984. A tragedy and a travesty! How could such a clean, classically graceful ship have suffered such a premature death?

When BSSM withdrew from Starman Shipping in 1984, *Starman Anglia* was sold to Atlanska Plovidba, Yugoslavia, and renamed *Lapad*. She survived until mid-2006 when she was broken up at Aliaga, on Turkey's Aegean coast.

And my last ship? *New Zealand Star* plodded along for many years. In January 1986, she was lengthened with a centre section of two-and-a-half holds inserted at her midships and another 35-ton deck crane was fitted to retain her fully self-sustaining capability. This work at Jurong Shipyard, Singapore, increased her container capacity to 1,151. During the refit, she was transferred to L&H and renamed *Churchill*. Five years later she moved back to Blue Star Line as *Argentina Star*. In 1993, she was an unwitting nail in the coffin of British-crewed, UK-registered, deep-sea merchantmen. NUMAST (National Union of Marine, Aviation, and Shipping Transport Officers, the officers' trade union) protested over BSSM 'flagging-out' their last such ship. The union lost the battle and the ship became Filipino-manned (albeit with a British Master, Chief Engineer, Chief Mate, Chief Refrigeration Engineer and Chief Electrician) and was re-registered in The Bahamas. She was also the last ship to sport the famous outsize Blue Star funnel. When Blue Star Line was sold to P&O Nedlloyd in 1998, she continued to trade until her final voyage to Shanghai, where she was scrapped in January 2002.

This was all heartbreaking for me because of the many brilliant and fond memories of each ship and the characters with whom I sailed the world: Masters, Mates, Engineers, Cadets and the crews (Barbadian, Chinese and British).

I was extremely fortunate and proud to have been a Blue Star man. Fate had pointed me in that direction via an advert I scarcely recall. Over 1,000 blokes had applied in 1980 and I was one of the lucky 13 selected.

I have no idea how many miles I steamed, but I certainly enjoyed visiting every part of the world I'd ever dreamt of seeing. Circumnavigating the globe on my first trip was brilliant. I had many adventures: going 'up the road' whenever possible; down the 'skids' in Santos at the 'Love Story Bar' and Rio's 'Scandinavia Bar' with drunken sailors and beautiful Brazilian whores; through narrow channels in the Amazon delta; under San Francisco's Golden Gate Bridge; numerous transits of the Panama and Suez Canals; up the Gulf; down to Ozzie and Kiwi. I saw a myriad places that people only dreamt about in those days. Today, it's far too easy and cheap for anyone to do likewise.

I loved the camaraderie on board every ship I sailed in and the wide spectrum of personalities. Party nights in the bar, occasionally too much beer, traditional curry lunch with condiments every Sunday, three excellent meals per day, ice cream for dessert every day if I wanted it, film nights (courtesy of Walport) in the mess or on deck, a white sheet strung between derrick samson posts.

As a deck cadet, I loved working with the 'deck crowd', particularly Mr Best the Bosun and his Bajan ABs on *ACT 5*, with their relaxed pace of life and laconic West Indian lilt. The Chinese crews, all old blokes with poor English, at sea almost constantly for decades, sending their wages home to family in Singapore. The wit and cutting sense of humour of British crews, accents dominated by Scouse, Geordie, and Jock, with some Cockney thrown in.

I loved all my ships but I have a particular affection for *ACT 5*, my first. I think any seafarer would concur with that sentiment. The beautiful *Mandama* and her distinctive Hallen 'D'-frame swinging derricks. The unique experience of *Starman Anglia* and her monstrous 300-ton Stülcken jumbo derrick. *Rockhampton Star's* classic graceful lines, wooden decks, and no air-conditioning. The rather top-heavy *Benedict* at the mouth of the Amazon. Even the box boats (*ACT 5, California Star*, and *New Zealand Star*) had a certain style and sleek hull, spoiled by the disarray of containers on deck, obscuring visibility from the bridge. Yep, I loved them all.

By chance, my trips encompassed every type of vessel managed by BSSM (general cargo, refrigerated cargo, containers, heavy-lift), and I sailed under every house flag, except Lean & Hungry.

There was an interesting contrast between 'at sea' and 'in port'. The leisurely cruising across the world's oceans at speeds of 20 knots, sometimes more; the hectic cargo watches in port, with short hops between each port 'on the coast'.

I enjoyed being busy, pacing up and down and across the weather deck, monitoring and noting the loading and discharge of cargo. I must have walked miles every cargo watch. Most of the time, tropical sunshine beamed down as I worked on deck in boilersuit or shorts and T-shirt, always shod in Doc Marten boots.

With the ABs, wearing safety goggles to chip vast expanses of deck, using traditional handheld chipping hammers or, with ear-defenders clamped to my head, the powerful, loud, pneumatic version. Then painting those same deck areas with red lead, primer, and topcoat, using rollers or brushes.

With the other cadets, dismantling, cleaning, greasing and reassembling all manner of stuff: hatch dogs, door dogs, shackles, blocks and tackles. Inspecting and scrubbing the lifeboats, mustering their rations and kit. Learning to rig stages and bosun's chairs; operating winches to open MacGregor hatches; and observing how derricks were rigged for single and union purchase. Holystoning *Rocky's* teak decks with Doddy.

At day's end, a sherbet or two on the 'patio' outside the officers' bar with shipmates as the sun set and the horizon glowed shades of red. Shoving my grubby, increasingly discoloured, boilie into the boiler suit washing-machine, then showering and dressing in Red Sea rig for dinner. Draping my rejuvenated white boilersuit over a guardrail in the oil-smelling, noisy, hot, vast cathedral-like engine room, full of interconnected pipes (like spaghetti) and ancillary machinery, as the engine rhythmically powered the ship through the ocean.

My favourite spot was right up forward, on the fo'c'sle, alone, listening to the relative wind whistling through the fairleads and bull's-eye. Sitting on the deck, back to the bulwark, among the bollards, winches, and windlasses. Bliss! On my knees, peering through the bull's-eye, down to the bulbous bow cleaving through the ocean, creating the bow wave and the ship's wake. Hypnotised by the endless turmoil below, almost magnetically drawn into it, certainly visually – but thankfully not bodily. Frequently joined by a pod of dolphins, 'flying' clear of our bow wave, and diving back into the water, or by schools of small, silver flying-fish with their delicate, almost transparent, gossamer wings. I was entranced!

On watch on the bridge, pacing endlessly across its width, continually checking everything, taking fixes, plotting our position on an Admiralty chart, adjusting course if necessary, monitoring the radar, and 'maintaining a proper lookout at all times'.

I loved the respite of sipping a mug of tea staring out through the centre line bridge window or, better still, leaning against the bridge wing dodger in the sun or on a warm tropical starlit night. During the day, distant echoes of the 'deck crowd' chipping on the weather deck carried to the bridge.

Absolute silence at night, save for the perpetual rhythmic pulsating throb from the engine room. I was lucky that most nights had a clear sky, the blanket of myriad tiny pinpricks of starlight untainted by light pollution. Trying to identify some of the 57 stars listed in the *Nautical Almanac* and looking for planets: Venus, Mars, Jupiter, and Saturn. In calm seas, the moon's bright light shimmering across the crinkled sea surface. In the right conditions, looking over the side and observing bioluminescence glowing in the sea directly beneath and trailing away in the ship's wake. It was captivating!

I'd heard about the singing of 'Bye, Bye, Blue Star' (to the tune of the 1924 jazz classic 'Bye, Bye, Blackbird') in the bar at the end of a deep-sea trip, on approaching a home port and about to pay off. Alas, I never had the experience:

No one in Blue Star Line understands me
The best thing they could do would be to land me.
I'll go to Aberdeen, be a British Tanker man.
Bye, bye, Blue Star

Pack my bags, pack my grip,
I'm not coming back next trip
Bye, bye, Blue Star.

No more turning-to on Sunday morning,
No more early stand-bys without warning
Soooo, up the 2nd, up the Chief,
All I want is my relief,
Bye, bye, Blue Star.

Pack my bags, pack my grip,
I'm not coming back next trip
Bye, bye, Blue Star.

The expansion of containerisation changed the merchant navy of the 1980s. I'd missed out on the heady days of spending months on the Ozzie and Kiwi coasts or in South America. Weeks berthed in port because loading and discharge went at a pedestrian pace, with civilised working hours. Endless parties on board with 'molls', waving them farewell on departure from the last port on the coast. What a full and exciting life that must have been.

Since my resignation, I've had no contact with Blue Star shipmates, until I started this project. Four decades later, it's likely that many of the Masters and senior Mates with whom I sailed have 'crossed the bar'. Some must still be kicking around in their eighties! The junior officers of my time must be approaching retirement in whatever career they followed post-Blue Star.

It saddens me very much that the renowned super-sized funnel, emblazoned with its famous big, bright-blue star within a white disc on a red background will never be seen again. It dominated in every port. Floodlit at night, it advertised Vestey's Blue Star empire and served as a beacon to get you home safe after a drunken night up the road.

In my era there was no internet, no email, no post, no phone calls (except via satellite phone at an extortionate cost), no women at sea, no

GPS, no mobile phones, no social media. We were just a bunch of highly qualified, experienced blokes, trading from place to place worldwide. We had a jolly good time, too. In so many ways, a much simpler, uncomplicated, enjoyable way of life.

Noel Payne's poem 'A Sailor You Be' captured the life and experiences of typical merchant seamen. I'm intensely proud to count myself among their number.

> Have you felt salt spray upon your face?
> Have you seen porpoise at the bow, keeping pace?
> Have you viewed sea birds, above the wake in flight?
> Have you fixed on a star, at sunset shining bright?
>
> Has there been a time, you saved a shipmate?
> Has the roll of the deck, ever kept you awake?
> Has the vastness of sea, left you feeling alone?
> Has a foreign port, made you wish you were home?
>
> If you have weighed anchor, from calm shelter
> If you have crossed the Equator, at noon time swelter
> If you have stood your watch, on a pitching deck
> If you have made a landfall, on the horizon a speck
>
> When you have secured the decks, for the night to turn in
> When you have mustered at sunrise, seen a new day begin
> When you have battened down hatches, in mountainous seas
> When you have known all these things, a sailor you be

Overall, I had an unforgettable, fantastic time with Blue Star. No regrets. My wanderlust triggered and engaged for the next phase of my life, by joining the Royal Navy.

References

Anon (1969). *Blue Star Line Spans the World: The Story of a Great Shipping Line*. Unknown publisher. Fraser Darrah Collection.

Clough-Smith, J. H. (1967). *Applied Physics: Notes and Examples in SI Units for Students of Nautical Science*. Brown, Son & Ferguson Ltd.

Clough-Smith, J. H. (1979). *An Introduction to Spherical Trigonometry*. Brown, Son & Ferguson Ltd.

Danton, G. L. (1972). *The Theory and Practice of Seamanship*. The Gresham Press.

Earl, Capt G. E. and Main, Capt F. L. (n.d.). *Munro's Navigation*. James Munro and Co., Ltd.

Eyres, D. J. (1972). *Ship Construction*. William Heinemann Ltd.

Frost, Capt A. (n.d.). *Practical Navigation for the Officer of the Watch*. Brown, Son & Ferguson

Hamilton-Paterson, James. (2011). *Empire of the Clouds*. Faber and Faber.

Hamilton-Paterson, James. (2017). *Gerontius, a Novel*. Faber and Faber.

Hordern, Miles. (2005). *Passage to Torres Strait*. John Murray

Karabell, Zachary. (2003). *Parting the Desert, the Creation of the Suez Canal*. John Murray.

Kinghorn, Capt A. W. (1983). *Before the Box Boats*. Kenneth Mason.

Kinghorn, Capt A. W. (1996). *Away to Sea. Life in Blue Star and Golden Line*. Abergavenny, P. M. Heaton Publishing.

Norie, J. W. (1977). *Norie's Nautical Tables with explanations of their use*. Imray Laurie Norie and Wilson Ltd.

Taprell Dorling, H. (1973). *Blue Star Line at War 1939-1945*. W Foulsham and Co. Ltd.

The Hydrographer of the Navy (1971). *The Mariner's Handbook*. HMSO.

Winchester, Simon. (2010). *Atlantic*. HarperPress.

Wright, C. H. (1977a). *The Efficient Deck Hand*. The James Laver Printing Co. Ltd.

Wright, C. H. (1977b). *Survival at Sea, the Lifeboat and Liferaft*. The James Laver Printing Co. Ltd.

Film

Snowbow. (2000). *The Great Liners (Episode 37) A Voyage to the Amazon*. Snowbow Documentary Productions Ltd.

Websites

Website. *Blue Star Line on the Web*. www.bluestarline.org

Website. *Blue Star Line & Associated Companies*. www.facebook.com

Bibliography

Clare, Horatio. (2015). *Down to the Sea in Ships*. Vintage.

Durrant, Graham. (2020). *The Sea, the 70s and the Passage*. Lulu.

Earl, Capt J. E. (2020). *A Bucket of Steam*. Arthur H Stockwell Ltd.

Smiley, David E. (2017). *Beyond the Blue Horizon – An Autobiography*. Amazon.

Ingram Content Group UK Ltd.
Milton Keynes UK
UKHW052145030423
419585UK00002B/3